The Kachina
and the
White Man

The Kachina and the White Man

THE INFLUENCES OF WHITE CULTURE ON THE HOPI KACHINA CULT

Revised and Enlarged Edition

Illustrated by the author

Frederick J. Dockstader

UNIVERSITY OF NEW MEXICO PRESS
Albuquerque

To
Fred Kabotie

in admiration for his artistry,
respect for his devotion to tradition,
and gratitude for his friendship.

Library of Congress Cataloging in Publication Data

Dockstader, Frederick J.
The Kachina and the White man.

Reprint. Originally published: Bloomfield Hills,
Mich.: Cranbrook Institute of Science, 1954
(Bulletin; 35) With new introd.
Bibliography: p.
Includes index.
1. Hopi Indians—Religion and mythology. 2. Katcinas.
3. Indians of North America—Arizona—Religion and
mythology. I. Title.
E99.H7D65   1985   299'.78   85-968
ISBN 0-8263-0789-2
ISBN 0-8263-0790-6 (pbk.)

Contents

Illustrations

PLATES

FIGURES

Preface

THE AIM OF THIS STUDY is to examine the possible origins and the development of the Hopi Kachina Cult, and in particular to analyze the changes or adaptations which have resulted from contacts with White culture. I have largely excluded consideration of influences reaching the Hopis through other Indians, even though many White influences were, of course, introduced to the Hopis by neighboring tribes.

Much of the content results from the gathering of loose threads; for many of the facts and opinions presented have been available previously in scattered or obscure sources. I have attempted, however, to weave these separate threads into a whole fabric—an ethnological weft on an historic warp. My own interpretations and original data are based on a long-time interest in Pueblo ceremonialism, particularly the masked dances. Starting by collecting "Kachina dolls," I eventually became familiar with the literature on the Kachina Cult. Real understanding, however, comes only with first-hand experience, and this I gained by field work between the years 1934 and 1941. During this period, I profited from intimate contact with the Hopis through frequent visits to the villages, travel in and around the Reservation, and occasional residence with the people themselves. In this phase of my work, no one was more helpful than Jimmy Kewanwytewa of Oraibi, who, indeed, was largely responsible for the growth of an interest that might otherwise have remained only a hobby. Other Hopi informants, in deference to their wishes, remain unnamed.

My activities in the arts, particularly silversmithing and woodcarving, have been of value in reaching an understanding of the Kachina Cult. I learned both arts through Indian techniques, and this provided a good foundation from which to investigate other facets of Indian art. In addition, I have made a collection of Hopi art that is especially strong in material related to the Kachina Cult. It includes a reference series of about 400 Kachina statuettes, some made by the Hopis, others by myself.

No one can undertake a survey of this character without incurring great obligations to those who preceded him and to those who helped along the way. These, in my case, have been so numerous that to adequately express my gratitude to them all would be to encumber this preface with expressions which are essentially personal. There are, however, several whose help requires some recognition here.

Dr. and Mrs. Harold S. Colton, of the Museum of Northern Arizona, influenced me more than they can know to follow my present course; their friendly help and many courtesies cannot be adequately acknowledged, and I have drawn heavily upon Dr. Colton's own work in the field.

My gratitude also goes to Dr. Mischa Titiev, who gave generously of his time in patiently reviewing the entire manuscript. He provided many helpful suggestions, and has given sympathetic interest throughout the preparation of the book.

Mr. James A. Beresford, of Bloomfield Hills, has been unsparing with time, encouragement, and invaluable suggestions.

Cranbrook Institute of Science provided a grant which made it possible for me to visit the major museums and libraries of the eastern United States, where I studied the collections of Southwestern artifacts and consulted unpublished material. A list of the custodians of these collections who took great pains to help me would be impracticably long, but special kindnesses require the following recognitions: Dr. George G. Heye and Mr. E. K. Burnett of the Museum of the American Indian; Miss Bella Weitzner of the American Museum of Natural History; Dr. Matthew W. Stirling and Dr. William N. Fenton of the Bureau of American Ethnology; Mr. John C. Ewers of the U. S. National Museum; and Dr. Frederick Webb Hodge of the Southwest Museum.

Others who took time out of busy schedules to see that the facilities of their several institutions were placed at my disposal include Dr. J. O. Brew of the Peabody Museum, Harvard University; Mr. Charles S. Nagel, Jr., of the Brooklyn Museum; Dr. Frank Setzler of the U. S. National Museum; Dr. George Quimby and Miss Agnes McNary of the Chicago Natural History Museum; Dr. John Alden Mason and Miss Frances Eyman of the University Museum, Philadelphia; and Dr. Ruth L. Butler of the Ayer Collection, Newberry Library.

Mr. Watson Smith of the Peabody Museum of Harvard University placed his files of illustrations and photographs of murals at my disposal, made numerous helpful suggestions, and permitted me to draw upon his own research for certain illustrations and points of fact that I have included here.

Dr. Frederic H. Douglas of the Denver Art Musem was unusually helpful with suggestions, and his informed discussion opened my eyes to several sources I had overlooked.

To the Forgotten People of Research—the many staff members of these various institutions and of the several libraries consulted—my sincere appreciation. Without them, no investigator could find his way through the vast collections of books, or the maze of storage cabinets, cases, and vaults.

An earlier version of this book, in dissertation form, was helped by the patient editing of Dr. Lyon N. Richardson of Western Reserve University and by many suggestions from Drs. Newbell N. Puckett and William E. Lawrence of the same institution.

I am grateful to Miss Marcía L. Dorwin, Miss Adèle H. Fridhandler, and Mrs. Emmy Irene Hesz for their zeal in helping to bring together source material, in typing, and in the many other tedious details prerequisite to publication; also to Mrs. Dorothy Carlin for her capable assistance and friendly suggestions. Mr. George Migrants and others of the Cranbrook Press were most helpful in the planning and execution of the book.

At the initiation of this project I was associated with Cranbrook Institute of Science, and the encouragement and guidance given by its Director, Dr. Robert T. Hatt, extended far beyond what would normally be expected.

To earlier scholars, to such giants as Alexander M. Stephen, Jesse Walter Fewkes, and Elsie Clews Parsons, recognition from me would be presumptuous. We who follow them add to their stature in the same measure that we take from their work.

To my wife, Alice, I extend grateful recognition for the many long hours she has spent in typing and reading manuscript. The book is better for the unassailable logic of her arguments, her enthusiastic persistence, and her capable aid in the preparation of illustrations.

Lastly, but most importantly, I acknowledge an over-all debt to the Hopis, whose stubborn determination to retain their own ways and ability to resist the abrasive culture surrounding them first won my interest and my respect. *Kwakwai, i'kwákwachim!*

FREDERICK J. DOCKSTADER

Dartmouth College
Hanover, New Hampshire
December 1, 1953

Preface to
the Revised Edition

IT IS RARE TO HAVE the opportunity to review an earlier work and to reevaluate one's ideas with the possibility of making any needed changes; the publication of this volume offers just such an occasion. In the thirty years since this book first appeared, the world of the Indian has changed radically, and the Hopis have not been overlooked. Many of the changes have probably been for the better, certainly in the field of civil rights. Economically, however, the results have been less favorable, and even in those instances where Indian lands have been leased for subsurface exploitation or for recreation, it is still uncommon to find a situation in which the tribe involved has received a completely equitable return for the use. There are exceptions, of course—but in general, most payments, such as they are, have been in cash royalties, while jobs have gone to outsiders. When the resource is gone, little remains but deep scars on the surface or in the soul. The native has not been well served by the bureaucrat (*see* Davis and Matthews).

With the Hopi, this is quickly apparent in the continuing exasperation over exploitative land leases, justifiable anger at the District 6 controversy (*see* page 2), and the continuing bitter confrontation over the Tribal Council role in Hopi life. Out of this frustration have come feelings of hostility, resentment, and indignation at being forced by outside pressures to adjust to obvious inequities. The religious life of the people, which also continues to face pressures to change, is no exception. In Chapter 10, I have made an effort to examine the contemporary record of the past thirty years. There is no question, however, that the final word has not yet been spoken— just as the Hopis have resisted the impact of outside forces, whether social, political, or religious, they have continued to demonstrate a remarkable resiliency, and in the instance of the Kachina, which is the central theme of this study, that element of survival is comforting, if still somewhat surprising.

Following the publication of this volume in 1954, I was called to other activities and could only keep in touch with reservation life by occasional contact. The great weakness of these later observations is the lack of a day-to-day, on-the-scene opportunity to watch the various modifications in Hopi culture over the years. I have, of course, kept as close pace with these as I possibly could; staying in touch with Hopi friends and non-Hopi students of the Southwest has enabled me to maintain a fair degree of awareness, as have my professional reponsibilities, which fortunately have continued to be closely related to these interests.

It is with deep satisfaction that I can evaluate the strength of the Kachina religion today and realize that it does not show as low a profile as seemed to threaten a quarter of a century ago. The Kachina has made yet another dramatic return in the face of external pressures. And this is no small feat, when one realizes the problems facing 8,500 people, standing against the population surrounding them. Their Navajo neighbors, to take one example, have become the largest American Indian group in the United States, numbering over 150,000 today, with a political strength proportionately effective. This in itself is a problem for the Hopis, and perhaps more than any other single factor—save perhaps the Hopi inability to unite and cooperate with each other—denies them equality in a public forum.

The question may be asked whether a new edition of this book is warranted. To me, the answer is simple: the original edition has long been unavailable, and it seems appropriate to reach another generation. I so firmly believe in the strength of the Hopi way of life and what it has done for its own people, admire the role it occupies in human life, and appreciate the beauty of its representation, that I have perhaps become something of a missionary in the desire to introduce more non-Hopis to a unique ceremonial tradition that actively survives in the midst of a world dominated by abrasive, fast-paced sociopolitical concerns. It is astonishing to realize that a fair-sized element of prehistoric America remains alive and healthy in these closing years of the twentieth century; that it has been able to maintain itself against concentrated efforts to eradicate it; and that, if the observations of this volume are at all accurate, the future suggests that it will be many years yet before the last Kachina dance is held. Moreover, a renewed interest in Indian arts has created a deeper, more sympathetic concern for precisely the esthetic values that are represented so superably in the costume, choreography, and social vitality of the Kachina ritual.

In the past thirty years, several good friends who had much to do with my early growth have put on the cloud mask. Notably, Jimmie Kewanwytewa, who first inspired my interest and taught me all I really know, remains a spirit mentor; Mischa Titiev, whose sensitivity to his Hopi friends far overshadows all others in contributing a real understanding of Hopi life; Eric Douglas, who developed my interest in the museum representation of other cultures and an understanding of the wealth of native arts; Frederick Webb Hodge, from whom I gained a sense of ethnohistory and who provided a treasured link with the past; and lastly, Tom Bahti, an unsung hero of the Indian art world, whose perceptive, witty, and shrewd observations were invaluable. They are not forgotten.

But new friends have stepped into their moccasins, helping me to grow, as well as providing the arena in which to debate ideas, form theories, and share interests; among these, certainly the most influential continues to be Robert T. Hatt, friend and mentor. He is closely followed by many to whom I am delighted to acknowledge my indebtedness: Fred Kabotie, Pál Keleman, Edwin Earle, Gene Meany Hodge, Sallie Wagner, Erik Bromberg, Mark Bahti, David Harner, and Nathan Shippee. Professionally, the supervisory hand of Luther Wilson and the editorial eye of David Holtby of the University of New Mexico Press cannot go unnoted; their friendly criticism and interest in working this volume into print are acknowledged with pleasure. The willing cooperation of Mary Davis and the staff of the Huntington Free Library provided the bibliographical assistance that is indispensable in such an effort; and the long-enduring patience and support of my wife, Alice, remains a comfort.

But in the last analysis, it is the Hopi people themselves to whom the greatest debt is due. Their strength in the face of tremendous internal and external strains, maintenance of their religious life at considerable cost in comfort, and the promise of a continuance of that culture, makes any writing of this nature presumptuous. If it serves as a recognition of the qualities of the people, and a means of expanding the awareness of others to a way of life which I deeply admire, this book has well served its purpose.

The Kachina
and the
White Man

I.

The Hopi World

PERCHED IN SPLENDID ISOLATION upon three mesas that jut into the Painted Desert of northeastern Arizona, some 8,755 Hopi Indians live on a Reservation set aside by presidential executive order in 1882 (Fig. 1). According to archeological evidence, the Hopis are the descendents of Pueblo Indians who have inhabited the southwestern United States since the dawn of the Christian era; 11 A.D. has been definitely established as a time of early occupancy (Smiley, 1951, p. 6). The Hopi language, belonging to the Uto-Aztecan linguistic family, suggests a relationship with the early Aztecs. For many centuries before settling in their present location, the ancestral Hopis moved from place to place throughout Utah, Arizona, and New Mexico. Examples of their architectural skill may be seen today in such National Monuments as Wupatki, Montezuma's Castle, Keet Seel and nearby Betatakin, as well as in many of the other ruins which dot the northeastern Arizona plateau area (Fig. 1).

The present-day Hopi villages are a mixture of extreme antiquity and modernity. Of the twelve villages now inhabited, two were established as recently as 1910, whereas the oldest, Oraibi, dates from about 1125 A.D.—therefore it can claim the distinction of being the oldest continuously-inhabited town in the United States.

There were, at various times, many other Hopi villages, of which Awátovi, Sikyatki, and Kawaika-a are the best known. These were abandoned for various reasons, but their number and distribution demonstrate the considerable importance of the Hopi people during their "Golden Age" (just prior to invasion by the Spaniards).

The surrounding country has affected Hopi life to such an extent that its geography cannot be ignored in any study of the people. At one time grass grew thickly on the area, but over-use of the land by an ever-increasing population has resulted in erosion to such an extent that the once lush ground covering is gone. Now, scrub bush and bunch grasses are seen, yucca is fairly plentiful, and cottonwood trees grow along the larger streams. To the west are extensive conifer forests, while south of the area, belts of piñón, cedar, and juniper are found. Growing at an altitude of about 6,000 feet, the flora of the Hopi area must subsist in a porous, sandy-clay soil on a rainfall of 10 to 13 inches per year. The temperature variation of the country is extreme: on the average, daily temperatures vary by about 30 degrees. The average annual growing season is only 130 days.

The whole Reservation area as set aside in 1882 was, even then, barely able to sustain the Hopi population—and this situation has become even more aggravated by the arbitrary establishment in 1943 of a subdivision known as "District 6," to which the Hopis were restricted (Fig. 1). The Indian Bureau gave the remainder of this land to the Navajos at the expense of sedentary Hopis who unfortunately could less easily move elsewhere, due both to their deep attachment to the mesaland, and (more importantly) the pueblo architecture. This limitation, in addition to the increased White settlement of the Southwest, has intensified pressures in the area to a point where neither Indian group is able to support itself adequately from the land.

The Hopis have been able to maintain a sedentary culture in this inhospitable environment only by developing, through years of experience, an ingenious and expert system of intensive agriculture. Fortunately, there are scattered areas of fertile soils which need only moisture to yield ample crops; but in this region moisture is life, and extreme drought is often imminent. In normal years, the Hopis can support themselves; in times of drought, they are in serious trouble.

In prehistoric times, the Hopis raised maize, pumpkins, kidney and tepary beans, and cotton, as well as various gourds. In more recent times, they have been introduced to peaches, chili peppers, watermelons, wheat, and squash, while the raising of cotton has been superseded by the White man's more easily obtained machine-made textiles.

The fauna of the immediate area is limited to the smaller game animals, including rabbits, prairie dogs, foxes, coyotes, owls, hawks, and eagles. Reptile life includes numerous varieties of snakes and lizards. Farther afield, in the forests to the west, are larger game animals, such as deer, elk, bear, and turkey. In early days, antelope

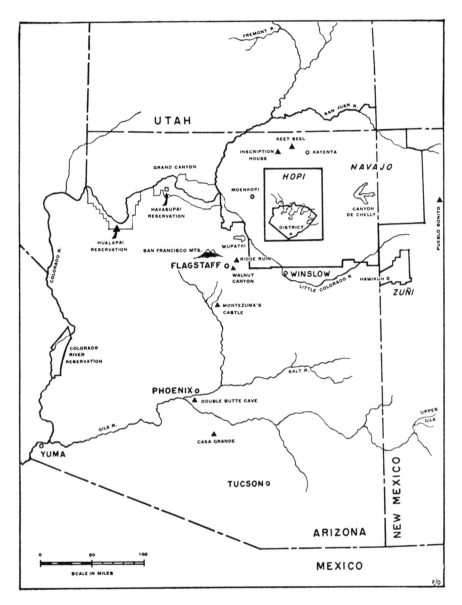

Figure 1. The Hopi Reservation and neighboring areas.

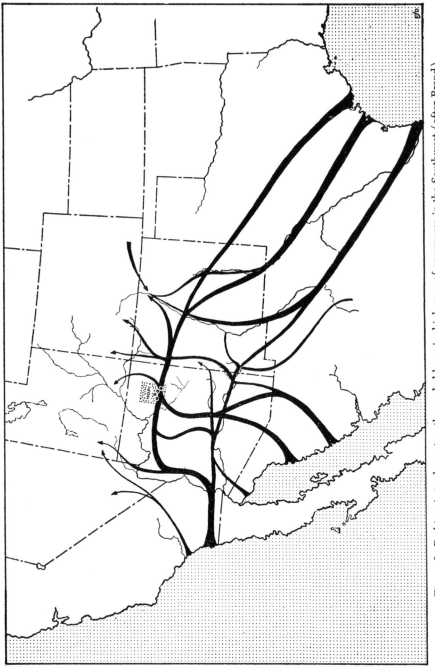

Figure 2. Prehistoric trade routes; the probable major highways of commerce in the Southwest (after Brand).

and mountain sheep were plentiful in the neighboring mountain and plateau areas, but the White man depleted their numbers; only in recent years has the game-management program stimulated their return. The Hopis are known to have domesticated the turkey and dog in prehistoric times, but cattle, horses, and the domestic sheep were unknown until brought in by the Spaniards.

During the centuries of nomadism over the Southwest, and the eventual establishment of their present settlements, and despite the continuing struggle against the forces of nature and alien peoples, a unique and lasting culture developed. The Hopis are unique among Amerind peoples in that they live in the "old ways" more than any other North American tribe. This presents the scholar with an opportunity unparalleled elsewhere in North America to study pre-Columbian Indian culture in action, and gives the traveler a brief view of one segment of America much as it was in 1492 A.D.

ALIEN CONTACTS BEFORE THE SPANIARDS: INTER-TRIBAL TRADE ROUTES.

In order to understand how the Hopis receive outside influences, it is appropriate that we examine the degree of contact they made with neighboring tribes in prehistoric times. These influences are today one of the most difficult problems facing the comparative ethnologist. Some contemporary intra-Indian influences can be fairly substantially demonstrated; but of the prehistoric exchanges we can only suggest which types of contact probably took place, and surmise the degree of resultant influence.

The geographical locality of the early Pueblo people embraces such a relatively limited area that the various tribal units must have known and visited one another fairly regularly. This is evidenced by the general uniformity of culture, certain obvious borrowings, and examples of cultural intermingling frequently recovered from excavations.

There was also regular, though less frequent, contact with Indians living in areas far afield from the Hopis. The latter, in the role of trading middlemen, traveled over several long-established trade-routes, which were recognized highways over which each group bartered with others for needed objects, giving in exchange their own products or articles which they had received in trade.

There seem to have been three major trading areas with well-defined routes (Fig. 2), and from each area the Hopis received certain objects in which that area specialized. These areas were: [1] the Pacific Coastal region, centering in Southern California, from which articles went to the Hopis via the Mojave, Huálapai, and Havasupai tribes; [2] the Lower California-Mexico area, from the mouth of the Colorado River, Gulf of California, and west coast of Mexico, from

6　which trade objects went north through the Pima and Pápago peoples; and [3] the territory along the Gulf of Mexico, centering along the southern coast of Texas. For the most part, objects traveling through this section were brought into the Hopi area by Río Grande, Acoma, and Zuñi tribesmen. There were many secondary routes, but these three highways seem to have carried most of the trade between Tusayan and outside tribes (Brand, 1938, pp. 3–10).

Of the above areas, the first specialized in the exchange of shells, pottery, textiles, and hides; the second featured shells, pottery, parrots and macaws (for their ceremonially-important feathers), stone, and copper articles; while the third, which seems to be the least important, was a source of exchange in shells, turquoise, lignite, and textiles (Colton, 1941, pp. 308ff.). That these routes were not short-range affairs is demonstrated by one remarkable find at Pueblo Bonito of a pottery bowl believed to have come from central Mexico—a distance of over 1,300 miles.

It should be pointed out here that one of the major points of Hopi contact was through the village of Awátovi. A glance at the map (Fig. 3) will show how the peripheral location of this village made it necessarily the outpost for Hopi contacts with the Eastern tribes, and it had the large population needed for commercial importance. The result was a cosmopolitan, sophisticated flavor far surpassing that of the other villages. Hence, it would not only be more receptive to new ideas, but would in turn be responsible for introducing many innovations to the several other Hopi towns—for, although the purpose of this inter-tribal trade was to barter material objects, it should be kept in mind that an equally important transfer of ideas, language, and other non-material culture took place.

Moreover, these trade routes continued well into the historic period; for Antonio Armijo, on his way to California in 1830, mentioned connecting with the "well-known trade route" which the Hopis used in trading shells with the Mojave Indians.

GROWTH OF THE HOPI RELIGION

The Hopi way of life represents the gradual establishment of an harmonious but precarious relationship between man and nature. Faced with the ever-present threat of water shortage, as well as with the absolute necessity of inducing the land to yield an adequate living, the Hopis were made fully aware of the need to adjust their lives so as not to disturb the delicate balance of nature in the Southwest.

With an economy whose equilibrium can be upset by many factors, such as unwise crop planning, drought, enemy raids, and (more recently, due to increased erosion) flood hazard, it is not surprising to find that the Hopis have a strong feeling of insecurity, or that they

have highly developed and maintained the bulwark of all peoples
faced with problems beyond their immediate power to solve—religion. The Hopi religious creed reflects all the varying needs of the
people, as well as the effort to compensate for, counterbalance, or
obtain protection against, the uncertainties of their society.

A detailed calendar of religious ceremonies has been evolved to
provide, at stated times, the needed supernatural aid and encouragement. Only four of these religious ceremonies will be emphasized in
this study, but it may be well to list briefly the year's major religious
activities:

December	Soyala	Winter solstice rites
February	Powamû	First major Kachina rites
July	Nimán	Last major Kachina rites
August	Chüchübtî	Rites of the Snake and Antelope fraternities, alternating with those of the Flute Societies
September	Maraû	Women's society function
October	Oáqöl	Women's society function
November	Wüwüchim	Tribal initiation ritual

While there are other religious rites of lesser consequence, these
seven are performed regularly. Earle and Kennard (1938, p. 3) have
pointed out that these ceremonies, in addition to their frequent observance, and their importance in Hopi eyes, warrant mention for
certain other aspects common to all seven:

Each is conducted by one or more chiefs whose offices are
hereditary. Each begins with an announcement at sunrise, has
eight days of secret rites and is concluded with a public dance
on the ninth day. Each has as its primary aim the production of
rain, fertility, and growth. Each imposes purification taboos upon its members. In addition, all ceremonies use the following
specific techniques: preparation and offering of prayer sticks,
building an altar of sacred objects, smoking, sprinkling medicine, prayer, song, and dance.

The Snake-Antelope (Chüchübtî) rites, a solar observance, are
perhaps the best known to White tourists, since they include the
highly-publicized Snake Dance. Unfortunately, this ceremony holds
such fascination for Whites that its importance has been exaggerated
far beyond its original place in the Hopi ceremonial world. This is
well stated by Earle and Kennard (1938, p. 1):

Although the Snake Dance . . . has attracted the most attention
and draws great throngs of visitors from the outside world no
such emphasis is placed upon it by the Hopi. For them it is but

one of many rites each of which has its fixed place in the calendar, and its eight days of esoteric activity are as secret to the uninitiated Hopi as they are to the casual visitor. The Kachina cult, however, is distinguished from the others in that every man, woman, and child is initiated into it and every man takes an active part in its dances throughout his life.

Alternating biennially with the ceremonies of the Snake and Antelope Societies are those of the Gray Flute and Blue Flute Societies which perform their ritual activities coöperatively.

The complicated ritual of the Wüwüchim ceremonies is also extremely important. It is at this period that "boys become men"; all males go through the ceremonies, usually at about the age of ten or twelve. In addition to the rite leading to the attainment of adult status, the Wüwüchim ceremonies are concerned with the Hopi genesis, life after death, war and hunting, and fertility.

A third group of important ceremonies is the Soyala, held in December, whose purpose is to induce the sun to start on the first half of its journey. Soyala activity is extended to almost all members of the village, although somewhat limited in the case of women. In some respects Soyala is the peak of ceremonial achievement for the lay Hopi. It is at these ceremonies that the Kachina season is opened; for after the appearance of Şoyál Kachina, other Kachinas may appear at any time during the next six months. In considering the religious life of the Hopis, it should be noted that whereas the other ceremonies are essentially of short duration, lasting usually for a set period of days, the Kachina "season" extends over a half-year period.

Each of the ceremonies discussed above concerns certain traditional functions. The pattern has been set by age-old usage, and the object of these rites is essentially the tribal welfare. There also seems to have been an early need for some religious activity in which each individual Hopi could not only work for the public good, but demonstrate his *personal* piety and devotion. This brings us, then, to a consideration of the Kachina Cult itself, for no other Hopi ritual offers the individual such opportunity for personal expression of devout adherence to the Hopi religion.

II.

The Kachina Cult

In MANY WAYS the Kachina Cult and its ritual are the most important ceremonial observances in the Hopi religious calendar. This prominence seems to have increased in recent years—an interesting fact in view of the prediction of many ethnologists that the Kachina was doomed to early extinction (e.g., Fewkes, 1901, p. 81).

The term *Kachina* means several things to the Hopis. Etymologically, it may mean "life father," or "spirit father" (*kachi,* life or spirit; *na,* father). However, many Hopis trace it to *kāchi,* "to recline" —thus, a "sitter," i.e., one who sits with the people (and among other things, listens to their petitions for rain and other spiritual and material blessings). The name primarily refers to supernatural beings who are believed to visit the Hopi villages during the first half of the year. These beings have the power to bring rain, exercise control over the weather, help in many of the everyday activities of the villages, punish offenders of ceremonial or social laws, and in general act as a link between gods and mortals. Their functions also extend to the non-religious sphere, since some Kachinas often appear for entertainment purposes, dancing and performing for the pleasure and amusement of the spectators.

The second meaning of the term is that which most White tourists have in mind and is almost coequal with the first in Hopi thinking: this refers to the masked impersonators who appear in traditional costumes at the various ceremonies. Not only is the term *Kachina* applied to each impersonator in the performance of his particular religious function, but in a very real sense the impersonators are regarded as taking on supernatural qualities (and thus *becoming* Kachinas) with the placing of the masks on their heads.

Just as a White religious participant believes that his own ecclesiastic hierarchs achieve something of a spiritual ennoblement when dressed in liturgical vestments, so a Hopi believes that when he wears the costume and mask of a particular Kachina, he loses his personal identity and is imbued with the spirit of that being. As he not only gains certain spiritual powers but assumes tremendous responsibilities, the role is one which is not lightly undertaken. He is subject to the requirements of pure thinking, pure action, ritual celibacy, and other proscriptions. If the ceremonies do not achieve the desired result, the fact is usually attributed to the human failure of the impersonators to observe the several tabus.

Often the statement is made that the term Kachina applies to the small brightly painted wooden "dolls" which are miniature representations of the masked impersonators. Actually, such a carving is called a *tihü* (a figurine), or *Kachintihü* when a more specific term is desired.

Neither the Hopis of today, nor those as far back as we have any reliable accounts, *worship* the Kachinas, nor is there any hint of idolatry in the Hopis' use of the *Kachintihü*. Kachina impersonators have no exalted status in their everyday life as a result of their participation in Kachina ceremonies, other than the temporary *noli me tangere* that accompanies the role, and the responsibility for adhering to tradition in order to secure maximum benefits for the people. The Kachina spirits cannot be termed "gods" in any correct use of the word. Their function is to listen to the priest, usually a tribal elder, who transmits to them the prayers of the people; and the Kachinas are expected to carry these petitions to the gods, thus becoming spiritual messengers for mortals. Kachinas are also regarded as representing the spirits of the dead—there seems to be a belief that some sort of occult communication exists between the living and the dead through the medium of the Kachinas.[*]

THE ORIGIN OF THE KACHINAS

According to one version of Hopi belief, the Kachinas were beneficent spirit-beings who came with the Hopis from the Underworld, whence came all people. The Kachinas wandered with the Hopis over the world until they arrived at Casa Grande, near present-day Phoenix, Arizona, where both the Hopis and the Kachinas settled for a while. With their powerful ceremonies, the Kachinas brought rain for the crops and were in general of much help and comfort. But all of the Kachinas were killed when the Hopis were attacked

---

[*]Although the correct plural, in Hopi, of *Kachina* is *Kachínam*, I use the more familiar Anglicized Kachinas for the reader's convenience. Likewise Kachinmámamt' is Hopi, whereas I use *Kachinmanas* throughout—and I believe it will be more useful for the English-speaking reader to read *tihüs* in place of the Hopi plural: *tit-hü*.

by enemies (now usually spoken of as Mexicans—a pre- or post-Spanish concept?) and their souls returned to the Underworld. Since the sacred paraphernalia of the Kachinas were left behind, the Hopis began impersonating the Kachinas, wearing their masks and costumes, and imitating their ceremonies, in order to bring rain, good crops, and life's happiness.

Another version says that in an early period the Kachinas danced for the Hopis, bringing them rain and all the many blessings of life. But eventually the Hopis came to take the Kachinas for granted, losing all respect and reverence for them, so the Kachinas finally left and returned to the Underworld. But before they left, the Kachinas taught some of their ceremonies to a few faithful young men and showed them how to make the masks and costumes. When the other Hopis realized their loss, they remorsefully turned to the human substitute-Kachinas, and the ceremonies have continued since that time.

While legendary accounts describe the origin of the Kachinas as a group, individual new Kachinas are introduced from time to time. Some developed from village history, such as Hühüwa and He-é-e Kachinas. Hühüwa Kachina is said to be the spirit of a man from Mishongnovi who died some seventy-five years ago (Colton, 1949, p. 49), while legend relates that He-é-e Kachina was a Hopi maiden who successfully defended her village against raiding Ute warriors. Some resulted from the invention of an individual Hopi. The traditional origin of Movitkúntäqä Kachina is illustrative of this method. A young Hopi had a dream, in which the costume and mask appeared to him. He related his dream, taught the songs he had composed to his kiva mates, and the result was a new Kachina. There are several which have developed from dreams in this manner.

A number were introduced by Hopis who had seen dances in other pueblos, or even in non-pueblo areas; and some were adapted from dances presented in the village areas by visiting Indians. Some admittedly and obviously were taken over from such neighboring pueblos as Zuñi, Acoma, or Jémez; and a few were taken from non-pueblo tribes such as the Navajo, Comanche, or Havasupai.

To my knowledge there is no Kachina which has been taken over from White culture that represents a White individual or White ceremonial functions.* Legendary accounts say that **Chákwaina Kachina** (Plate 1) represents Estebán, the Negro or Moor guide, who led Fray Marcos de Niza to Cíbola in 1539 and was killed at Hawikuh for his arrogant behavior and molestation of Indian women (Colton, 1947a, p. 47). The appearance of this Kachina and the fact that Chákwaina is known in all the pueblos as a horrible ogre, support this legend. Estebán would be remembered because of the

---

*Some Hopis claim that Ahöli Kachina represents a Catholic bishop, reminder of their 1680 victory over the Spaniards "to put the bishop in his place [as secondary to the Kachinas]." If so, this is certainly a very modern idea, since only priests were in the Hopi country, until 1680, and almost none, especially bishops, came into the area subsequently. The visual similarity of the costume, though impressive, would seem only coincidental (see Fig. 14).

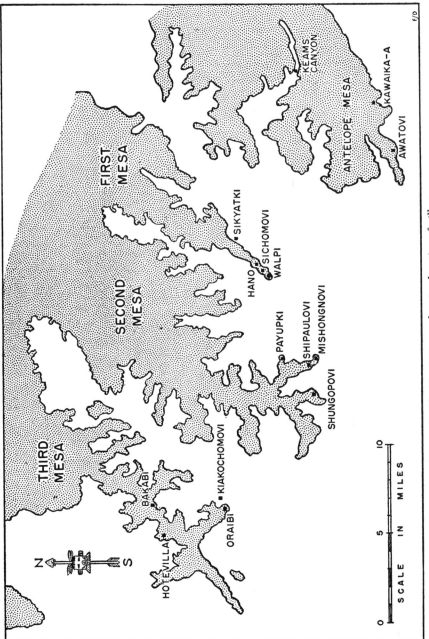

Figure 3. The Hopi Mesas; showing location of villages.

color of his skin, because he was the first non-Indian seen in Cíbola, and because of the circumstances surrounding his fate.

There are several Kachinas which have been created as a result of the introduction of European material culture. Some of these betray their foreign origin by their names: Wakás, the Cow, whose name obviously derives from the Spanish *vaca;* Kavayo Kachina, the Horse, from *caballo;* and Kanela Kachina, the Sheep, from *carnero.* These three animals were unknown to the Hopis prior to 1540.

A few other Kachinas which can be traced to alien sources by some obvious characteristic of costume, function, or nomenclature, include Tsilî (Chili Pepper) Kachina, Kowako (Rooster) Kachina, and Pichoti (Pig) Kachina.

If the first few performances of a newly-introduced Kachina are usually followed by good weather, rain, and fertile crops, he is adopted for regular performance, and becomes an integral part of the Cult; if, on the other hand, severe storms, drought, or poor crops follow, he is "put on the shelf," and rarely, if ever, appears again. Doubtless many have disappeared into oblivion in the past in just such a way. A modern example of this is Movitkúntäqä Kachina, whose power seemed too dangerous in Hopi minds. Whenever he appeared, hail or sleet storms ensued, so he is now rarely presented, although Movitkúntäqä *Kachintihü* are still carved.

There seems to be a fairly free attitude of acceptance on the part of the Hopis in taking over new or alien Kachinas, although there is a natural feeling that the original Hopi Kachinas are superior in power, prestige, and dancing skill. For the most part, those Kachinas which are freely admitted to be created recently or derived from other tribes are of a more social nature, and appear to have a less marked aura of sanctity than those which are regarded by the Hopis as being ancient and truly native. An exception to this seems to be Hümis Kachina: he is generally regarded as originating at Jémez Pueblo but is held in extreme reverence. The Hopi attitude toward Añákchina, probably the most frequently presented of all Hopi Kachinas, is one of thorough acceptance and respect. The mask and costume of Añákchina is similar to the Zuñi *Kókoshi,* but if he is of Zuñi origin, the borrowing happened so long ago that the fact has been completely forgotten.

SECONDARY ELEMENTS IN THE CULT

The Underworld, whence came the original Kachinas, is a concept common to all the Pueblo Indians and constantly encountered in their folklore. It is the place where the spirits or shades live: the newly born come from there and the dead return there.

14   Beings of the Underworld are thought to follow a pattern of existence similar to that of the living:

> There seems to be in the minds of the Hopi priests a recognition that the life of the Katcinas or ghostly inhabitants of the realm of the dead is somewhat like that on earth and that their sociological condition reflects the same. The inhabitants of the lower world are arranged in clans the same as on earth. Legends indicate that the deceased Hopi plant and harvest, that the dead have ceremonies and altars, or, in other words, that the customs of those who occupy the abode of the dead resemble those living on earth (Fewkes, 1922, p. 490).

Thus the Kachina concept contains a vague connotation of the spirits of the dead and the Kachina ceremonies include a hazy idea of memorialization of the departed. It may be said with some truth that the multitudes of departed ancestors have come to be regarded as Kachinas. But for the most part, there seems to be no individualization in such ancestor memorialization: the names by which the Kachinas are known have apparently little traceable connection with dead individuals. There are two or three Kachinas who supposedly represent definite individuals, but the accounts of these are rather hazy. Examples are Hühüwa and He-é-e Kachina mentioned above.

A few Kachinas function as clan ancestors: the names by which some of the ancient Kachinas are known are the same as clan names, and living clan members claim that the Kachina of the same name as their clan is also their clan "ancient," or ancestor (*wöye*). Usually the *wöye* masks are kept in the custody of their respective clan mothers, who see to their safe-keeping, and ritually feed them regularly.

The totemic aspect is present, but very few of the Kachinas that are traditionally regarded as the most ancient have any marked totemic character—most of the apparently totemic Kachinas seem of more recent origin, and some are of recognizably alien provenience, either alien-Indian or White.

Fewkes (1901, p. 91) clearly expresses the subtlety of these two elements in the Kachina Cult:

> Katcina worship . . . is not that of an animal, plant, or other object which has given a totem, name, or symbol to a clan. It is not what is ordinarily called totemism, nor, strictly speaking, ancestor worship, for in a system of clans with matriarchal

---

Plate I. Chákwaina Kachina
The "monster Kachina" who reputedly represents Estebán, the first European to enter the Pueblo area.

descent, the male ancients are not parents or ancestors of the living members of the clan. They are simply ancient members of the same; their sisters are literally ancestors of the worshippers.

Other elements are interwoven into the Cult, many of them even more difficult to isolate. For example, sun worship is discernible in the Kachina Cult, notably in the performance of Ähül Kachina. The development of this phase has been traced by Fewkes (1920). The fact that several mask designs parallel the Tawa (Sun) Kachina mask is of interest, and will be discussed more fully in Chapter III.

However, a Hopi does not analyze the Cult. As Earle and Kennard (1938, p. 2) point out:

> Hopi interests . . . are centered much more upon the actual appearance and performance of the Kachinas in the village than on the ideological background. While any Hopi can describe in detail the costume, songs, dance steps of a great number of Kachinas he remains comfortably vague on the subject of their relations to the forces of the universe, the nature of their power, and the fate of the soul after death. Frequently, members of other cult groups hold beliefs at variance with those of the Kachina cult. All ceremonies are for rain and the correct performance of numerous ritual acts brings the desired result . . . There is no tendency to develop a unified conception of the universe, to identify specific deities of their mythology with natural forces, nor to arrange them in a hierarchical system.

And Titiev (1944, p. 129):

> The complexities of their Katcina worship are of little moment to the Hopi. They make no effort to systematize or to classify their beliefs, but are content to regard the Katcinas as a host of benevolent spirits who have the best interests of the Hopi ever at heart.

THE DANCE AND ITS RITUAL

Kachina ceremonies and other Hopi rites take place in a *kiva* or *kísonvi*. A kiva is an underground room, rectangular in shape, with entry from above by means of a ladder. The floor is of packed earth or of flagstone, and is raised eight or ten inches at one end to provide a platform for spectators during ceremonies. The lower portion,

---

Plate II. Hümis Kachina
Frequently mis-called Nimán Kachina, *because he is commonly seen at the rituals held to celebrate the Hopi Nimán Ceremony.*

usually about two-thirds of the room space, is a "stage" for cere-monial performances. The kiva serves primarily as a place in which to hold regular ceremonies. Some of these are secret, others are not particularly esoteric but are held in the kiva because of unfavorable weather. The kiva is also a "lodge hall," or men's club, where the members may return to weave, do other handiwork, prepare cere-monial artifacts, carry on conversation, or escape from domestic worries. Each village has several of these sanctuaries, in which wom-en are only occasionally allowed.

The kísonvi is the court or plaza, usually in the center of the vil-lage, surrounded by houses on at least three sides. Entrances to this area are openings between buildings or covered entryways four to five feet wide. Normally rectangular in shape, and measuring about 100 by 150 feet, it provides a ground-level area where ordinarily the public daytime performances are held.

With the close of *Wüwüchim* (initiation) ceremonies in late No-vember, the stage is set for a completely new ceremonial organiza-tion. One of the Chief Kachinas (*moñkachinas*), Şoyál Kachina, rep-resenting great antiquity, opens the Kachina cycle. He appears on the day following the close of Wüwüchim and sixteen days before the *Soyala* (winter solstice) ceremonies. Since the Hopi believe that the Kachinas are sleeping in their Underworld homes or in caves on the slopes of the neighboring San Francisco Mountains, this first Kachina of the year to arrive at the village expresses by his behavior the torpid walk of one who has slept too long. He acts like a weary old man, staggering uncertainly, as if too weak for the exertion re-quired, and singing feebly in a very low voice (Şoyál songs are re-garded as being too sacred to be overheard by the spectators).

He totters over to Chief kiva, where Soyala rites are conducted (the Şoyál Kachina is usually impersonated by the chief of the Şoyál group), and performs the ceremonial "opening" of the village and the kiva for the *Soyáliiña*. On the last day of the ceremony, other Ka-chinas appear and "open" the other kivas. (On Third Mesa, a group of Qöqöqlö Kachinas perform this ritual opening of the kivas.) Thus begins the Kachina season.

Whereas the other religious ceremonies of the Hopis have certain set dates and rites to observe, the Kachina ritual is very flexible both in date and formula. Of the host of beings included in the ritual, only a handful of the most important have set times for their appear-ance—the others may perform at the pleasure of the village inhabit-ants. After the ceremonial opening of the Kachina season, any indi-vidual Kachina or group of Kachinas may be selected for presenta-tion. This selection is very informal: any Hopi may ask the Village Chief for permission to sponsor a ceremony. If there is no objection,

such as a conflict in date, consent is given. This fact is soon made
known to the village, and each kiva head selects the particular Kachina which his group will impersonate. Thus is inaugurated a series
of night dances in the various kivas—relatively short performances
in which the primary emphasis is visual. These dances are performed
quite freely between the time of Soyala in December and the beginning of Powamû in February.

Powamû, a nine-day ceremony, is the major ritual of the Kachina
Cult, during which other dance performances are suspended. Several
functions of varying importance are embodied in this ritual, including initiation into the Kachina Cult and (separate) initiation into
the Powamû fraternity. While any male initiated into the Kachina
Cult may participate in Kachina dances, only Powamû members may
act as kachina'amû (Kachina father or dance leader). There is also a
ritual to promote germination and fertility in the approaching season. Forced crops of beans are grown in the kiva and carried out into
the village by members of the fraternity. Dramatic performances
portray Hopi mythology in the appearances of certain wöye (clan
ancestor) Kachinas, such as Eótoto, the father of the Kachinas. The
importance of such village leaders as Şoyál Chief, Hónaû (Bear
Clan) Chief, and other clan officials is emphasized. Young initiates
are made acquainted with the many aspects of the Kachina myster-
ies. And finally, there is the curing or healing function (which has
not received adequate consideration in many studies of the Hopi
Kachina Cult), for Powamû is regarded as having strong medicine
for the cure of rheumatism (Stephen, 1936, p. 156). Powamû marks
the end of the first division of Kachina activity, for it completes the
period during which the Honáni (Badger) Clan has control of activities; at this time authority is tranferred to the leader of the Kachina
Clan.

Now night dances return for a while, and in large part the previous
activities under the Honáni Clan control are repeated, although additional Kachinas are frequently impersonated. It is during this
period that the Pálülükoñ (Horned Water Serpent) Ceremony is
performed, which, rich in symbolism, requires more ritual paraphernalia and preparation than any other Hopi religious observance.

The Pálülükoñ Ceremony is not to be confused with the Snake
Dance, which has no connection with the Kachina cycle and takes
place in August—long after the Kachinas have departed for the
Underworld. There is a close connection in the Hopi mind between
the Powamû and Pálülükoñ ceremonies. The main elements of similarity seem to be: the repeated use of forced-growth plants; the
drama of germination, crop, and harvest; the traveling from kiva to

18   kiva (a reflection of the all-inclusive quality of the Kachina?); and the replastering of the kiva walls (Titiev, 1944, pp. 114–120).

By the time these several ceremonies have taken place, it is early April, and winter has given way to milder weather, thus permitting day-long Kachina dances in the kísonvi. These are the most familiar to the non-Hopi, and they are among the most colorful dramatic performances of all North American Indian tribes.

As with the night dances, any man may sponsor a day dance; he need merely apply to the Village Chief. Usually permission is given, and the sponsor proceeds to select the Kachinas he will present. While any initiated male may participate, usually the dancers and officials for the ceremony come from the sponsor's kiva. Each man makes his own costume and mask, borrows whatever jewelry and finery he needs, and is responsible for making a good presentation.

Rehearsals are held in the sponsor's kiva, and since many of the steps, dance patterns, and formulae are traditional, not many practice sessions are needed. The sponsor composes new songs for the coming dance and teaches them to his mates. These songs, however, follow a general traditional pattern, so that learning them is somewhat akin to learning a new popular song in White culture. Finally the public ceremony is ready for presentation: rehearsals have been completed, prayer-sticks (paho) have been made, an all-night prayer and rehearsing session has been completed just prior to tíkive (the dance day), and the chaákmoñwi (crier) has made his announcement to the village.

On tíkive morning, the performers, painted and costumed, proceed to one of several shrines outside the village, where they ritually don their masks. In the regular dance pattern, there may be from thirty to forty performers, all costumed alike. With them often appears a group of several masked Kachinmanas (Kachina maidens), or female Kachinas, who are thought of as the sweethearts, or sometimes sisters, of the Kachinas (Plate XIII). These manas are usually men dressed as women. As the sun rises, they start for the village where they are met by the kachina'amû, usually an old man not in costume, who has the function of encouraging the dancers, guiding them, and offering to them the prayers of the villagers.

The typical organization and performance most commonly seen in the villages is as follows: the kachina'amû leads the dancers into the kísonvi, single file, along a path which he has created for them by sprinkling a line of sacred corn meal. (This ritual path represents symbolic feeding of the dancers to give them strength; frequently during the performance the father walks along the line of dancers, "feeding" them by sprinkling meal on their shoulders.) The dancers are led to the south side of the kísonvi, where they line up in single file, facing east. In this position, the leader of the dance group (who is always in the center of the line) shakes his rattle, starts the song, and the dancers on each side of him join in, one by one taking up the song and rhythm. Generally each dancer comes in on cue, down to both ends of the line, where the poorer singers and the neophytes are placed. This same pattern follows throughout the various songs which have been selected for the dance.

Upon completion of one rendition, the kachina'amû leads the dancers to the second position, along the east side of the kísonvi, facing north. The songs are repeated, and the dancers move to the north side, facing west. After the songs are repeated in this position, the dancers leave the kísonvi and go to a secluded section of the mesa, where they unmask, smoke, eat, and rest for a while. Following a brief rehearsal of the next song-set, they mask and return to the village for another round of dancing.

This sequence continues from dawn until sundown, with a longer break at noontime for lunch which is brought to them by women of their own clan. The major responsibility for providing this food rests upon the family of the dance sponsor.

A second type of dance performance adheres more closely to the Río Grande pattern. The dancers, costumed alike, do not sing; instead, as in the eastern pueblos, they are accompanied by a drummer and a "chorus," ordinarily composed of a dozen or so singers (usually older men) who are dressed in everyday clothes.

Usually the Kachina dancers bring various gifts on their first entrance, which they place in the center of the kísonvi. At the completion of the third song-set, the dancers break ranks and distribute the gifts to the spectators before leaving for their rest-period. These gifts are either from the Kachina impersonators or from non-participants who have requested a dancer to give an article in their behalf. Gifts vary, but a bow and arrow for a boy and a tihü for a girl are traditional; other items, such as food, store goods, and so on, are common nowadays.

During Kachina dances, very often a number of Táchüktî appear (Fig. 4).* These clowns, commonly called "Mudheads" because of their peculiar masks, participate at dances on a voluntary basis. There are several organized clown groups who may decide to take part, but individuals may also elect to give an impromptu show. Many of the clown pranks are satires aimed at Whites, or pantomimes of Hopi individuals; often they burlesque the Kachina dance. Some pranks are frankly obscene, and many are marked by gluttony.

---

*Although *Táchüktî* is their correct Hopi name, these masked clowns are more commonly known by the Zuñi term, *Koyemşi*—even in the Hopi area, strangely enough.

Usually they are of excellent dramatic quality, and the spectators howl with laughter at the absurd comedy.

The Táchükti have a privileged position in the Kachina observances. Not only do they have *carte blanche*, but supernatural power is attributed to them. They are immune from the tabu which forbids a lay spectator to touch a Kachina impersonator, and if a performer's costume shows signs of disarray, repairs are made by the Táchükti.

Another type of Kachina performance is the individual dancer. Kachinas of this class come into the village, not in groups of thirty or forty costumed alike, but singly, in pairs, or in small bands of half a dozen or so. These are frequently less dignified and less beautifully dramatic than the more "orthodox" beings—they are the "character actors" of the drama. Some have distinctive actions or calls

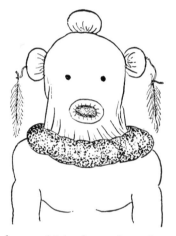

Figure 4. *Táchükti*. One of several types of "Mudhead" clown mask. Commonly called *Koyemşi*.

from which they often derive their names; others are known for unique costuming, while many are named for local animals or plants. They may come at almost any time during the Kachina season, even while the regular Kachinas are performing, or in Mixed Dances where many Kachinas, all costumed differently, appear (Plate XIV). But the greatest number are seen during the Powamù rites, when there is a regular "Kachina parade" (*qöqöntinumya*). On that particular occasion as many as fifty or sixty different Kachinas appear for the brief time of the parade, during which they roam through the village, each performing in his characteristic manner. Often the individual Kachinas come at odd times; for example, at the annual village coöperative activities such as spring cleaning. One group of Kachinas which appears at this activity, and also in conjunction with certain other regular or mixed performances is the Racing, or Wáwaş Kachinas. (Plate XII). These appear irregularly, usually early in the spring, and challenge the male spectators to a race. If the man wins, he is given a gift—but if he loses, then the Kachina may whip him, cut off a lock of hair, strip off his shirt, or inflict some other indignity on him, depending upon which Wáwaṣ the performer represents. The races are short—usually just across the plaza area, or around the village (For a good article on the whole aspect of Hopi racing, including the Wáwaṣ, *see* Titiev, 1939b).

Precisely what *is* and what *is not* a Kachina is sometimes difficult to determine. It is impossible to make a dogmatic statement, for there are several beings upon which not all Hopis agree. Parsons (1939, p. 730) has expressed it this way:

> A mask makes a kachina, but a kachina does not make a kachina ceremony, for kachina appear at the winter solstice ceremony or at the ceremony of a curing society, in fact on almost any ceremonial occasion, and almost any impersonation can be converted into a kachina [i.e., Buffalo dancers become "kachina" when wearing Buffalo Kachina masks, but are social dancers when appearing unmasked]. It is only when the kachina organization dominates the scene that we may consider the celebration a kachina performance.

However, it should be added that not all Kachinas are masked; for example, during the kiva Powamû ceremonies, the Powamû Kachina appears without a mask, yet is considered a fully qualified Kachina.

THE KACHINAS "GO HOME"

As the summer solstice approaches, the dance season draws to a close, and the final act in the Kachina drama begins. The Honáni Clan ushered in the Kachina ceremonies at Soyala, but the Kachina Clan has charge of the Kachinas' ceremonial departure from the villages to return to their legendary dwellings, there to rest from their ritual labors and take care of their own crops until the following winter, when the cycle begins all over again.

This *Nimán* (Going Home) Ceremony usually comes in July, and in many ways is the most dramatically impressive of the kísonvi dances. The Nimán observances are of sixteen days' duration, beginning four days after the summer solstice. Any Kachina may be selected; Hümis Kachina (Plate II) has come to be such a favorite that he is popularly known as "Nimán Kachina," although there is in fact, no such Kachina *per se*. Two other very popular Nimán performances are those of Añákchina (Plate III) and Táṣap Kachina (Plate IV). It is interesting to note that these three are quite distinctly "foreign"

Kachinas. (Hümis is derived from Jémez Pueblo, Táşap from the Navajos, and Añákchina comes from Zuñi.)

Each village has its own Nimán ceremony. The dance is often performed by different Kachinas at different villages—the village of Mishongnovi may decide to present Hümis Kachina, Añákchina will perhaps perform at Hotevilla, while Walpi may say its farewell with Malo Kachina. But the dance date does not differ greatly, since it is solstice-controlled.

The Nimán dance routine is much the same as that described above, except that it is usually performed with greater solemnity and more gifts are distributed. The Nimán ceremony has been likened to Christmas, since especial care is taken that no child shall fail to receive a gift at this time (Dockstader, 1944).

Just before the Kachinas leave the kísonvi for the last time, the kachina'amû, as tribal representative and spokesman, gives a long farewell speech in which he thanks the Kachinas for their blessings and benefits and prays for continued help and for rain. (A translation of one version of this farewell speech may be found in Earle and Kennard, 1938, pp. 37–38.) After a brief ceremony symbolizing the end of the Kachina season, the dancers unmask and return to their village homes.

The kivas are all ceremonially "closed" the next morning with a ritual performed by Eótoto Kachina and clan leaders. From then until Şoyál Kachina opens the season the following fall, no masked ceremonies may be presented. As with most Indian ceremonies, there is an exception to the rule—for Masaû Kachina occasionally appears during the closed season.* This is quite logical, for Masaû Kachina represents death, among other things—and the Hopis well know that death can come at any time.

The Number of Kachinas

Just what the total number of Kachinas is we do not know, for well-informed Hopis cannot agree. The usual estimate is that there are about 250 in all. In his classic study of Hopi Kachinas, Fewkes (1903) secured the services of what he considered to be both the best artist and the best-informed man among the Hopis at that time. By cross-checking this man's work with other Hopis, Fewkes was able to obtain information and pictorial material on about 185 Kachinas, plus some 35 additional beings whose nature was not entirely clear. During his 1882–94 First Mesa stay, Stephen (1936) listed some 140 Kachinas as appearing at various times, while the recent study published by Colton (1959) mentions 245, plus 21 for which

---

*For a vivid description of one such appearance, see Titiev (1944, pp. 236-238).

he has little or no information. My own material includes slightly
more than 400. Of this number, there are some on which I have little
data other than the fact of their existence and a pictorial representation. While Colton lists primarily those Kachinas which may be considered to be currently functioning, my listings, as well as those of
Fewkes and Stephen, include many which are not known to present-
day Hopis.

It seems probable that the number of Kachinas familiar to and
fairly regularly impersonated in the several villages today would not
include more than about 200. And, not all of the Hopis would be
able to identify all of these; the amount of "Kachina lore" possessed
by various individuals varies tremendously. This latter fact has con-
tributed greatly to the large amount of misinformation which exists
today concerning the Kachina.

For several reasons the number of Kachinas tends to be very flexible, making any summary survey very difficult. Although the majority by far are known and closely duplicated in all of the villages,
some may appear only at one mesa, and there are a few which are
observed apparently only in a single village. Furthermore, the same
name may be used in different villages to indicate totally dissimilar
Kachinas; or, conversely, the physical appearance of the Kachina
may be the same in two villages, but different names may be applied.

A few examples will serve to illustrate how complicated the situation can become. The First Mesa Kahaila Kachina has no similarity
in appearance or function to the Second Mesa being by the same
name; whereas Hótoto Kachina, although appearing in the same role
at First and Second Mesas, does not have the same mask design in
both areas. Ahülani, an important being at First Mesa, does not
appear at Third Mesa, while Qöchaf Kachina apparently appears
only at Second Mesa. Ota Kachina is similar in appearance and function to Kwasa'itäqä Kachina, and the same similarity exists between
Qáö Kachina and Avách'hoya Kachina. Many other instances of this
type of confusing duplication of nomenclature could be given.

Many Kachinas may be "multiplied" by color alone. Some preserve
the same mask design and the same name, modified only by a term
descriptive of the color variation. The mask color usually indicates
the compass direction whence comes the Kachina. Thus, there is not
only a Hónaû (Bear) Kachina, but there may also be Şakwa Hónaû
(Green Bear), Kücha Hónaû (White Bear) Kachina, and so on,
depending on where he is presumed to live. These are often called
merely "Hónaû Kachina," but they represent different beings to the
Hopi mind.

Moreover, the variation in individual ability must be taken into
account. Even though trained from boyhood to observe and continue

an artistic pattern (i.e., Kachina costumery), different Hopis will vary in their ability to paint mask designs and other ceremonial symbolism. Some will do an excellent job, while others may lack that skill to such an extent as to make important differences. Usually these are corrected by older men present; but occasionally they are not. A few will undergo slight changes at the hands of an esthetics-conscious Hopi; usually this is the result of outside schooling, or due to something seen in another village. There is, then, not often a series of masks painted in *exact* duplicate; and this, extended to its limit, may result in "new Kachinas." We can only guess to what extent this type of secondary invention has happened in the past.

This variety in mask design is not confined solely to the individual-type Kachinas, for I have seen instances where the regular group dancers demonstrate several variations of the same Kachina mask. One instance was in an appearance of Hote Kachinas in which some twenty-five were costumed with the conventional yellow masks; but in the same line dance were two white-masked dancers and three blue-masked dancers, all similarly costumed. Another variation in a line dance was noted in the performance of a group of Kachinmana who appeared together, but with some wearing white masks and others blue masks. Also, while most of the masks had black beards, three appeared with white beards.

At the risk of belaboring a point, this should be made clear: that although there is a strong respect for, and adherence to, tradition among the Hopis, this is not inflexible. The many human factors, such as artistic ability, convenience, materials at hand, quality of memory, and even a streak of individuality (albeit disapproved in Hopi society), often result in such wide variants in mask design that any attempt by non-Hopis to fully catalogue the Kachinas is inevitably confused by a fringe of enigmatic beings which seem to fit into no logical classification.

The more ancient Kachinas seem to persist fairly well, but the many individual types come and go, apparently rapidly. Many have disappeared from Hopi usage even in the brief fifty years since Fewkes made his classic study. On the other hand, almost an equal number of new beings have been created in the past half-century: Stephen (1936), for example, makes frequent reference to Kachinas which have been introduced recently, or which he had been told were "brand new."

VALUES INHERENT IN THE KACHINA CULT

To summarize all of the values inherent in the Kachina Cult is not easy, for many are so subtle as to escape analysis. Preëminent, of course, is the fact of universal participation—the Kachina Cult is the

only phase of Hopi religious life to which all belong. There is no
sense of exclusiveness or limited privilege. True enough, the Kachina
performances are essentially an all-male affair, and women are excluded from most of the ritual aspects of the Cult. Yet women may
participate as masked Kachina dancers in a few limited roles (e.g.,
Pachavuin Mana); they are all members of the Kachina society by
initiation and have a very real part in the activities. Their functions
also include supplying performers with food, holding custodianship
of the *wöye* masks, and maintaining ritual relationships through their
matriarchal activities.

The place of the child in the Cult is not inconsequential. Even
when still too young for initiation he figures importantly, receiving
gifts at the ceremonies and a careful education in Kachina lore.
Formerly, initiation for both boys and girls took place at about the
time of puberty, which had much the same maturity significance to
the Hopi as the magical age of twenty-one in White culture. But
today, school attendance, in particular, has made an adjustment
necessary: since the Hopis feel strongly that their children should be
initiated before their entry into the White world is complete, this
ritual may take place as early as eight or nine years of age. (Eggan,
1943, has written a penetrating analysis of some effects of this initiation on Hopi personality.) Young boys are given an early opportunity to participate on an adult level in the Kachina dances and are
accorded the same respect as an adult performer. One role, that of
Kókoşori Kachina, is traditionally reserved for young boys, while
several others, notably the Wáwaş Kachinas, are frequently impersonated by youths.

The Kachina Cult is in no sense an individual matter, but reflects
the coöperative character of Hopi life. Although the individual is
initiated, he derives only secondary benefit from this fact; the primary good accrues to the clan, or to the fraternity, and hence to the
tribe as a whole. The Kachinas bless the whole group, not the individual. While the Kachina may bring a material gift to a particular
child or adult, his important gifts—life-giving rain and assurances of
good crops—are given to the village at large. Even when Kachina
ceremonies are performed in order to cure a sick individual, this
benefit is interpreted as extending to the group. The ritual observances of the Kachina season, such as the system of sponsorship in
which one kiva opens and closes the season and other kivas function
in the interim, strengthen the sense of coöperative activity and internal cohesion. Thus there is provided a needed link between groups
which are often otherwise detached from each other; and each individual is given a sense of group security and defense against the
forces which beset him.

26   In addition, the Kachina calendar is well-integrated with the other religious activities by the coupling of the first masked appearances each year with the Wüwüchim and Soyala ceremonies, by Powamû initiations, and by the duplication or inclusion of other ritual observances within the Kachina framework.

In many ways, the Kachina Cult is a reflection of Hopi everyday life, thereby permitting the people to review ceremonially their own activities. There are the same family relationships, e.g. the Nataşka Kachinas (a family of mother, father, son, daughter, grandparents), and so on. Clan relationships are represented by a few traditional Kachinas, such as Ahül Kachina of the Patki Clan, Honáni Clan's Nakyacho Kachina, and Sítoto of the Piva Clan—although not all Kachinas belong to clans. Each of the daily concerns of the Hopi has one or more protagonists among the Kachinas: the Kachinmana grinds corn; Wáwaş Kachinas perform in athletic contests; procreation is represented by Mástop Kachina and Hehea Kachina; and there are others much too numerous to mention.

The disciplinary character of some of the Kachinas also helps to integrate the Cult with everyday life. When group work-parties are announced, usually one or more Kachinas accompany the group to encourage the workers and goad the lazy. At other times, certain Kachinas discipline youngsters, threaten or punish adults, and aid the Village Chief in maintaining peace in the village. During Kachina ceremonies, some Kachinas act as guards to keep away the uninitiated or to control the crowds at the public dances.

The fact that a Kachina can die out or be newly-introduced without disrupting the basic strength of the Cult is a further tribute to its flexibility. It is this ability to absorb the shock of change which has had much to do with the Hopis' unique talent in adjusting in their own way to the problems of living in a White world.

Curing is an added feature of the Cult. The Kachinas do not supplant the Hopi "medicine man," but they are empowered to cure (specifically, rheumatism); they may also inflict that same ailment upon those who transgress Kachina restrictions.

The pure fun-making aspect of the Cult should not be minimized. A people who are as prone to laughter as the Hopis would never flourish under a fearsome, doleful, Calvinist religion. Therefore the Kachinas who enact the roles of funmakers and clowns, playing tricks, acting out absurd pantomimes, or cleverly mimicking spectators, have as important a function in Kachina religious activity as joy and laughter do in Hopi daily life. Further, the burlesque drama and impersonations are opportunities to strike back at Hopi oppressors, for example the White man. This affords a psychological release that is important for a people such as the Hopis, who have a strong

inclination for peaceful living, and whose nature it is not to advocate 27
armed revolt unless the oppressive forces become as intolerable as
at the time of the 1680 Revolt.

The limited opportunity in Hopi life for individual expression, or
for the attainment of personal eminence, has often been mentioned.
A person who achieves prominence in the village through expression
of his own abilities or talents may be criticized by his neighbors, or
in extreme cases, may even be accused of being a witch. Likewise,
teachers have found that one sure way to failure in dealing with Hopi
students is to praise an individual highly, or to select one (or a few)
and elevate him to a prominent position as exemplary to the balance
of the class. This almost never succeeds, and usually results in un-
happiness for the selected student.

This constant pressure to conform to an accepted norm has its
psychological toll, and I believe that the pseudo-anonymity of the
masked dance may have a certain small measure of release worth
noting. Although the identity of the dancer is of course well known
to most of the village, when he dons the mask he is transformed into
the character of the Kachina he represents. In this secondary role,
he may demonstrate his every talent, "show off" to a certain extent,
and have little fear of criticism—in fact, may be silently commended
by the spectators. Even here, however, he is limited: he must observe
the traditionally-established characterization of the particular Kachina he impersonates, and if he goes too far in his individuality, he
risks being blamed should the dance fail to achieve the desired result.

Finally, to a group as artistic as the Hopis, I believe that the color
and pageantry of the Kachina Cult are not the least of its many posi-
tive values. As Titiev (1944, p. 129) says, "To impersonate . . . [the
Kachinas] is a pleasure, to observe them a delight. Quite apart from
its more formal features, the operation of the Katcina cycle brings
more warmth and color into the lives of the Hopi than any other
aspect of their culture." The Cult permits the expression of their
esthetic abilities in dance, drama, music, and visual arts to a far
greater degree than most religious ceremonials. Significant in this
connection, I think, is the fact that the Hopi's "popular songs"—those
he sings most frequently in everyday life—are the Kachina songs.

All in all, then, the Kachina Cult represents to the Hopi Indian an
unusually full experience; within its structure he can find ample
opportunity to express any emotion or idea that arises in his daily
life. Not only does it provide full expression for the religious and
spiritual needs of the people, but it also affords a satisfactory outlet
for the many social needs—neighborliness, behavior control, humor,
satire, burlesque, the "sacred and profane" aspects of sex, and finally,
the universal desire for esthetic expression.

A religion which demands a great deal of sedentary time for preparing costumes, masks, and other ceremonial objects, and for rehearsing songs and dances, could prosper only if this demand could be satisfied without upsetting the regular economy. The period during which the Kachina Cult flourishes is also the season during which Hopi economy makes the smallest demand; and in the farming season (late summer and early fall) the men are free to devote their full attention to crops. Thus the Hopis have been able to take care of all the needs of the Cult, and at the same time fulfill the requirements of daily life; both Cult and economy flourish under a system in which neither makes demands which interfere with the functions of the other.

KACHINAS IN OTHER TRIBES

It should not be thought that only the Hopi tribe observes the Kachina Cult in its religious calendar. With the possible exception of Taos, all of the other Pueblo villages in the Southwest observe the Kachina ritual in one way or another, even if this observance is quite sketchy in some areas. Zuñi has the nearest duplicate to the Hopi Kachina organization, and in many ways the two coincide so closely as to indicate a close relationship in the past. Many Hopi Kachinas carry Zuñi names, retain Zuñi legends, and are acknowledged by the Hopis as being of Zuñi provenience. Likewise, the Zuñis admit several of their own *Koko* as having come from the Hopis.

And indeed, the very use of the Zuñi word *Koko* is of help in tracing some of these Hopi beings, for a few bear names suggestive of hybrid origin. Kókopölö, Kókoṣori, Kokoshshóskoya, and perhaps Qöqöqlö, are examples of Hopi Kachinas now fully accepted, which seem to indicate this incorporation.

It is not difficult to name many other Kachinas of probable Zuñi origin, but it is exceedingly difficult, if not impossible, to establish when these might have been introduced. A few can be traced through accounts of some of the older Hopis; Stephen (1936), and Fewkes (1903, p. 125) have mentioned a few of the more recently-introduced beings from Zuñi. But many of those Kachinas which show evidence of Zuñi genesis, and are so accounted by the Hopis, may have been introduced at any time during the past several centuries of contact between the two tribes.

Which of the two Kachina organizations, Hopi or Zuñi, was developed first, is not possible to say at this time. There are contradictory legends on this score, and archeological investigation has not been able to answer the question so far. The Hopis have built their Cult into a more elaborate ritual and seem to have a greater sense of drama and artistry than the Zuñis. On the other hand, the latter

have developed a more sizeable folklore concerning their *Koko*.
There seems more discernible White influence in the Zuñi Cult, whereas the Hopis have thus far been able to resist this influence more successfully.

Since this study is not concerned with influences on the Kachina Cult exerted by other Indian tribes, we need not go into details of interchange. But it should be pointed out that through this avenue may well have come some White influences. For, although the Hopis were resistant to innovations of the White man, those same innovations, introduced under cover of Zuñi custom, would not be suspect.

Plate III. Añákchina
The "Long-Hair Kachina." This being represents one of the most commonly-performed Kachina dancers.

III.

Origin of the Kachina

WELL-SUBSTANTIATED ARCHEOLOGICAL EVIDENCE has established the occupation of Tusayan by Hopi or proto-Hopi peoples for well upwards of two thousand years, and definitely as early as 11 A.D. The earlier Puebloid folk may have differed slightly in physical or cultural characteristics, but they were essentially similar to the Hopis of today. They developed the basic cultural expressions upon which contemporary Hopi life was built; and although this culture changed, just as the Hopis themselves changed, the fundamental similarities can clearly be seen. Parallel features in the religious life of prehistoric and contemporary Pueblo peoples have been fully demonstrated by archeological investigation. The prehistoric origin of the Kachina Cult, however, has often been denied. For example, the theory has been long maintained by many authorities that the Kachina complex was but an outgrowth of Catholic hagiolatry interwoven with Pueblo religious practice. In fact, Elsie Clews Parsons, one of the most eminent scholars of Pueblo ceremonialism, strongly supported this view for years (Parsons, 1930), although she gradually changed her opinion as additional evidence was brought to her attention.

In order to establish the definite existence of the Kachina Cult prior to the arrival of the first Europeans in 1540, and to trace its early growth, it seems advisable to group the evidence and to follow each division to its logical conclusion.

Plate IV. Táşap Kachina
  This "Navajo Kachina" is very popular, and takes his name from the Navajo tribe, from whom he is reputedly derived.

Evidence of prehistoric origins of Indian cultures is in most cases fragmentary. Only when the materials include artifacts constructed from the more durable stone, clay, or metal substances do we have adequate data upon which to base conclusions, for articles of wood or fiber decay rapidly. It is in the arid Southwest alone that these perishable materials are found in any quantity in North American archeology; even here the finds are usually in such poor condition that their original function can only be theorized. The leather or cotton cords holding the various parts together disintegrate; insects and the action of the elements destroy the basic substance, as well as any surface decorations which might have aided identification. In fact, this class of material was so perishable that earlier archeologists perforce tended to pay less attention to it; their tools and techniques were such that quantities of such objects were necessarily lost upon recovery. Not only did the scientific investigator incline toward selectivity in what he saved, but he also looked rather definitely for specific artifacts. Durable materials were set aside and carefully numbered, for stone or ceramic artifacts were the prizes sought. Since materials of fiber, wood, or leather usually deteriorated almost immediately after exposure to the air, they not infrequently escaped the eye of the investigator.

By about 1930, however, technology brought many new preservatives to the field worker. Because of this, as well as more thorough basic training, widening interests and knowledge, and improved excavation techniques and transportation facilities, the recovery and preservation of such fragile materials has now become customary. It is not improbable that more will come to light as work progresses.

The difficulty is well-illustrated by a recent survey of masks in ethnological collections.* I found about 500 Pueblo Kachina masks gathered in less than a dozen institutions. Only some 200 of these masks were Hopi, most of which were made during the past seventy-five years; in no case did they antedate 1875. And yet these represent practically all that have been obtained from the untold numbers of Hopis who have lived in a limited area for the past thousand years. A great majority of these masks are in such poor condition, or are so adulterated or re-worked that they are almost useless for ethnological purposes. (Undoubtedly the original collectors were able to obtain the masks solely because they *were* in such unidentifiable condition!) I doubt that more than 100 masks in usable, excellent condition could be gathered from the Hopi collections at present known to me.

------

*I am greatly indebted to Dr. Frederic H. Douglas of the Denver Art Museum for his assistance in this survey.

It has long been argued that the most telling point against presuming an indigenous origin for Kachina ceremonies is the lack of definite prehistoric evidence concerning the Cult. In the words of Parsons (1930, p. 594), then a stout opponent of the Indian-origin theory: "It is highly significant that no archaeological Pueblo mask material has been found." There is much logic in this argument—it may well be expected that any cultural activity with a considerable amount of ceremonial paraphernalia should leave some traces, if it attained any great importance in the life of the people. That there are, in fact, such traces will be demonstrated in this chapter, but it may be well to review briefly the various causes for the paucity of material remains from earlier Kachina ceremonies.

(1) The early form of the Kachina Cult presumably represented that of any inchoate ritual. It probably started on a small scale, with its direction concentrated in the hands of relatively few advocates. Therefore, the quantity of masks and ritual paraphernalia at first probably would not be very large.

(2) If we can proceed from the assumed parallel of today's Hopi custom, the archeologist should not expect to find masks in graves. Today, many clans possess a mask, or masks, which they call their *wöye* (old man); kept within a maternal family in the clan, it is passed on at death to a ceremonial heir within this family. While the *wöye* masks are repainted whenever necessary, they are used only for the respective individual Kachinas which they represent. In the case of the regular *kütü* masks, these are personal property, but the masks are not buried with the owner. He may own several, if he is quite active in Kachina rites, but the masks are inherited by his son, brother, or nephew. These masks may be repainted to represent various Kachina beings, as desired. When they become too badly worn out to allow further use, any useful parts (ears, snouts, etc.) are salvaged and the rest is discarded—usually in such condition as to be unidentifiable. Parts from one mask are often used to patch up another, thus further completing the process of rendering identification impossible.

(3) If we may again assume that the early peoples followed the same practice as contemporary Hopis, the place of the masks in the Cult would have much to do with their absence from ruins. Contemporary masks, particularly the *wöye* type, are very carefully preserved and ritually fed daily. Under no circumstances are they supposed to leave the custody of their clan owner except for ceremonial use, and they usually occupy a special niche or space in the owner's home. This feeling is so strong that in many cases (particularly in the Río Grande area) outsiders are prevented from even learning where the masks are housed. The *kütü* masks, though less sacred in

34   Hopi eyes, are also carefully tended, often being stored in niches
built for that purpose in the kivas. If this attitude of care obtained
in prehistoric days, as seems logical, it cannot be expected that masks
would have been disposed of lightly. Thus, although many villages
were abandoned in ancient times—and in a few that desertion seems
to have been precipitous—it may be said with some certainty that
masks would have been the last thing the inhabitants would have
left behind. Therefore it does not seem very reasonable to expect
them to be found in ruins, even in their customary kiva niches. As for
pueblos abandoned in haste under hostile attack, too few sufficiently
undamaged to permit adequate research have yet been discovered.*

(4) Another reason that masks have not been found in abandoned
pueblos and other excavations lies in the repeated *autos-da-fé* which
the Spaniards held almost annually. One such example was during
the abortive attempt by Otermín to reconquer the pueblos two years
after the Pueblo Revolt (*see* p. 59). Special efforts were made to
destroy the Kachina ceremonial, which was apparently regarded by
the priests as comprising the heart of the Pueblo religion. Whenever
ceremonial paraphernalia, masks, and costumes were found, they
were immediately seized and burned. As a result the remaining masks
would be few, and zealously guarded; all new masks made since
that period would be given the same protection from prying or
censorious hands.

(5) Most of the paraphernalia used in connection with the Kachina Cult are extremely perishable. It is probable that the early
ceremonial costumes were made from fibers, skins, wood, and feathers—all subject to rapid deterioration. Thus, whatever discarded
materials might have been left, have long since decayed.

Petroglyphs and Pictographs. In the absence of actual Kachina masks
left from prehistoric times, we naturally look for portrayals of masks
or Kachina figures. To distinguish representations of Kachinas from
representations of animals and of the human face and figure among
Indian pictographs is not always a simple matter. The line of distinction is difficult to draw; but mask designs have developed characteristic stylizations in treating eyes, ears, mouths (or noses) to such an
extent that with familiarity it is possible to speak with some degree
of confidence in interpreting pictographs. Eyes on masks are usually
one of three types (although not necessarily matching); non-masked
faces commonly show only "dot" eyes, or occasionally may attempt
realism. In portraying the mask mouth, or nose, several styles are
used; these organs in the human representation are usually a dot, or

*An excellent review of the various theories attempting to account for the abandonment of
the many prehistoric villages, with critical comment, is given in Brew (1946), pp. 298-301.

sometimes altogether missing. But it is the ears which seem to provide the most definite clue: in the gravings of human faces, the ears are frequently missing or form a very minor feature. In depicting masked beings, however, the ancient artists usually emphasized the ears, in close similarity to the large, wooden ears commonly attached to the Kachina mask today. Other elements—mask shape, mask ornament or headdress, horns, and body costume or attributes—all help in the distinction. With these differences as criteria, it is possible to select certain pictographs as definite attempts to portray masked figures. (see Reagan, 1935, for suggestions pertinent to this problem.)

This type of art, however, offers at once the most tempting and the most frustrating evidence available. Indisputable representations of masked dancers too numerous to mention have been found distributed widely over the Southwest, from Utah and Nevada south through Arizona, New Mexico, and west Texas. Unfortunately for research purposes, only a few of these can be dated with any degree of accuracy. It is possible in some instances to establish relative dating; but this at best is only accurate to within a century or so, and usually includes a much longer span. The petroglyphs, therefore, are of little value except as supporting evidence, for dates of rock gravings found in the area outlined cover the past thousand years. In some instances these gravings parallel contemporary mask designs; and they are spread over such a wide area that they offer interesting possibilities for speculation concerning the prehistoric spread of masked ceremonies.

Although the total number could be extended to unwieldy lengths, I have arbitrarily selected a few gravings which seem to contain elements strongly suggestive of the masking complex—bearing in mind the restrictions set down above.

The mask shown in Fig. 5a is from Fall Ranch, Arizona, and is, as Steward remarks (1929, p. 158), "highly suggestive of some of the kachina dance masks of the Pueblo Indians." He also illustrates (ibid., p. 183) another extremely interesting petroglyph which he found north of Kayenta (Fig. 5b). This is notable for the close similarity to one of the apparently masked beings in the Kuaua murals (see Fig. 9b).

Jackson (1938, p. 17) reproduces one of the few pictographs which unquestionably depict a mask (Fig. 5c). Located near El Paso, Texas, the design is executed in red and green. In Plate CCLXV of the same work, he reproduces three facial designs which are not only strongly suggestive of masks but contain elements which can be demonstrated in current Hopi usage (Fig. 5d–f). These four would seem to indicate that masks were known at least this far southeastward.

36

Figure 5. Pictographs suggestive of masked beings:
a-b, Arizona; c-f, Texas; g-h, Utah; i-n, New Mexico
(a-b, after Steward; c-f, after Jackson; g-h, after Morss; i-n, after Sims).

Figure 6. Pictographs of Kachina masks located near the Hopi villages (after Fewkes and Stephens).

38   Two petroglyphs reproduced in Morss (1931, pp. 34ff.) from the Fremont River area, Utah, offer possible evidence of masked figures in this area, due north from the Hopi villages (Fig. 5g, h); and Reagan (1931) presents additional specimens from the same area. Sims (1950, Plate V, VII) illustrates several obviously masked figures from San Cristóbal, of which I reproduce six here (Fig. 5 i–n). While some of these are less convincing than others, they offer interesting parallels to certain figures in the Awátovi-Kawaika-a murals as well as present-day Kachinas. Especial note should be taken of the conical cap (Fig. 5j) and the speculative depiction of a *hürünkwa* (warrior feathers) (Fig. 5m).

To return our attention to the area of the Hopi villages, it seems desirable to consider such mask petroglyphs as may be seen in the Tusayan area. These cannot be definitely dated, and undoubtedly cover a long period of time; but their undeniably Kachina quality merits mention at this point. The first group was collected by Fewkes (1892a, Plate I) adjacent to First Mesa, and includes several recognizably contemporary Kachina masks (Fig. 6a–h). A similar group, collected in much the same area by Stephen (1936, pp. 1012–1029), shows several obvious masks, plus a few which are less readily identified (Fig. 6i–n).

Interesting as these stone artifacts are, they are much too limited in what they can tell us. They give no satisfactorily accurate dating, little detailed factual information, and are useful primarily as suggestive evidence for the possible widespread knowledge and performance of masked ceremonies.[*]

Ceramics. Almost as durable as stone, but more widespread and much more plastic in its expression, is the art of the potter. Pots and potsherds have long been among the most valuable evidence that the archeologist has had to work with; and the whole science of Southwestern archeology owes much of its knowledge to this art.

Examples of mask decoration on pottery are not very numerous, although specimens have been found in scattered excavations. With all the potter Nampeyó's searching in the Sikyatki ruins, few pieces of pottery were found bearing Kachina-like designs. This lack impressed Fewkes (1898a, p. 633), who stated:

> Although we can not definitely assert that this cultus [the Kachina] was unknown at Sikyatki, it is significant that in the ruins no ornamental vessel was found with a figure of a *katcina* mask, although these figures occur on modern bowls.

To him this was further evidence that the Kachina Cult did not become known to the Hopis until after the fall of Sikyatki.

---

[*]In 1960, at the Hooper Ranch Pueblo in northeastern Arizona, Dr. Paul Martin discovered a remarkable carved and painted stone figurine that suggests strong design parallels with certain Hopi deity effigies, but I doubt it is truly a Kachina figurine (Martin, 1962).

There are several probable reasons for this scarcity: (1) The technical skill of the earlier artists, as well as their ideas of art, tended more towards geometric patterns; anthropomorphic designs do not become common until later. (2) Zoömorphic figures, especially bird forms, are frequently encountered and apparently seemed more appropriate for the decoration of pottery. (3) If the Cult developed slowly, as seems logical, it was probably localized, quite restrictive, or practiced somewhat secretly; thus it would have been less familiar to "lay" ceramists than it is today. (4) There may have been a tabu against decoration of utilitarian articles with religious figures. (5) Women probably did the decorating of pottery and were prohibited from activity in the masked ceremonials, as obtains today; thus they would not be likely to paint the "forbidden" designs on

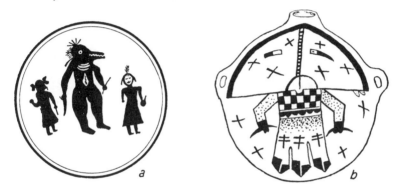

Figure 7. Kachina figures on Pottery:
    a. Oraibi bowl, bearing designs of *Nataşka* family;
    b. "Hopi area" canteen, possibly *Wüwüyomo* or *Ahül* Kachina (from Martin and Willis).

their ware. It has only been in very recent years that there has been any marked tendency for potters to use Kachina themes in their craftwork. (Compare the strong feeling by Navajo artists against incorporating Yeibitchai figures in their weaving—which work is also done by women. This has been overcome only in recent years, and against tremendous opposition.)

It is interesting to note here that the Snake Dance, although usually regarded by ethnologists as one of the older Pueblo ceremonials, has likewise rarely been a subject for pottery decoration. To my knowledge, but one prehistoric bowl has been excavated showing an unmistakable design of Snake Dancers in action (Parsons, 1940, p. 541).

I have been able to locate very few specimens of early pottery which bear apparent Kachina subjects. However, three interesting

40   examples in the collection of the Chicago Natural History Museum
warrant consideration. (For details concerning these pieces, *see*
Martin and Willis, 1940.) The first (Fig. 7*a*) shows what is unmis-
takably a group similar to the Nataşka trio today. This was found
in a ruin near Oraibi, but the circumstances of its excavation are not
entirely clear, and it probably dates no earlier than the mid-1800's.
The second (Fig. 7*b*), a canteen unquestionably of Hopi workmanship, is of special interest because it has a definite connection
with a Kachina which will be discussed more fully in a later section.

Figure 8. Bowl design. From
Homolovi, a prehistoric
Hopi village north of Wins-
low (from Martin and
Willis).

Figure 9. Mural Figures from Kuaua:
a. Ceremonial being in full costume;
b. Figure with conical headdress (from
photographs).

Little data accompanies the piece beyond the fact that it was found
"in the Hopi country;" it therefore has little value beyond the design
and the fact that it can be presumed to have been made prior to
American entry. The final specimen (Fig. 8) is a pre-Spanish bowl
from Homolovi, dating about 1350. The design has not been identified, but the facial decoration strongly suggests a masked being; although it may be zoömorphic, the tail could be the fox pelt which
hangs from the belt of a Kachina dancer.

A few examples of Mimbres pottery have been cited occasionally
as depicting masked figures; but most of these are so controversial
that they do not warrant inclusion here. They could be face paintings, decorative animals done in a conventionalized manner, or any
of several similar anthropomorphic forms. (Superb collections of
Mimbreño ware are illustrated in Cosgrove, 1932, and Fewkes, 1925a
and 1925b. For a recent definitive study, *see* Brody, 1977).

Wooden Implements. For the most part, the relatively few prehistoric wooden artifacts which have been discovered in the Southwestern area are in such poor condition that their original function
is extremely difficult to determine; this is particularly true of objects
made for ritual use, since most of their identifiable characteristics
are painted designs which soon fade, peel, or chip off. However, a
few specimens have been recovered from excavations with sufficient
traces of the original decoration remaining to permit a cautious investigator to postulate their intended purpose as definitely ceremonial.

Rather than examine here the entire literature of those archeological excavations from which wood materials have been recovered, I
have elected to mention only a few of the more striking parallels
with recognized Kachina mask or costume accessories. There are
many other specimens known, I fully realize, but since their use *is*
presumptive, I feel it will better serve the present purpose to indicate the variety in types, rather than quantity in numbers.

One of the most interesting series of finds has been made in the
Upper Gila region of New Mexico (Cosgrove, 1947), where numerous painted yucca slabs have been recovered. The general configu-
ration of these slabs suggests strongly the present-day slat-headdress
called *nakchi*, and one in particular (*ibid.*, Fig. 126k) was cut so as
to fit over the head, just as present day *nakchi* are fastened to masks.
Another (*ibid.*, Fig. 126g), has the center cut out in the step design
which is seen very frequently today in the pueblos. A third, called
a *tablita* by Cosgrove, is very interesting because of its form and condition (*ibid.*, Frontis. *b*). However, I am inclined to question this
identification; a lack of any means of attachment to the head, and
the over-all size of the specimen (7 in. by 6 ¾ in.), would suggest
that perhaps it was carried in the hand, used in some other way as a
costume accessory, or formed part of the decoration of an altar or
shrine. A final intriguing item depicts a face painted on a yucca-wood
slab (*ibid.*, Fig. 126o). While it cannot be called unquestionably a
masked face, the eye, nose, and mouth elements can be found in use
today on several Hopi masks.

Staffs, wands, and canes have been found in profusion. Most of
these are in such poor condition that little can be told from a study
of them, other than their physical similarity to the currently-used
staff (*ñatyüñpi*), or wand (*ñülükpi*). However, in one remarkable
find, several wooden ceremonial staffs and wands were recovered
(McGregor, 1943, pp. 286ff.). Although many of these cannot be
called obvious Kachina paraphernalia, three wooden sticks, each
having a carved deer or antelope hoof at one end, deserve special
mention. Originally, the shafts were colored red, with the hoofs
painted in blue or green. McGregor identifies these as ceremonial

42 wands, with which I am in complete agreement. However, I should also like to suggest that the carved hoof may be indicative of an earlier practice of imitative magic. Since these hoof-carved staffs are quite short, they may not have been used in precisely the same way as Kachina personators use such staffs today; but it is interesting to note that Pañwû (Mt. Sheep), Sowíiñwû (Deer), and Chüb (Antelope) Kachinas, as well as many other animal beings, carry short staffs in their hands, symbolic of quadrupeds. May it not be that in earlier times such Kachina sticks terminated in carved hoofs similar to the Ridge Ruin specimens? Today these ñatyüñpi usually lack any special carving, since the personators often use whatever sticks are handy.

Wooden figurines and possible prototypic Kachintihü are difficult to identify, since the wooden tihü and the wooden idol often appear isomorphic. The most remarkable find in this type of artifacts is undoubtedly the Double Butte cache discovered by the Hemenway Expedition in 1888 (Haury, 1945). This material is discussed in detail in Chapter VII, infra.

The Graphic Arts. The existence of examples of the Pueblo painter's art has long been known. As early as 1610, painted murals were reported from Nuevo México (Villagrá, 1610, Canto XV). Other individuals saw murals throughout the Southwest, and later archeological work uncovered many of them to demonstrate the universality of this art form (Roberts, 1932, pp. 79ff).

Four great mural excavations, all made in the last two decades, have revealed excellent examples of the art which answer several questions that have long plagued ethnologists, and which prove the prehistoric evidence of the Kachina Cult beyond all doubt.*

In excavations at Kuaua, Kawaika-a, and Awátovi, scholars found colorful wall paintings of geometric designs, ceremonial paraphernalia, costuming, and dancers dating from as early as 1300 to about 1630 A.D., or to that era which is classified by archeologists as Pueblo IV. These are true murals, painted in rich earth colors upon the walls of various kivas.

Since the architectural construction of the prehistoric kiva is in every way similar to that of today, and since materials found in the kiva rooms closely parallel modern ceremonial artifacts, it may be assumed that the purposes of these subterranean chambers were much the same then as they are today. Not only do the contemporary kivas contain the same niches, sípapü openings, banquettes, raised platforms, and so on; many are also decorated with wall paintings.

---

*A fourth, at Pottery Mound in New Mexico, included designs similar in style and chronological period, but apparently lacked any examples which are obvious representations of masked beings (Hibben, 1975).

The first of these three recently-excavated murals, at Kuaua, are those described by Villagrá. In a good state of preservation, they are a dramatic illustration of prehistoric art. Although a complete report has not yet been published on these paintings (two brief articles are Hewett, 1938b, and Sinclair, 1951), I have been able to examine a few photographs which indicate that they are representative of the style of art found in the Tusayan pueblos. Hence the artistic expression of the two areas would seem to have been paralleled in early times.

Of the several examples recovered from the Kuaua excavations, two in particular are informative about early costume details. One (Fig. 9a) shows what seems to be a masked individual. In facial treatment, the use of feathers across the forehead, and the head-shape, it closely resembles the contemporary Hopi Şálako Kachina.

Another mural (Fig. 9b) shows an individual wearing what seems to be a conical cap, similar to those often seen in pictographs (Fig. 5b) as well as in contemporary Kachina costuming (Fig. 14).

In discussing his work in excavating the Kuaua murals, Gordon Vivian (1935, p. 115) has this to say:

> The murals, so far exposed, are principally of masked figures in Pueblo dance costume. Colors represented are black, white, red, yellow, brown, and green. So far there has been no indication of Spanish influence in the paintings.

The second set of murals was excavated at Kawaika-a, near First Mesa. Here we find evidence closer to our needs. Executed in mineral pigments, they have retained much of their original coloring, and graphically portray the beauty and richness of design in early Pueblo costume. It is apparent that most of the subject matter is ceremonial in nature, and there are several parallels to contemporary religious practice. As a result, some deductions relative to prehistoric cere-monialism can be drawn from studying them.

Although none of the Kawaika-a murals yet excavated show definite examples of masked individuals, the importance of the discovery lies in the close relationship between Kawaika-a and adjacent Awá-tovi. Since these villages were coexistent for a period of several hundred years, there can be no doubt that their customs would have been very similar.

This brings us to Awátovi and the third set of murals excavated, and in these we finally find conclusive proof of the prehistoric existence of masked ceremonies.

When the Peabody Museum Awátovi Expedition started work in 1935, all that was known of the murals was brief mention by archeologists working at the turn of the century. Nothing was known of the extent of the paintings, nor of their content, until Watson Smith, of the Peabody party, discovered a small section of a mural painting on a kiva wall in 1936.

Subsequent examination revealed other murals hidden in layers beneath the topmost, and Smith turned to the task of recovering as many as possible, developing a technique which enabled him to peel back the various layers without losing the detail. Unfortunately, the destruction of Awátovi in 1700, plus two and a half centuries of erosion, had damaged the top portion of each wall; so that, for the most part, only the lower two-thirds still existed.

While all of the murals at Awátovi and Kawaika-a have not been fully recovered owing to the intervention of World War II, Smith has been able to remove and mount some 150 murals and mural fragments which have been preserved for further study.* (Many of these recovered fragments may be seen at the Museum of Northern Arizona, Flagstaff, where they have been placed on permanent loan.)

A study of the murals demonstrates the many changes which took place in Awátovi art techniques, but it is not within the scope of this study to deal with this problem other than to mention that several phases of art expression are shown in the decorations. One, presumably earlier than the rest, was a quite simple "primitive" style of work, with little attempt to portray recognizable, realistic forms. Another seems to represent the art ideals of a different era, and is much more complex, incorporating a multitude of geometric patterns.

As realism began to develop, many zoömorphic creatures were represented, together with articles evidently of ceremonial significance. A further development of skill resulted in portrayals of the human form in both everyday and ceremonial costume. The final layers depict what was evidently the height of mural art in the prehistoric Southwest, for they display an extremely sophisticated use of design with a polished technique and use of color.

The various designs portraying human forms in costume are primarily of interest to us. In studying this group we find many which are obviously paintings of warriors or priests with faces painted ceremonially. Others are quite possibly supernatural beings, or perhaps human beings wearing masks; or they may be merely elaborately painted faces drawn in very stylized fashion. Other, quite dramatic, designs are obviously intended to portray deities of various sorts, and are drawn in such a manner that they are not necessarily masked impersonators. However, there are several figures which present undeniable evidence of the existence of masked ceremonials.

---

*I am deeply indebted to Watson Smith for many discussions concerning the details of his work at Awátovi and for the privilege of examining the murals. At the time of this writing, his monograph was not yet available.

The most conclusive (Plate V) is one of the few which include the upper portion of the being.

That the design cannot be considered merely a painted face, or a warrior decoration, is quite apparent on careful study. The facial features are identical with those of modern mask design, indicating a long carry-over of art elements; the shape and style of the ears are very similar to the wooden ears attached to many contemporary masks. The necklace and the decorative armbands have their duplicates today in the shell-and-turquoise jewelry and painted leather armbands commonly in use. It is interesting to note, however, that no collar is shown on the figure, although today an evergreen or fur ruff is customarily worn by this personator. The materials used at Awátovi can only be surmised, but since wood, deerhide and cotton were available, it would seem probable that these substances were commonly used.

The feather pendants find their duplications today in the use of feathers piercing the ears of many Kachinas (Plate VIII), or attached in other ways to the horns or ears of other Kachinas. In addition, it should be noticed that the feathers surmounting the head of the Awátovi figure are not the usual full-crown type of headdress, such as the feather bonnet of the Plains Indian; instead, the feathers seem grouped in a fan-shaped arrangement, or *shürüadta*, like that worn by many contemporary Kachinas (Plate X). It is significant that several masks of this type show a three-feather arrangement, which the mural figure suggests may also have been true in early times.

Not only is this mural of interest because of the clearly-depicted mask, but also because the mask is almost exactly like several Kachina masks still in use in the Hopi villages. These are built today on a woven basketry base, usually covered with canvas, and painted in the design characteristic of the particular Kachina. The various designs vary from one village to another, chiefly in color and minor details, but the relationships are quite apparent upon study (Plate VI). Each of these masks employs a substantial portion of the basic elements found in the Awátovi mural mask. These several Kachinas vary greatly in importance, but the present emphasis is on the similarity in design, since we have no idea of the function of the older being. The following comparison is offered as a possible basis for identification of that being.

The first for comparison, Ahül Kachina (Plate VIa), belongs to the Kachina clan, is one of the chief actors in the Powamû ceremony, and seems to be definitely identified with the sun. (The solar ceremony in which Ahül participates is fully described in Fewkes, 1920, pp. 493–526.) The mask is very similar to that of the Awátovi figure;

minor differences can be seen in the absence of ears, the presence of a nose, and the full-feather headdress instead of only two (or three?) feathers (For the full-costumed figure, *see* Plate VII).

The next to be considered, Wüwüyomo Kachina (Plate VId), is a Badger Clan Kachina who performs in Powamû, blesses the plants, and at certain times appears in a quartet. The mask of this Kachina is not only quite similar to that of the Awátovi mural, but two additional characters are parallel: instead of a full-feathered headdress, Wüwüyomo wears only three feathers' and he has a white cotton robe (*kwáchkyabû*) over one shoulder and under the other arm. Unlike the older being, he lacks ears and has a peculiar hooked gourd snout, painted blue and yellow with a cotton-wrapped red base. The black line in the Awátovi painting may represent a staff, and Fewkes (1903, Pl. V) shows an example of Wüwüyomo bearing just such a *ñatyüñpi*. This characteristic may have changed in the past few years; those which I saw in 1936 carried a sheep-scapula rattle (*kaláhainiadta*) in one hand and a spruce branch, or feathers, in the other. Colors on the mask vary somewhat, not only from those of Awátovi, but also from village to village today. The name is an interesting suggestion of antiquity: "Wise Old Man." Earlier mention has been made of pottery bearing a design similar to this Kachina mask, found in the Tusayan area (*see* Fig. 7b).

Another Kachina frequently seen today is Wüpamo (Plate VIc). Even though the colors and design of his mask vary greatly from those of the Awátovi figure, he is included to illustrate the persistence of feather headdress and divided-forehead elements.

If there is Sun symbolism in the Awátovi figure, as seems to be suggested by the apparent parallels between it and Ahül Kachina, it is appropriate to include in our comparisons the mask of Tawa, the Sun Kachina (Plate VIb). Although at first glance there may seem to be little reason for regarding the two as having any close relationship, analysis demonstrates several features in common. The design on the forehead of the masks shows the same bisected feature, each has a similar rayed headdress (according to contemporary account, indicative of the sun's rays), and finally, Tawa Kachina masks of recent times have a painted triangular mouth. This latter feature is much smaller in proportion to the total face than that of the Awátovi being.

The exact design on the mask of Tawa Kachina, is not rigidly fixed; variations are often seen, and one which has come to be used almost as much as that in Plate VI is that illustrated in Figure 10. The feature of interest is the mouth, which reverses the triangle upon itself, giving an hour-glass shape. Usually this shape is in two colors, red and black. It is very common today both in mask design and as body decoration—not only in Pueblo, but also in Navajo usage.

In examining other possible derivations from the Awátovi symbolism, Stephen's (1936, Plate VIII) illustrations of a variant of the Ahül mask should be noted (Fig. 11). The central design is of especial interest, for it is found in certain other Kachina masks, notably Añwüşnasómtäqä Kachina (Plate VIIIa). Commonly called Crow Wing Mother, Añwüşnasómtäqä Kachina is an important participant in the Powamû initiation ceremony.

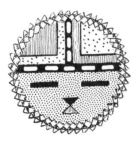

Figure 10. Mask of *Tawa*, the Sun Kachina; The Hopi "Sun Shield." See Pl. VIb.

Figure 11. *Ahül* Kachina mask variant (after Stephen). See Pls. VIa and VII.

Colton (1949, p. 66) mentions an Ewiro Kachina as being "an old type of Third Mesa Kachina." He gives no further information, and it is included in this group only because of the bisected mask design and the incorporated star symbolism similar to the Awátovi being (Plate VIIIc). I have seen two tihü, both dating from about 1900, which show variants of this design and represent a Kachina known by the same name (Plate VIIIb).[*]

It is tempting to postulate not only a common origin for these several beings but also a development of design from the Awátovi being (perhaps a basic Sun-being?) to the contemporary Ahül or Wüwüyomo, for more of the Awátovi characteristics appear in these two Kachinas than in any others. The design, headdress accessories, and costume (to the extent that we can judge from the mural fragments remaining) all support this theory.

Another support for the theory is offered by clan relationships. As previously mentioned, Wüwüyomo Kachina is a Honáni (Badger) Clan being. According to Hopi tradition (Stephen, 1936, p. 944) there were large numbers of Honányümü at Awátovi, apparently immigrants from Zuñi, who, after the destruction of Awátovi, went to

---

[*]One, in the Museum of the American Indian, was collected at Oraibi by H. R. Voth, who catalogued it as "Awiri Kachina." The other is in a private collection.

Figure 12. Awátovi mural fragments (after Smith).
a. A Ceremonially-robed Warrior (?);
b. Beings similar to *Pókoma* and *Kókopölö* Kachinas.

Walpi and Mishongnovi. Many of these later established the "Walpi suburb" of Sichomovi, where they live today. To my knowledge, Wüwüyomo Kachina is no longer performed at First Mesa, and may also be dormant at Second Mesa. In the minds of inhabitants of both areas, the concepts of Wüwüyomo and Ahül seem to have become mixed.

A second Awátovi mural group shows a being whose costume includes several features suggesting parallels with contemporary usage (Fig. 12a, right). Whether this being is wearing a mask cannot be definitely established—this may only be a representation of an individual with a painted face. However, the designs are of especial interest, for many Kachinas today have hand (or paw) prints on the mask or body, similar to that on the face of the mural figure. One example, Sivü-i-qiltäqä Kachina, features this white hand design on a black background (Fig. 13). The conical cap has a counterpart in the similar usage by Ahöli Kachina, the being which today accompanies Eótoto Kachina on his trip through the village during the Powamû ceremony (Fig. 14). A similar headdress may be that of the Kuaua figure (Fig. 9b).

A further similarity to Ahöli Kachina is the fact that the Awátovi mural figure is undoubtedly wearing a painted robe of deer or buffalo hide. Today, Ahöli wears just such a robe (now sometimes woven cotton), painted with a symbolic half-man, half-bird being, Kwátaka. Since this monster's body has a long 'eagle tail,' the dangling bunch of feathers on the mural figure's robe might well be a similar representation. Ahöli today carries a long ñatyüñpi, instead of the bow and arrow in the hand of the mural figure.

I do not claim that the Awátovi figure is necessarily a prototype of Sivü-i-qiltäqä or Ahöli Kachina. In the first place, it is not at all certain he is masked. In the second place, the black body and face paint, conical cap, decorated buckskin robe, etc., are strong evidence to support the belief that this is an early representation of Pü'ükoñhoya, the elder War God. Although today this being usually wears a porópta'nakchi (pointed woven cap) in place of the conical cap, and has two vertical white lines on the face instead of the hand imprint, the general character of the costume bears out this opinion. The marks on the Awátovi figure *may* represent animal paw prints (although such marks usually are less "hand-like"). If so, they are doubtless bear-paw prints—and there is a close connection between the Bear medicine and war.

The point is that in this one individual are several features which apparently have continued in ceremonial use from at least as early as 1625 or so, and are frequently found in Kachina costumery.

Two figures shown in Fig. 12*b* particularly seem to have contemporary Kachina parallels. The inverted figure may or may not represent a masked being; there are two Kachinas known today which incorporate characteristics of his facial design: Pókoma Kachina and Hoho Mana Kachina. The first, Pókoma, is called the Pet Kachina, since it concerns all domestic animals (Fig. 15*a*). Often confused with Pohko, or Pok'kachina (Dog Kachina), the mask of Pókoma includes several features of the mural being. The second, Hoho Mana, is less strikingly parallel, but does include the zigzag-and-crescent feature (Fig. 15*b*). One other Kachina, Sio Avách'hoya, also includes this (Fig. 15*c*), and it is notable that the latter two have design parallels in several Zuñi *Koko* (Bunzel, 1932, Plates 21, 29, 47).

Figure 13. *Sivü-i-qiltäqä* Kachina; often called *Matia* Kachina. See Fig. 12*a*.

Figure 14. *Ahöli Kachina.* See Fig. 12a.

The two figures just below the inverted being are of interest for two reasons—costume and history. The erotic aspect of the male figure almost certainly suggests Kókopölö Kachina, who appears occasionally at Kachina dances. His mask is usually black, with a vertical white stripe; he is represented as humpbacked, with an erect penis. This latter, in dances today, is of carved wood or a gourd tied around the waist (Fig. 16). It is notable that the Awátovi figure is somewhat humpbacked, and has a cord around his waist which would seem to hold the erect phallus in place. Kókopölö Kachina

dashes about the kísonvi simulating intercourse with various femi-
nine spectators, as the mural figure suggests. The mural female may
possibly represent Kókopölö Mana, although I doubt it, since she
lacks any of the distinguishing elements of costume by which Kókopölö Mana is known today. I am of the opinion that the figure merely
represents an Indian woman with whom Kókopölö (if it be he) is
carrying out his traditional role.

Figure 15. Contemporary "zigzag element" masks. See Fig. 12*b*.
    a. *Pókoma* Kachina;
    b. *Hoho* Mana;
    c. *Sio Avách'hoya* Kachina.

However, there are several interesting historical references to early
Kachina dances which describe this activity in graphic terms. It
seems quite apropos to quote one such reference at length, both for
its parallels, and for the possible indications of ceremonial changes
in the last three hundred years. The dance described below was observed by the Spanish in 1660; it was reported as being held at Tesuque, Puaray, and Isleta. In many respects it demonstrates remarkable similarities to present-day custom (Hackett, 1937, pp. 207–208):

> . . . Before dancing the first kind [of Kachina dance], the Indians
> fast two or three days; the fast being concluded, comes the day
> of the dance. Appearing naked, they put on their faces a kind
> of hood, or mask, having a small hole through which they can
> see a little. The masks are made of cloth or of elk-skin. They
> also put on other masks which are dyed black. The ones who
> put on these are the most idolatrous; before they appear in pub-
> lic they rehearse in their underground council-chambers. When
> they come out before the public one of them puts the offering

in the place where the dance is to be performed. The other participants dance around the offering, using a language which is not understood, even by the Indians, or else they will only say that it is the language of the devil. If they are asked why they perform these dances, they say that it is to obtain possession of the woman they desire, that the devil may give her to them; or, they ask that corn may be given them, or for some personal favor. . . . Sometimes they go away from this dance, enter whatever house they wish and have carnal intercourse with the woman whom they desire. In the second variety of this dance no fast occurs, although there is sometimes a ritual in the form indicated, but always they keep their masks on, and perform the dance to the singing of that unknown language. After dancing they go to whatever house they desire and have intercourse with women who are relatives within the degree of kinship mentioned . . .

Figure 16. *Kókopölö* Kachina; the costumed *mana,* the mask, and the male personator.

There is too little detail in this description to say definitely that it concerns Kókopölö Kachina, but the mention of a black mask is interesting, plus the fact that the dancers appeared naked, as did Kókopölö formerly. The "language of the devil" is reminiscent of the Kachina language today, which is supposed to be unintelligible to the lay spectator. The underground council-chambers were obviously kivas, fasting is still a customary observance, and the "intercourse" with female spectators may quite possibly have been simulated, as it is today.

One other questionable incidence of masking in the murals may be found in the white-faced individual to the right of the Awátovi masked being (Plate V). Viewed obliquely, this fragment suggests an early version of Şótüq'nañwû, the Hopi Sky God, who appears today in a white mask and costume, wearing one horn on his head-dress. The nearest diety in the Hopi pantheon to the Christian God, Şótüq'nañwû is not considered to be a Kachina, but a god in the full sense of the word. The only other Hopi deity who might be con-sidered in this connection is Aloşaka (also called Müí'yiñwû), the Germ God. Aloşaka wears two horns on his mask, has a white face, and may also be the modern version of this figure.

The sequence of layers of the murals makes it possible to suggest a fairly certain chronology, which, while perhaps not completely accurate, does establish the seriate relationship of one with the other. Watson Smith estimates that the Awátovi murals were made about 1600–1625. Superimposed on the layers we have just discussed were four later murals, the last of which was probably applied in 1627 or 1628. It is very definite that this last painting was completed before the church of San Bernardo de Aguátubi was built over the filled-in kiva containing the murals (1629).

There can be little basis for any theory of Spanish influence upon this particular mural work. Although we do not know the exact dates for the founding of Awátovi and Kawaika-a, McGregor (1941a, pp. 372–373) gives 1332 for Awátovi and 1357 for Kawaika-a. The vil-lages, then, were about two hundred years old when the Spaniards arrived, and their cultural life was matured in every respect. Fur-ther, Spanish religious activities in Tusayan were irregular and in-effective prior to the establishment of San Bernardo. The use of crosses on the Awátovi mask cannot be interpreted as indicating Christian symbolism, for this design is an age-old symbol in Amerind art, and has been found wherever geometric Indian art styles are known. In Pueblo Indian art, these crosses are commonly used to symbolize stars, and support the theory that the Awátovi being rep-resents in part a Sun complex wholly free from Christian influence. To pursue this analogy somewhat farther, the dichromatic design of the mask definitely suggests a night-and-day symbolism—the choice of alternating black-and-white colors offers a final bit of support for this argument.

Although a Zuñi origin is asserted for the Awátovi Honáni clan, and though Zuñi and Hopi Kachinas frequently parallel each other both in design and theology, there are, to my knowledge, no Zuñi *Koko* whose masks are similar to Wüwüyomo, to Ahül, or to the Awátovi figure. Nor am I aware of any other Pueblo masked beings with designs of this particular type.

It has been suggested by many students of Southwestern cere-monialism that much of Navajo ritual has been adopted from Pueblo

54 custom. This theory is in part supported by a similarity between the Awátovi mural and the mask of Thōbādzhìstshíni (Fig. 17). This Navajo Yei is one of the Twin Heroes, who represent light and darkness; Thōbādzhìstshíni, the younger brother, is darkness and moisture. His mask is covered with small hour-glass figures, similar to those on the body of Chákwaina Kachina (Plate I), and a fringe of red hair is fastened around the edges. But the central design holds most interest—for here again is the black inverted-triangle motif, much as in the Awátovi mural being. His brother Nayénezganî is the Yei of light and heat. The legend of the creation of the Twin Heroes, and the place of these Yei in Navajo mythology is given in Matthews (1897).

Figure 17. *Thōbādzhìstshíni* ("Born-from-water"), The Navajo Yei whose mask combines several design elements of the Awátovi mural being. See Pl. V.

EVIDENCE FROM FOLKLORE

Hopi folklore has yet to be completely reported. In the few collections gathered to date, references to Kachinas are frequent, although those legends which detail the origins of Kachinas are quite uncommon. Such versions as do exist, however, tend to agree fairly well with each other. Two of the traditions accounting for the origin of the Kachinas have been given elsewhere (see pp. 10–11); there are other versions which differ in detail. But in no case in these legends is origin admitted as being non-Indian; those Kachinas regarded as non-Hopi in origin are regarded as having come from other tribes, notably the Zuñi. In general, there seems full agreement among the Hopi that the Kachinas came to their present abode from the east or the south (depending upon the version given). Considering other evidence presented in the fields of mural art, archeological excavation, and historical documentation, the conclusion seems inescapable that in this case legend contains more than just a seed of truth.

Insofar as folklore accounts now available are concerned, the Hopis ascribe origins of most of the Kachinas to activities well within the period of their own history (roughly the past one thousand years). Furthermore, some Hopis claim that many, if not the majority, of those Kachinas known today were "invented" in the past century— a further tribute, if true, to the remarkably fluctuating character of the Cult. (The most complete collection of Hopi legends yet published is found in Voth, 1905.)

THE WRITTEN RECORD

The early exploring parties in the Southwest described in the following chapter have fortunately left several excellent accounts of their travels; and, of especial interest to this study, they include some valuable comments on the religious ceremonies of the Pueblo people as they existed at the time of the European invasion. Since these observations were usually made by soldiers or priests, their ethnographic value is often small; but in spite of the unsympathetic point of view of the Whites, there is enough information to allow the student to form certain conclusions.

In his report, Pedro de Castañeda, the chronicler of the Coronado expedition of 1540, makes no mention of Kachinas or masked dances. This fact has frequently been pointed to as evidence of the post-Spanish origin of masked ceremonies. Parsons (1930, p. 594) for example, stated:

> It is highly significant that . . . the early Spanish chroniclers [do not] refer to mask dances. It seems unlikely that had Benavides, for one, seen masks among the "thousand superstitions" he would not have mentioned it.

But Bandelier (1890, p. 151) offers this observation of Spanish psychology of the period in refutation:

> The [masked] dances of the Pueblos were therefore no surprise to the whites; they had seen far more striking displays of the same nature, and unless a calisthenic feast showed features which farther south they had not seen, it was passed over in silence or slightly noticed.

Beals (1932, p. 168) adds a further note in comment:

> The Spaniards, as anyone who has read the early accounts has discovered to his exasperation, rarely mentioned anything which was the same or similar to Mexican customs.

There could be much truth in this; through prejudice and interest in other things, there was little inclination on the part of the early

Spaniards to comment at length on the native customs, unless they were of such spectacular moment that there might be a possibility of stimulating interest in further exploration. The instance of Bernardino de Sahagún's sincere interest and accurate ethnographic reporting on the Aztec civilization is a rare exception.

When the Espejo expedition went into the Southwest in 1582, a careful account of the trip was kept by a member of the party, Diego Pérez de Luxán, in which this statement occurs:

> Throughout this nation they have many masks which they use in their dances and ceremonies. (Hammond and Rey, 1929, p.79).

This, the earliest reference to Pueblo masked ceremonies yet known, would seem to settle the question of early existence of masked ceremonies. And, significantly, there is only one earlier Spanish document recording travel in the Pueblo area—that of Castañeda.

Masked ceremonies are known to have existed in Spain and Mexico prior to 1540 and, since a whole generation had grown up in the time between the arrival of Coronado and Espejo, it may be argued that masks, or the knowledge of masks, had been brought in by the Coronado party, and their use had developed during the fifty-year interval. I think this is hardly possible. In the first place, since the major aim of the Coronado party was to seek information about the area, and possible sources of treasure, any cultural interchange would have been largely incidental. Priests accompanied the group, and it is unlikely that they would have tried to introduce anything other than orthodox religious ritual—they would, in fact, have opposed any introduction of non-Catholic observances among a population whose conversion was their primary goal. Moreover, the use of masks had become such a serious problem in the eyes of the Church that their use was frowned upon, for a law was enacted by Spain early in 1553 prohibiting them throughout the Spanish world (Parsons, 1930, p. 597). There is even less probability of such introduction among the Hopis. The main Coronado party at no time entered Tusayan—only a small party of about twenty men made the journey. These men were horsemen (i.e., of Spanish ancestry, therefore not likely to be carriers of native Mexican practices), accompanied by one priest, Juan de Padilla, and three or four footmen (Winship, 1896, p. 488). Considering this personnel, and the brief time the party spent in the Hopi villages, it is hardly possible that marked influence of any kind could result.

Furthermore, the Coronadoans had not entered Tusayan under the most auspicious circumstances; the Spanish soldiers had shown their disposition in several skirmishes in which natives were killed or wounded, and were for a time resisted by the Awátovi people.

with affection.

There is one point which deserves consideration in connection with the effect of Coronado's expedition upon the Kachina Cult. Since the recent discovery and publication of the complete roster of the Coronado expedition (Aiton, 1939) it is now well known that this party included a considerable retinue of Indian menials. It would seem that if any alien religious practices were to be introduced via exploring groups, it would have been through the intermingling of these Mexican Indians with the Pueblo people—contact between the Spaniards and the Pueblos would not be on the fraternal level that one would expect to characterize the meetings between the two Indian peoples.

The degree of influence resulting from these Mexican Indians who came into the Pueblos certainly warrants further study; but for the present problem, there are, in my opinion, two strong arguments against the supposition that the Indians with Coronado had any hand in introducing masked ceremonies into the Pueblo area. First, as mentioned above, it seems quite improbable that the priests who accompanied that party would have allowed the large-scale display of masks or masked ceremonials necessary for the introduction of a new Cult.

Secondly, there is a very marked difference between the art styles of the Pueblo and Mexican areas—a consideration which is of extreme importance. There remains sufficient pottery and mural art upon which to base a comparison of the sixteenth century art styles of these two groups, and they show no parallels to support a theory of Mexican origins for such an elaborate art expression as that practiced by the Hopi and Zuñi mask makers.

The whole philosophy of art design of the Spanish-Mexican masks is completely unlike that of the Pueblo masks. The Spanish-Mexican designers seek to mould facial features in their work, and regardless of the painting and ornamentation, the physical structure of the head is still retained in recognizable, naturalistic form. The Pueblo artists, on the other hand, make little effort to retain the sculptural qualities of the face—their painting is extremely conventionalized, the face-surface is normally flat, and facial organs are not treated realistically. Isolate an eye, ear, or mouth design from the rest of a Pueblo mask, and it often can not be recognized as such—it could be any of several art symbols or designs. An eye, nose, or mouth detached from a Mexican mask, however, is still an eye, nose, or mouth.

While it is possible that the Pueblo artists might tend to re-create these Mexican designs in their own way, a Mexican flavor of realism would surely be retained—and none is visible today. Even those

Hopi masks which have a slightly-moulded character, such as Yüche, Wó-e, or Píptüka, have conventionalized features which cannot be called Mexican (*see* Fig. 18).

This same objection applies to the possible pre-Spanish introduction of masking from Mexico into the Pueblo area, via the intertribal trade routes discussed in Chapter I. Although it is not within the scope of this book to deal with wholly Indian influences on the Kachina Cult, recognition should be made of the argument that the masking complex may have come into the Southwest through this

Figure 18. "Realistic" Hopi masks:
Yüche Kachina; *Wó-e* Kachina; *Píptüka* Kachina.

avenue of commerce as part of an interplay of Indian cultures. Parsons (1929, p. 155) in particular has repeatedly raised the question of Mexican mask usages as a source of this exchange and influence. Also, Alfonso Caso (1929, pp. 111ff.) has suggested possible Aztec origins; but it seems to me that the examples presented by Covarrubias (1929, pp. 114–116), and the more contemporary situation discussed by Toor (1929, pp. 127–131), refute most of his arguments. The types of masks used in Mexico are not only completely different in physical form and artistic concept, but the spiritual attitude of the wearer and his purposes for masking apparently differ from those of the Pueblos.

An additional argument holds that the period of the Kachina ceremonies, which begin in the winter, coincides with the Spanish advent, since Coronado spent the winter near Zuñi; if, then, the Spaniards introduced masking rituals during their winter stay, this winter ceremony of the Kachina return would be more than coincidence. I cannot agree that this proves anything—not only do agricultural folk throughout the world observe the solar seasons ceremonially but they usually observe the solstices with especial care. And this is particularly true of people like the Pueblo tribes who are completely dependent upon agriculture. Therefore, any such coincidence of the ceremony with the Spanish winter residence would seem to be wholly fortuitous.

In 1682, two years after the Pueblo Revolt, one of Otermín's lieutenants, Mendoza, was sent to Puaray where:

> ...they made a house to house search and found...a great many "masks *de cacherias,* in imitation of the devil, which are those that they use in their diabolical dances." All of the latter were collected and burned. (Hackett, 1916, p. 63).

This statement is not an isolated specimen: many similar comments are to be found in the documents of the period, indicating that the Cult had assumed considerable size by the end of the seventeenth century. Of especial interest is the use of the word *cacheria*—an obvious reference to Kachina. This word is frequently encountered in early Spanish documents, and suggests that even in these early days the Cult had attained no little importance, and that the term was well understood in reference to masked ceremonies. While negative evidence is weak evidence, it should be noted that the Spaniards themselves noted no similarities nor any relationship between the masked ceremonies and their own religious customs.

Although a thorough search of documentary evidence has not been possible, such material as has been available to me has revealed at least several score references in early Spanish documents to masked ceremonies or dances in the several Pueblos. Of these, at least half specifically employ the term Kachina, or an obvious phoneme.[*] The earliest written use of the word that I am aware of is a 1615 reference to *Caçina.* Moreover, I have been able to establish documentary evidence of the performance of masked ceremonies as early as 1660 in the following pueblos: Hopi, Zuñi, Quarai, Tesuque, Chililí, Isleta, San Ildefonso, San Juan, Cochití, Las Salinas, Tanos, Galisteo, Sandía, Jémez, San Marcos, La Alameda, Puaray, Pojoaque, Santa Fé.

---

[*]These spellings are most commonly seen in early documents: cacheria, cachina, cacina, caçina, casina, catina, catzina, cazina, cusina, kasina, tininia, etc.

IV.

Earliest White Arrivals

THE FIRST NON-INDIAN known to have penetrated the Pueblo area was Estebán, the Moorish slave. As a guide for Fray Marcos de Niza in 1539, he went as far as Hawikuh, near present-day Zuñi (Fig. 1). In southern Arizona, Estebán had been regarded as a Black God, and was loaded with gifts of turquoise and women, which latter were especially pleasing to him. Hence, on arriving at Hawikuh, he arrogantly presented himself to the village leaders and demanded the same privileges. But Estebán had not reckoned with the different psychology of the Pueblo folk. Noting with distaste his conduct, as well as realizing from his costume (part of which had been given him by the Indians farther south) that he was not a god, they temporized with him. Holding a council the night following his arrival, they decided to refuse him admittance. In the ensuing mêlée he was killed by arrows, and the southern Indians who had accompanied him fled.

Fray Marcos had followed Estebán some two day's journey behind, and when Estebán went into Hawikuh, the priest ventured only close enough to be able to see the village from a distant knoll (A thorough study of the history of this village is in Hodge, 1937). From there, he reported, he could see the gleaming walls and streets of gold of the "Seven Cities of Cíbola." When the frightened retinue deserted the slain Estebán and rushed to tell Fray Marcos what had happened, he scuttled back to Mexico City to report his adventures to the Viceroy, Antonio de Mendoza. His account, based on reports related by frightened Indians and his own long-distance observations, could scarcely be accurate. His desire to tell a good story caused him to exaggerate the size of the village, although it must be admitted that in contrast to the *xacal* and *wikiup* dwellings he had seen farther south, the well-built pueblo buildings must have seemed luxurious indeed. The desire for gold, plus the staggering wealth that had already been found in Mexico, made the priest's auditors perfectly willing to believe his optimistic report. (However, Hallenbeck, 1949, believes that Marcos was not only optimistic, but a chronic liar as well.)

Impressed by the vision of golden cities and hosts of heathens, both of which could be brought into the Spanish fold, Mendoza commissioned Francisco Vásquez de Coronado to lead an exploring party into Pimería Alta, as the Southwest was then called. Coronado set out in 1540 at the head of a well-equipped expedition, and proceeded to the heart of Cíbola, visited Zuñi and Acoma, and sent out minor parties to explore the neighboring areas.

One party, led by Pedro de Tovar, was dispatched to visit the distant Hopi villages and to learn whether the rumored gold might be in this area. This expedition stayed in the Hopi villages, probably at Awátovi. (A well-written account of their reception by the Hopis is in Bartlett, 1943.)

Hearing of a "large river" to the west, Coronado sent a small expedition led by García López de Cárdenas with a few Hopis as guides, and they became the first known Whites to see the Grand Canyon. Finding no treasure, they returned to tell Coronado of these Indians, whom they named Moquis, and whose lands they called Tusayan.* Because nothing of value had been discovered by Tovar or Cárdenas, Coronado had no further interest in the area.

With the return of Coronado to Mexico City, reporting the failure of the party to find any rich cities, Spanish interest in Nuevo México as the new territory was named) subsided. In 1565 Francisco de Ibarra attempted to explore the area, but met with such extreme hardships in northern Sonora that his party abandoned the venture and turned west to Chihuahua (Hammond and Rey, 1927, p. 241). Then followed the second Spanish entry: the expedition of Fray Augustín Rodríguez and Captain Francisco Chamuscado in 1581 and 1582.* After exploring the Río Grande area, this party went as far west as the Zuñi pueblos, where they were told that "two days

----

*The orthographic variety found on early maps and in documentary references is not only extremely wide, but somewhat confusing: Tocayan, Tonteac, Tonteaca, Tontonteac, Totanteac, Totonteac, Totonteal, Totontoac, Tototeac, Tucan, Tuçan, Tucano, Tuçano, Tucayan, Tuçayan, Tuçayán, Tuchano, Tusan, Tusayan, Tusayán, Tusean, Tusyan, Tuzan, Tuzayan, Tuzayán, etc. They are all regarded as referring to the same Hopi homeland.

Plate V. Portion of an Awátovi Mural Fragment
Based on a restoration by Watson Smith.

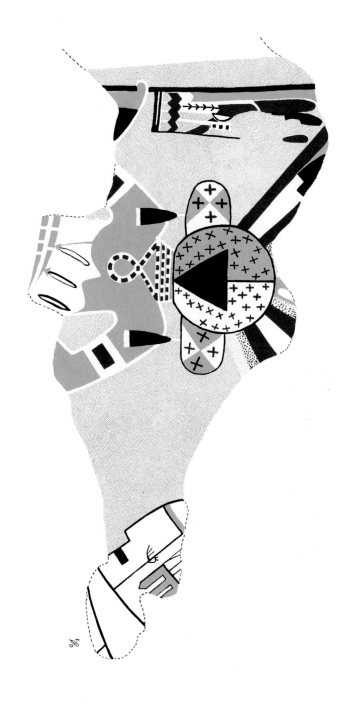

from there were five pueblos and a mineral deposit" (Hammond and
Rey, 1927, p. 356). A heavy snowfall and insufficient provisions prevented them from visiting the Hopi villages, to which this unquestionably refers. However, the account of the party does mention
Pueblo ceremonies which parallel in great degree contemparary
practices, including the earliest known mention of a Snake Dance.

The next year saw the entry of Antonio de Espejo into the Hopi
villages. This expedition is the first to record the use of masks in the
Southwest, as previously noted (p. 56). It should be mentioned that
Espejo found three Mexicans living at Zuñi—whether these were
"leftovers" from the Coronado or Rodríguez-Chamuscado parties is
unknown.

The next Hopi-Spanish contact was the 1598 expedition of Don
Juan de Oñate. He records the costume of the people and their
dance, which he calls *mitote;* but masked ceremonies are not specifically mentioned. While in Tusayan, Oñate dispatched Captains Far-
fán and Quesada in a vain effort to locate the legendary Tusayan
mines. At this same time, the Hopis were "assigned" to the ministra-
tions of Fray Andrés Corchado, but whether or not this prelate ever
personally exercised his primacy in Tusayan is not known. In this
same year, the first English map to outline the Hopi area by name
was published in London (Hakluyt, 1598), indicating that knowledge of the tribe had spread far beyond Spanish borders. In 1604,
Oñate again came into the pueblos enroute to California, seeking the
legendary South Sea; his mention of "Rancho de los Gandules" is
possibly the first reference to Moenkopi on record. The following
year, he made a brief contact with the Hopis on his way back from
California.

THE FIRST CHRISTIAN CHURCH

For the next twenty-five years, Hópi relations with the Spanish
were sporadic; we have no knowledge of the extent of White activities in Tusayan, other than a few scattered references (see Appendix I). In 1629 thirty friars were sent to Nuevo México from Mexico,
doubling the number of religious personnel, and making possible the
long-desired attempt to convert the Acoma, Zuñi, and Hopi pueblos
(Scholes and Bloom, 1945, pp. 69ff.). As a result of this added personnel, Franciscan Missions were established at Awátovi, Shungopovi

---

Plate VI. Contemporary Masks Similar to the Awátovi Being
    a. Ahül Kachina—*One of the "Return Kachinas."*
    b. Tawa Kachina—*The Sun Kachina.*
    c. Wüpamo Kachina—*Long-Snout Kachina.*
    d. Wüwüyomo Kachina—*One of the Ancient Kachinas.*

and Oraibi, and *visitas* were assigned to Mishongnovi and Walpi. That full success was not achieved during the period, however, is dramatically illustrated by the poisoning of Fray Francisco Porras at Awátovi in 1633 (Brew, 1949, pp. 11f.).

From 1540 until the establishment of the church of San Bernardo de Aguátubi, Awátovi had been slightly more conscious of the Spaniards than the other Hopi villages; the only difference in isolation was that the more easterly inhabitants naturally heard more about White activities in Cíbola. However, with the erection of the large church in 1629, European religious beliefs soon began to exert their influence in the village. Deliberately choosing a site directly above the main kiva in Awátovi, the Spaniards forced the natives to fill in that sacred chamber and build the church over it. All native observances were rigorously suppressed, all ceremonial paraphernalia were destroyed, kiva wall paintings and other decorations were obliterated by overpaintings, and every effort was made to supplant the Hopi faith by the new foreign religion. (An excellent account of the building of the church, together with an architectural study of its construction, can be found in Montgomery, Smith, and Brew, 1949.)

The village population took favorably to Catholic teachings, not unwillingly coöperated with the various priestly demands, and voluntarily surrendered most of their ceremonial objects. In fact, this friendliness was such that in the later Pueblo uprisings, one priest was sheltered from other Hopis intent upon killing him.

The Spanish religious activities in Tusayan for the next fifty years were confined largely to the missionary work of the various priests serving in the seven villages. Their number was never very large, usually not more than three to five; and Awátovi continued to be their headquarters, for it was here that the Catholics had the greatest success. Hopis in the other villages resented the presence and continual interference of the Whites, if we can judge by comments of the Spaniards, and the mesas were apparently in a continuous state of unrest.

THE PUEBLO REVOLT

By the middle of the century, Indian feeling throughout the Southwest was becoming more and more aroused against the conduct of the soldiers and the tyranny and venery of the priests. The Indians at Taos planned an uprising, but the Hopis refused to participate, and the plan was abandoned.

One cause for this ferment grew out of a long struggle which had been going on between Church and State for control of Nuevo México, and came to a head in the 1660's. (For an excellent account of this rivalry, *see* Scholes, 1936.) The complete story can not be told

here, for little of it concerns this study, but one event must be mentioned. The governor, one Bernardo López de Mendizábal, sought
by every means to discredit the clergy. One of his efforts included
encouragement of the forbidden *catzina* dances, even to the extent of
having a "command performance" held in Santa Fé (Hackett, 1937,
pp. 207–208). One consequence was undoubtedly a revival of Kachina ceremonies, which had in all probability never completely
lapsed. Another result is some of our most complete descriptions of
early Kachina dances, suggesting parallels to contemporary performances which are so startling as to warrant quoting a few random
examples. (All are from Hackett, 1937):

> ... in that kingdom [Tusayan] the Indians were accustomed to
> perform a dance, which consisted of their coming to the plaza
> in very ugly masks, each one bringing in his hand some of the
> fruits which they eat ... and depositing them ... in a circle in
> the plaza. The Indians then put on masks representing aged
> persons and walk among the fruit, making ridiculous figures.
> [Any] Indian ... who dares enter the circle to take the fruit,
> does so; he seizes what he wants, and flees. The Indians in the
> masks try to stop him and strike him with little paddles which
> they carry (pp. 141–142).

Today, these acts are paralleled by the bringing of food to the
kísonvi and placing it thereon; the Píptüka and several other clown
groups wear grotesque masks suggesting aged people, and perform
ridiculous antics. In Wáwaş performances, there is a similar challeng-
ing and racing—with the loser being whipped by the Kachina.

> ... There are other dances called *catzinas*, in which many people
> come out with masks on, to dance in the costume of men and
> women, all of them being men (p. 165).

Of importance here is evidence that, this early, all masked Kachina
performers were male—apparently women occupied the same role
then as now in the Kachina Cult.

> ... They did [the Kachina dance] after this fashion: Ten or
> twelve Indians dressed themselves in the ordinary clothes which
> they commonly wear and put on masks painted with human fig-
> ures of men; then half of them, with timbrels, such as are com-
> monly used in New Spain, in their hands, went out to the plaza.
> The others carried thongs, or whips, in their hands. They placed in
> the middle of the plaza four or six watermelons; ... [then] those
> who were dancing continued to do so noisily, sounding the tim-
> brels crazily, as they are accustomed to do, and saying, "Hu, hu,
> hu." In this fashion they circled around the plaza ... (p. 223).

Several contemporary Kachinas dress in "everyday clothes," and some wear masks bearing human features (or zoömorphic designs which can easily be mistaken for humans). The use of timbrels is not far from today's customary rattles; and watermelons, seen frequently, are a favorite Kachina gift. It is of considerable interest that whip-bearing Hú Kachina derives his name from his cry, "Hú!"—and, finally, the Kachinas still "circle" the kísonvi.

Spanish activity in Tusayan did not cease, in spite of the preoccupation with civil affairs—we have several documentary accounts of contact, plus observations of Pueblo customs made during this period (*see* Summary, p. 147). However, the far-reaching result of the clash was, in my opinion, one of the most important influences on the expansion of the Kachina Cult.

For the Indians were not slow to take advantage of this fight between their White oppressors. There had been other attempts at revolt, but each had lacked a strong leader. Finally, in 1679, a San Juan Indian named Popé began to work among the Río Grande tribes, planning an uprising to force the Spaniards out of their homeland. Among other things, Popé had been embittered by the punishment dealt out to him and to forty-six other Pueblo leaders by Governor Treviño in 1675 (Hackett, 1942, pp. 289–290). Other tribes soon joined, until all of the Pueblos were in full coöperation. The Hopis were urged to participate, and a date was set in 1680. Word of the plot leaked out, and it became necessary to advance the date; but the Pueblo Revolt, when finally set in motion, was successful. Every tribe performed its set task, killing or driving out all of the resident Spaniards—an example of tribal coöperation rare in Indian history. Many of the Whites who were forewarned were able to escape; but some 250 were killed. (The best comprehensive account of the Pueblo Revolt is told in Hackett, 1942.)

In the Hopi area, the only resident Spaniards were four priests, and these the Hopis merely tossed over the cliffs. From 1680 on, no Spanish priests were reëstablished in the Hopi missions except for a temporary sojourn at Awátovi.

The Pueblo Revolt left lasting and important influences in Tusayan. In the first place, the Hopis were fearful of a Spanish reinvasion. While they had had only a slight taste of Spanish warfare, they had heard of the vengeance wreaked on Acoma when that village had killed a few soldiers in 1599. Some 500 captive Indians were sentenced to have one foot chopped off, and to serve twenty years at hard labor (Hammond, 1927, pp. 122–123). Since two Hopis captured at the time were given a similar sentence as a warning to their tribe, there would have been little doubt as to what would happen should the Whites succeed in reëntering Tusayan.

To avoid such an attack and the same treatment, the Hopis left
their vulnerable sites on the valley floor and moved to the top of
neighboring Black Mesa. At this time, Awátovi and Oraibi were both
in their present locations; Walpi had recently moved up atop First
Mesa from its earlier, lower, site, and Mishongnovi and Shungopovi
moved to their present Second Mesa sites. At about this same time,
some Hopis left Shungopovi and founded Shipaulovi north of Mishongnovi (see Fig. 3). The primary reason for this latter move was
that the Hopis were afraid that the Spaniards might destroy the
more vulnerable Shungopovi; thus Shipaulovi, located in a less acces-
sible part of the mesa, would be a stronghold for the preservation of
ceremonial paraphernalia and traditional ritual.

A second result of the general fear of the Spanish was that many
of the Río Grande people fled westward to the Hopi villages for
sanctuary. These established the towns of Hano on First Mesa,
Payupki on Second Mesa, and indirectly, Sichomovi, the Walpi
"suburb" (Fig. 3).

As a consequence of these several moves, not only did many of
the Hopi towns have the task of settling in new locations, but were
also infused with new blood and new ideas. We can only guess at
the specific results of this mixing of cultures, but physical build,
language, customs, traditions, and concepts of both peoples were
undoubtedly modified tremendously.

The shock of the Revolt so disorganized the Spanish colonists
that they were unable immediately to reconquer their lost lands—an
expedition under Governor Antonio Otermín set out in 1681 to wrest
control of Nuevo México from the Indians, but failed to accomplish
anything more than the destruction of a few small villages.

However, the documents which record Otermín's attempted reconquest provide us with considerable information concerning masks
and masked ceremonies in the pueblos at that time. One example
which is also revealing in the detailed description given, as well as
recording the fact that there were, this early, "Kachina families," can
be found in the following description of the situation at Sandía
convent (Hackett, 1942, II, p. 225):

> [The cells] have been made into a seminary of idolatry, and in
> the third cell there is hanging from the whole circumference of
> the walls, arranged very carefully, after their barbarous custom,
> a large number of masks for *cusinas,* representing both men and
> women, and other small ones representing children.

It must be remembered that Otermín was away from Santa Fé
(and control of the province) for less than a year after the Revolt; it
therefore seems that the custom could not have sprung up again in

so short a time. Rather, it would seem that the encouragement they received from Mendizábal in 1660 had only encouraged the Pueblos to continue something which I suspect had never really died—and the success of the Revolt only strengthened their tenacious hold on masked ceremonies.

THE SPANIARDS RETURN

The failure of Otermín to achieve an immediate victory dissuaded the Spanish from other attempts for ten years, until Diego de Vargas was dispatched with a much better-equipped expedition. Arriving in the Río Grande area in 1692, he completed the subjugation of the several tribes by 1694, and reëstablished full Spanish control (Espinosa, 1942). A second attempt at rebellion was quelled in 1696, and Spain remained in power until the Mexican Revolution in 1821.

Many of the New Mexicans, especially the Río Grande people, fled from the De Vargas party and sought safety in the Hopi villages, now securely established atop the mesas. These Pueblo folk remained in the Hopi villages for well over half a century (many of their descendants are there to this day), and this stay likewise resulted in many cultural interchanges and influences.

In Tusayan, Spain was less successful. In 1692 De Vargas visited the four westerly villages of Awátovi, Walpi, Mishongnovi, and Shungopovi, and obtained promises of loyalty from them, but this allegiance lasted only as long as the Spanish force was in the vicinity. With the sole exception of Awátovi, the Hopi villages refused to have anything to do with the sporadic attempts of the clergy to reënter, scorning their missionary efforts. Subsequently, Spanish military parties were sent out occasionally to force the recalcitrants to submit to Christian authority; but the inhospitable nature of the country, as well as the incompetence of the leaders made every effort futile.

Following the collapse of the 1696 revolt, the harsh treatment meted out by De Vargas to the rebels caused the Hopis to send representatives to Santa Fé in 1700 to forestall possible Spanish retaliatory expeditions. It is not clear just which villages were represented by the ambassadors, but that same year three missionaries were sent to Awátovi, regarded as the main Hopi village. Just before these priests were dispatched, the Hopis tried to ward off their reëntry by offering the Spanish a pact, one provision of which was that each nation would retain its own religion, but Governor Cubero refused to agree to such a treaty (Bancroft, 1889, pp. 221–222).

On the basis of legends and archeological findings, it seems evident that the Awátovi folk received the priests kindly, and were somewhat inclined to follow their teachings. It must be remembered that because of its exposed location, Awátovi was a more cosmopolitan, and therefore probably more sophisticated, village than the other Hopi towns, and would presumably have many inhabitants who would be attracted by the exotic novelty of Christianity.

In any case, the other Hopi villages looked upon this favorable reception with concern, fearing that it would be only a matter of time before the Spanish would be back in force. They were not unnaturally aroused and fearful of the results of this welcome extended to the Spaniards. This, plus jealousy of the importance enjoyed by Awátovi, political intrigue, and inter-village strife (a paramount Pueblo cancer even today), resulted in a concerted attack. Late in 1700 a picked group of warriors from Walpi and neighboring villages descended upon Awátovi, killed most of the inhabitants, and totally destroyed the village. Some of the inhabitants who knew special ceremonies (and undoubtedly this included Kachina priests) or were possessed of particular skills, were taken as captives to Walpi and Shungopovi. Stephen (1936, p. 944) claims that some were also taken to Mishongnovi and Oraibi—thus all three mesas acquired involuntary ambassadors of the cultural practices of other villages.

From that date on, Awátovi remained a total ruin, and for years was overlooked by explorers and archeologists in their search for early sites. When it was finally located and excavated, the evidence supported the legendary accounts as told by the Hopis themselves. Fewkes (1893) gives a detailed account of the discovery and preliminary excavations of Awátovi in recent times, and (*idem*, 1898a, pp. 603–605) presents a version of the destruction of the village as told by a descendent of the Awátovi people.

V.

"Isolation"...1700-1875

In Nuevo Mexico, the eighteenth century marks the beginning of a more thorough integration of the Catholic religion with the Pueblo ritual. The Río Grande tribes, especially, became nominal Christians, even to the extent of adopting Spanish names and Christian practices in an effort to please the Catholic priests; and consciously or not, assimilated Catholic religion to such an extent that it became an indistinguishable part of native ritual. This was less true of Zuñi and Acoma; these towns resisted with much more vigor the attempts of the priests to convert them, and never gave more than lip service to the Franciscans.

Although there are several reasons for the collapse of Río Grande resistance, the primary factors seem to have been the following: (1) The unity which Popé achieved in organizing the Pueblo Revolt melted away almost immediately after the Spanish were driven out in 1680, and many of the tribes fell to squabbling among themselves. (2) The apparent impotence of the ancient gods to withstand the reëntry of De Vargas overcame some of the opposition to Christianity. (3) Undoubtedly the greatest factor was the Spanish diligence in searching out and executing the leaders of the rebellion—for most of these latter were ceremonial, as well as secular, leaders.

This situation, however, did not obtain with the Hopis in Tusayan. There was no reëntry of a successful Spanish military expedition, nor were there any effective results from the continued efforts of the Catholic priests to reëstablish themselves in the villages. Sporadic attempts were made to induce the Hopis to permit a renewal of religious activities and a few punitive expeditions ventured into

Tusayan, but the consequences were nil. The visits in every case were extremely brief, conducted under hostile conditions, and for the most part touched at only one or two of the villages. (With the razing of Awátovi, Walpi and Oraibi became the most important and best-known Hopi towns.)

HOPI "ISOLATION" AND KACHINA GROWTH

As the Summary (p. 147) indicates, the Hopis did not enjoy true isolation during the eighteenth century, as commonly supposed; the Spaniards were conscious of these stubborn apostates, and frequently considered means of recovering Tusayan. But geography, politics, jealousies within the Church, economic factors, and a new threat from the northeast combined to confine most of these efforts to words rather than deeds. Those few parties which did succeed in implementing the words were faced with an intransigent refusal. This attitude was so widespread that, towards the end of the century, efforts all but ceased.

As a result, although there were intrusions from time to time, the pressure from the Whites diminished to a point where they were no longer the primary threat they once were considered.

The only really concerted effort of the religious orders to regain the Hopi area during this period came as a direct result of the contest between the Jesuits and Franciscans which had begun with the Pueblo Revolt. This contest centered around a fight for the right to proselytize in the Hopi villages—the Jesuits blamed the Franciscans for the failure in Tusayan, and the Franciscans had to point to such evidence as they could muster in order to keep their franchise. The repeated efforts of Delgado from 1741 to 1745, for example, grew largely from this need—and, incidentally, retained the field for the Franciscans. The King revoked the temporary permit given the Jesuits, and from 1745 on, the Franciscans were left in unenvied possession of a field which had suddenly become strewn with plough-breaking boulders.

And the plough did break; for no sooner had the Franciscans been assured of their right to work the Hopi area, than they seem to have lost their sudden interest. There are records of only five major attempts of the gray friars to enter Tusayan from 1745 to the end of the Spanish era.

In spite of the occasional periods of drought, disease, and attack from neighboring Navajo and Ute Indians, the Hopis seem to have been able to maintain their independence, broken only by inter-village warfare. Lezaún (Hackett, 1937, p. 469) says:

> ...of some nine pueblos, ...due to continuous wars among them there remain only five, containing more than 8,000 Indians.

The province is the refuge of the Christian Indians [in the eastern part of Nuevo México] when they are tired of working for
the governor and the *alcaldes mayores;* at such times they retire thither, and, uniting with the Moquis, do great damage to
the cattle and horses of the Christians [the Whites].

Therefore, due to this relative isolation, and no doubt as influenced
by the more-or-less constant flow of Pueblo refugees into Tusayan,
the era 1750-1875 is, in my opinion, the period during which the
Kachina Cult expanded into its present importance and activity, becoming firmly entrenched in Hopi culture. Quite probably it had
previously been only one of many ceremonial rites, and may well
have been as exclusive as the Snake Fraternity is today, since Pueblo
prestige is largely measured by the amount of secret ceremonial
knowledge held by the society or individual.

However, since the Pueblo Revolt was a successful coöperative
venture, and since in Hopi eyes the Kachina figured prominently in
its success, I believe that the subsequent expansion of the Cult was
accompanied by an extension of membership to include all Hopis, as
obtains today. And there is evidence that some of the other religious
ceremonials were incorporated into its compass—Ancestor Worship,
Sun Worship, and the Warrior Cult observances, for example, all of
which have become extinct as separate observances in recent times.

Because the Kachinas had been the target for especially severe
attacks by the priests, as attested by innumerable documents of the
period, the success of the Revolt undoubtedly was interpreted by a
majority of the Indians as a clear indication of the supremacy of
Kachina over Saint. Since the Hopis were able to prevent the Spanish from returning in any considerable degree, their success was
credited to religious preëminence. Had there been any pitched bat-
tles from which Hopi warriors emerged victorious, the result might
have been credited to military superiority; but with the major clash
between the two cultures coming in the field of religion, the triumph
was quite naturally interpreted in theological terms.

But, although this successful expulsion of the White god greatly
strengthened Hopi religious belief and accelerated native ceremonials, it must not be overlooked that the Kachina ritual was undoubtedly infiltrated with some elements of White culture and religion.
Some were taken over directly from things the Hopis had seen themselves; but, in view of their attitude towards the Spanish, it is more
likely that a majority of these innovations came in by way of Zuñi
and the Río Grande tribes, thus losing the Hispanic taint offensive
in Hopi eyes.

A second equally important avenue of infiltration was through the

Río Grande immigrants. We can gain some idea of their numbers by noting that in 1742, Fray Carlos Delgado took 441 "Hopi" back to the Río Grande to reëstablish the pueblo of Sandía. This episode, as reported by Delgado in his diary, is related in Kelly (1941). With them went many of the "Hopi-ized Tigua" refugees from De Vargas' vengeance following the 1696 rebellion; as a result, Payupki was abandoned, never to be reinhabited. It is reported that many more would have returned, except for the fact that the Spanish could not escort a larger number safely through the lands of the hostile Navajos, who would have welcomed an opportunity to raid such a party. Hackett (1937, p. 31) credits Delgado with inducing, in all, more than 2,000 "Hopis" to go to the Río Grande settlements; thus the total number of refugees clearly was of such size that their influence upon their hosts would have been considerable.

The Tewas who had built up Hano, on First Mesa, however, were unwilling to leave—and to this day they remain staunchly Hopi, albeit still bilingual. They retain their own Tewa tongue; and their religious ceremonials, though essentially Hopi, have a strong flavor of Río Grande practice.

There were other effects of the Revolt in the Southwest. One, felt throughout the whole Pueblo area, was an extreme revulsion against everything Spanish, as demonstrated by destruction of all Spanish documents, materials, religious articles, and whatever else could be detected as coming from the hated Whites. This loss of documentary information is by far the most unfortunate result of the Revolt.

Much of the Indians' reaction against the Spaniards can still be seen in the pueblos—a reluctance to speak Spanish, a refusal to admit Mexicans to many of the villages or village activities, and a careful distinction between English- and Spanish-speaking Whites.

Although there was bitter hatred of the Whites after the expulsion of the Spaniards in 1680, many White influences had nevertheless become thoroughly integrated into Pueblo life. Innovations such as foods (chili, peaches, watermelons), animals (sheep, horses, cattle), textiles, and metals became a part of Hopi culture. From these substances new Kachinas were created, costuming was affected, and manufacture was greatly facilitated.

While the general Hopi attitude of hospitality was changed to one of hostility toward things Spanish, an even closer contact developed between Tusayan, Cíbola, and the several villages of the upper Río Grande. This contact, which originated in the trading expeditions of early days, was strengthened by the coöperation during the Pueblo Revolt, and the temporary residence of eastern Pueblo refugees in the Hopi villages. Although in time these friendships fluctuated, both groups learned new ideas that affected the Kachina Cult, and this

added intertribal contact resulted in even more elements of Spanish culture, unobserved as such by the Hopis. I believe that in this
way came many of the less easily noted material culture influences
now observable in the Kachina Cult. The situation has been summed
up by Fewkes (1898b, p. 194) as follows:

> ... The growth has been a development by addition of new and
> an evolution and modification of existing elements. Every in-
> coming family has added its peculiar rites, while neighboring
> pueblos which have been conquered have contributed their
> quota, making a complex ritual unexcelled in any tribe still
> living in the United States.

This determined stand of the Hopis had two near misses—both
due to "circumstances beyond their control." In 1777, the same year
that the eastern American Colonies were opposing George III of
England, a disastrous drought occurred. The smallpox epidemic
which followed nearly depopulated the villages; some Hopis fled to
the Río Grande, while many others were reported living with the
Havasupai Indians. Governor de Anza tried to take advantage of
this opportunity to regain Tusayan, but was prevented by the obsti-
nate refusal of the Oraibi people to leave, and a last-minute break in
the drought. De Anza remarked that the seven villages had been re-
duced to five, and that of the 7,494 Hopis reported by Escalante in
1775, only 798 were left alive when he visited them (Thomas, 1932,
pp. 236–237).

The second occasion was in 1819, following repeated attacks upon
the villages by the neighboring Navajos. Five Hopis went to Governor Melgares at Santa Fé to request his protection against the marauders, and indicated their grudging willingness to recognize Spanish sovereignty and receive Catholic priests once again. Though they
still had the Navajos to contend with, the Hopis were saved from
the Spanish in the nick of time, as it were, by the successful conclusion of the Mexican Revolution.

TUSAYAN AND THE REPUBLIC OF MEXICO

When Mexico achieved independence in 1821, Spanish officials
no longer held political power, but the Mexicans were not sufficiently
organized to make a smooth transition to authority. This was especially true in Nuevo México. Such remote outposts as Santa Fé were
left largely to their own devices, so that the several Indian tribes
were almost completely disregarded. During the quarter-century of
Mexican sovereignty, there is no evidence of Mexican contacts with
the Hopis, although we do know that the Mexicans were well-aware
of their existence (see p. 6).

Mexican political affairs were such that little attempt was made to extend active control to the remote outposts. Such distant areas as California and Nuevo México, although nominally under governors appointed by Mexico, continued otherwise in much the same conditions as in Spanish days.

The entry of William Becknell into Santa Fé in 1821 heralded the later arrival of many more Americans over that Trail; we do not know whether any of these early traders went on to Tusayan. It was shortly after that event that the Hopis saw the first "American" White men of whom we have record. These were a part of the Pattie fur-trapping expedition, which visited the villages in 1826; they left only slight mention of their trip (Pattie, 1905, p. 130). The second known entrant was one "Willians" [sic] (probably "Bill" Williams, the famous trapper), who spent much time in the villages in 1827 (Yount, 1923, p. 20). An excellent description of Hopi life was recorded by George C. Yount in the year following. In this account, which is the first detailed "American" commentary known, he claims that other Americans were also there in that same year (Yount, 1923, pp. 19–23).

The conduct of the next known group of American Whites was unfortunately more characteristic of the usual pattern of White-Indian relations. In 1834 a party of fur-trappers headed by Frapp and Jervais, accompanied by Meek, entered the Hopi country and discovered their small gardens. While raiding them, the Whites were challenged by the Indians attempting to protect their property. In the ensuing quarrel (it can hardly be termed a battle, since the Hopis were armed with only hoes and clubs), the Americans fired on the Indians, needlessly killing between fifteen and twenty (Victor, 1870, p. 153).

During the Mexican War (1846–1848) there is little record of travel in the Hopi country; but with the acquisition of the Mexican Cession, public curiosity about the new area resulted in several articles which discussed the Indians, including the Hopis, with varying degrees of accuracy. Not all of those who wrote these articles actually visited the Hopis, however; many relied upon earlier reports for their information (see Appendix I).

TUSAYAN IN THE UNITED STATES

With the increased interest in the Pacific Coast resulting from the Mexican War, the newly acquired Cession lands, the Gold Rush, and the expanding transportation facilities, it was only a question of time before Hopi isolation would come to an end. Numerous Government parties were sent out for military exploration, and railroad groups came to survey possible routes. Many of these visited the

Hopi villages, made cursory inspections, and then left. Since their main interest was in locating sources of food and water, the meager resources of the Hopis dissipated any interest in the tribe. A few Gold Rush stragglers, if Hopi legends can be accredited, wandered into the villages, were re-oriented, and left.

Antoine Leroux, the famous trapper and guide for many expeditions, is known to have been in the villages in 1850, at which time he estimated their population at 6,700. This same year also marks the practical end of Hopi isolation. In the preceding 50 years Whites had only occasionally entered Tusayan; in the following 50 years there were, to my knowledge, but two, 1855 and 1856, in which there was not at least one White man known to have been in the villages. These people include the previously mentioned exploring parties, plus Indian agents, school officials, traders, missionaries, and scientists intent upon learning what they could of Hopi civilization.

This period also saw publication of an early mention in the United States of the Hopis—a population estimate made in 1846 by Charles Bent (1850, p. 193), the first Governor of New Mexico. His figures of 2,450 Hopis agrees substantially with later census counts made by Government parties and scientists.

The first Government agent to leave a detailed record of Hopi life was Dr. P.G.S. Ten Broeck, who visited them in 1851-1852 (Schoolcraft, 1854, vol. IV, pp. 83–85). This includes the first American description of Kachina ceremonies, and mentions masks, costumes, and dance ritual as seen at Walpi. His account lacks sufficient detail to make definite identification possible, but it would appear that he witnessed a performance of Hümis Kachina, accompanied by Hümis Mana. This may have been a Nimán ceremony, although the dating (April 1st) seems unusually early for this. Ten Broeck mentions an "imp" who appeared at the dance; the description and illustration, drawn from his notes, suggests this was Kókoṣori Kachina. However there are some details mentioned which would also apply to Avách'-hoya Kachina—and since Hümis is regarded as the uncle of Avách'-hoya, and the latter often appears at Hümis performances, this alternate identification seems equally possible.

The next report mentioning the Kachina Cult is also the first-known serious attempt to devote any considerable space to a description of Pueblo ceremonial activity (Klett, 1879, pp. 332–336). This "study" was written in 1873 as part of an extensive Government survey of the Far West, and includes not only excellent descriptive material, but also color drawings. An interesting point in connection with this article is that while the particular dance discussed by Klett took place at Zuñi, and concerns the Zuñi *Kókoshi*, the discourse is titled "The Cachina"—evidence that at this time, even in the Zuñi area, the Hopi term was in common use, in place of the Zuñi word *Koko*. Thus there is a record of usage from 1660 to 1873 to 1953.

The third report of interest is that of Lt. John G. Bourke, who was detailed by military authority to visit and report on the various Western tribes. Bourke spent some time in the Hopi area, and as a result of his visit wrote what is still one of the better descriptions of the Snake Dance. In this book he included several references to other Hopi ceremonial activities, although the Kachina season was closed when he was in the villages. But his observations of Kachina paraphernalia leave no doubt that the Cult was a major factor in the religious life of the Hopis at this time. Some of his comments are worth quoting not only to illustrate the similarity to present-day custom, but also to indicate the prevalence of the Kachina Cult:

> Here [Hano] we found three cylindrical masks of buckskin, painted green. Around the eyeholes were heavy circles in yellow; the noses in two cases were made of black wooden pegs, and in the third was shaped thus, T.
>
> Each mask was provided with a necklace of cornshucks and cedar leaves, perfectly concealing the identity of the wearer (Bourke, 1884, p. 131).
>
> In the same room with this cast was a false head of black sheep-skin, untanned, and with wool still on; the face was of buckskin, painted red, with round holes for eyes and mouth,— altogether a very good piece of work (*op. cit.*, p. 135).

In another section of the book, he gives a good description of several types of masks he had seen:

> Masks are used in every dance and dramatic representation, and cover not the face alone, but the head and neck also. These masks have various shapes, the favourite one being a cylinder of buckskin or cardboard, painted green, crested with feathers, and trimmed at bottom with a necklace of cedar. Eyes, nose, and mouth are put in arbitrarily, the first being frequently bulging balls of buckskin set astride of a nose shaped of wood like a bird's beak; others again are altogether of sheepskin, the wool left on in the parts to cover head and neck, but denuded where the face is to be rudely represented by small circles for eyes, nose, and mouth (*op. cit.*, p. 239).

Plate VII. Ahül Kachina
   A being who appears at Soyala and Powamû, to celebrate the Kachina return, and to assist in the solstice rites.

a

b

c

Bourke was a careful observer, and his use of the term "cardboard" to describe the mask foundation is difficult to understand, for this substance has never, to my knowledge, been used for this purpose. The function of the cylinder type of mask would make cardboard quite unsuitable since the moisture from the breath and the sweat of the wearer would soon cause it to lose its strength. I am inclined to believe that he mistook painted leather for cardboard.

Bourke "quotes" from the early Spanish in a mistaken effort to give the origin of the term Kachina. Apparently he did not realize these same Spanish records regard the word as of native origin:*

> . . . D. Diego Vargas, . . . insisted upon the discontinuance of the dance in honour of the idols, called by the Castilians the Cochino or Pig, from its ugly snout, but known among the Zunis, who still practise it . . . (Bourke, *op. cit.*, p. 43).

Bourke's book (Plate XXIX) also presents one of the earliest illustrations of a Kachina mask, but details are so altered (apparently by the artist who prepared the drawing for publication) that the original effect has been largely lost. It is not identifiable.

In 1866–67 the Hopis suffered a severe smallpox epidemic, introduced by soldiers in a Government military party. The deaths resulting from this disease were so numerous that a large number of Hopis went to Zuñi to escape the pestilence. This migration affected the culture of both tribes, for there is a very marked change in the quality and decoration of pottery which continued to be noticeable until about 1900, when White influence began to cause even greater changes (Bartlett, 1936, p. 36).

Although this temporary sojourn at Zuñi had a strong affect upon ceramic art, influences of greater importance to this study were wrought upon the Kachina Cult. When the Hopis came to Zuñi, they brought their own religious customs with them, particularly their own Kachinas; many of these beings found a welcome in Zuñi practice, took root, and were adopted into the Zuñi *Koko* complex. In her

---

*As one Spaniard commented in 1661: ". . . the name [*catzina*] was given by the Spaniards, who perhaps took it from some of the languages of the Indians of those provinces . . ." (Hackett, 1937, p. 157). However, Kroeber (1916, p. 272) presents other evidence: ". . . *kachina* [is] a term that the Zuñi know but regard as "Mexican" and refuse to employ."

Plate VIII. Masks Incorporating Awátovi Being Elements

    a. Añwüṣnasómtäqä Kachina—*"Crow-wing Mother," who takes part in the initiation ritual.*

    b. "Awiri" Kachina—*Warrior Kachina (from Voth).*

    c. Ewiro Kachina—*A Warrior Kachina (from Colton).*

80   excellent study of Zuñi masked ceremonies, Bunzel (1932, pp. 837–1086) has described several such examples.

Nor was this a one-way street. There is considerable evidence that the returning Hopis brought back several Zuñi personages, whom they introduced into their own Cult, and who are regularly presented today.

VI.

The Modern Era

1875 - 1900

AT THE BEGINNING OF THE MODERN ERA, the Hopis were living in eight villages. Seven were atop the mesas, and are still inhabited today: Walpi, Hano, and Sichomovi on First Mesa; Shungopovi, Mishongnovi, and Shipaulovi on Second Mesa; and Oraibi, the largest, on Third Mesa. Moenkopi was some forty miles west, near Tuba City (colonists from Oraibi had reëstablished it in the 1870's on the ruins of a former village, taking advantage of the permanent water supply of Moenkopi Wash).* The total Hopi population in 1893 was estimated by Stephen (1936, p. xxv) at 1,950 individuals.

With increasing invasions by various military and civilian surveying parties, the Hopis gradually became aware of a new culture. Since these new Whites did not enter by force, but paid for what food, water, and fuel they needed, the Indians soon made a distinction between the Americans and the Spaniards (including the Mexicans, who had inherited the hostile feeling against the Conquistadores).

By nature a pacific people, the Hopis welcomed the *Bahana*, as they called the Americans, and freely offered them such hospitality as they had. Relatively few Whites entered the Hopi country during this period; and, since the Hopis were not possessed of resources valuable in White eyes, the violence and preëmption of lands was absent. Hence, there was not the sudden cultural dislocation characteristic of most Indian areas invaded by land-hungry White men. Finally, in many cases, the presence of military personnel acted as an effective bulwark against Ute or Navajo marauders.

---

*An excellent guidebook to the Hopi country, detailing travel routes, background information and history concerning the villages is Colton and Baxter (1932).

Thus, on the whole, American relations with the Hopis from 1850 to 1900 were better than with Indian tribes of other areas. Federal services to the Hopis were extremely irregular during this period, although it is surprising to note that the first Indian Agent for the Hopis seems to have been John H. Moss, appointed in 1864 at the height of the Civil War (Donaldson, 1893, p. 36). When Arizona became a separate territory in 1863, territorial Indian agents were supposed to have been responsible for local tribes, but this never seems to have worked very well. One reason may have been the ignorant handling of Indians by the Whites: when a delegation of Hopis went to Prescott in 1866 to see the governor, they were unaccountably thrown in jail! This inhospitable reception undoubtedly had an effect back in the villages, since the delegation had been sent to ask for relief from the famine brought on by the drought of 1864.

The Hopi agency was established in 1870, but it was not until 1874 that buildings for the agency and a Federal school were built at Keams Canyon (Donaldson, 1893, p. 36). Unfortunately, owing largely to a lack of knowledge and interest in the area and its inhabitants, both were discontinued and reëstablished three times before the creation of the definite reservation in 1882.

One basic reason for the eventual establishment of a reservation was the fear of Mormon activities in the Southwest, which had been magnified by Eastern hysteria. Although Mormons had traveled in and around the Hopi country since the arrival of Jacob Hamlin in 1858, no permanent settlement was made until a small Mormon community was established at Moenkopi about 1875 (Barnes, 1935, p. 281). Another factor which had much to do with the enclosure of the Hopi country was the construction of the Atlantic and Pacific Railroad, which entered Arizona in 1881 (Bradley, 1920, pp. 220–224). Although the railroad route was more than sixty miles south of the Hopi villages, it nevertheless facilitated White migration, and soon large numbers followed the route, scattering and settling over a wide area, effectively "fencing in" the Hopis.

Even after the official establishment of the Hopi Reservation in 1882, there was little consistent Federal contact until 1887, when the agency at Keams Canyon began active and continuous operation. The primary results of this seem to have been the introduction of more White material products, since trading was facilitated,* and a limited exchange of new ideas, which increased as the school made

---

*By this time several Whites had settled in the area adjacent to the Hopis for the purpose of trading. They included Thomas V. Keam (after whom the canyon was named), Don Lorenzo Hubbell, Hermann Wolff, and others. These men were for a long time the main "commerce highway" in and out of the Hopi country, particularly for the flow of White goods, and had a tremendous influence among the Hopis and Navajos.

itself felt to a more marked degree (Jones, 1950, p. 22). Yet even in the face of such apparently solid evidence of alien authority, the Hopis were not, until long after 1882, outwardly conscious of being surrounded by an invisible but operative and alien cultural wall.

PROTESTANT MISSIONARIES ARRIVE

Another force, and one which was ultimately to have perhaps the strongest effect upon the survival of Hopi culture, was the entry of Protestant missionaries. Led by the Catholics, whose early history in the area has already been treated, and the Mormons (who had been working for the past two decades), other denominations sent out workers to reap the harvest. A Moravian Church mission was founded at Oraibi shortly after 1870 (Parsons, 1939, p. 862); a Protestant missionary school was in operation at Keams Canyon by 1875, according to Bancroft (1889, p. 547); and the Baptist Sunlight Mission was established about the same time at Mishongnovi (Nequatewa, 1936, p. 108).

The effects of these several missions varied, and at first were relatively slight. The Catholics had never been able to reassert themselves after the Pueblo Revolt; even today their activity is largely confined to the Navajo tribe. Although the Baptists have made the most converts, their conduct has made them generally unpopular. The Mormons have probably earned the most enviable reputation, due largely to their more intelligent attitude in working among the people. Even so, there were estimated to be only about 30 converts to Christianity as of 1944 (Thompson and Joseph, 1944, p. 137).[*]

The Mennonite mission requires special attention for it has had the greatest effect upon Hopi life to date, not because of numbers of converts, but because of the disruption which followed its establishment at Third Mesa. In 1893, H. R. Voth established a new Mennonite mission at Oraibi which was to have a far-reaching effect upon that village. Although Voth was fully devoted to extending his religious views, he spent considerable time studying Hopi ceremonial life. Unlike most other missionaries in the field, he learned the language well enough to use it freely, which furthered his understanding of the people. In order to support himself, he sold from time to time written observations and collections of artifacts obtained by various means; today they form all, or a great part, of what we know of certain phases of Hopi ceremonial life of that period insofar as Oraibi is concerned.

DISSENSION IN ORAIBI

Voth had little success in converting the Hopis, but his activities on Third Mesa, coupled with Governmental policies, eventually brought a long-standing feud to a climax. For some time there had

---

[*]Although the number of converts to Christianity has increased slightly over the past quarter century, they still represent a small minority of reservation Hopis.

been two groups in Oraibi who differed over matters of internal politics. They struggled for ceremonial control of the village, and were opposed on the question of acceptance or rejection of White civilization. Titiev (1944) has discussed this struggle thoroughly, presenting a penetrating analysis of the whole problem of the frequent splitting-up of Pueblo villages. It is quite evident that Voth had a not inconsequential part in this Oraibi feud, although he can scarcely be charged with having been the whole cause.

By the end of the century, Oraibi was divided into two factions bitterly hostile to each other. These came to be known as the Friendlies (who today would be called Liberals), who welcomed White ways, and the Hostiles (or Conservatives), who wanted to have nothing to do with outsiders.

In 1891 Governmental pressure to force the Hopis to send their children to school at Keams Canyon had resulted in a refusal on the part of the Hostiles to comply. It is significant that when the Federal troops came up to Oraibi to enforce Governmental orders, they were confronted by Masaû Kachina, dressed in his customary blood-spattered costume. Unfortunately, this time the Kachina did not conquer his oppressors; a half-dozen Hostile leaders were arrested and taken to Fort Wingate, where they were imprisoned for a while—which only increased their antipathy for White culture (Nequatewa, 1936, pp. 60ff.). This affair had its culmination in the tragic Oraibi split fifteen years later.

SCIENTIFIC INVESTIGATORS

A third group, White students of Indian life, began to filter into Tusayan about this time. Never numerous—there were rarely more than one or two of them in the villages at any one time—they seem to have been present fairly continuously from about 1880 on.

The ethnographic work of these scientists, as exemplified by Alexander M. Stephen and Jesse Walter Fewkes, is of such merit that it has not been surpassed since. Due in part to their early arrival in the field, to the happy coincidence of their working in the most coöperative of the three Hopi mesas, and very largely to their superior ability as observers, they have left extremely valuable records of Hopi life at the turn of the century. Since these men were allowed free access to nearly all phases of Hopi life (Stephen, for example, was initiated into full membership in three Hopi ceremonial organizations), their carefully-written observations are a firm foundation for later comparative studies.

One of the earliest scientific projects in this area was the dispatching of parties to collect artifacts for exhibition and study. Individual collectors, such as Keam and Voth, had already been providing

considerable material, but three other groups brought back quantities of Hopi art and crafts to Eastern institutions. The first of these,
the Stanley McCormick Hopi Expedition, was subsidized to collect
Hopi material for the Columbian Exposition in Chicago in 1892 and
1893. Under the direction of George A. Dorsey, many artifacts were
accumulated and exhibited.

An equally important expedition was the 1891 Hemenway Southwestern Expedition, under the leadership of Jesse Walter Fewkes.
This party not only collected a large number of Hopi artifacts (now
housed in the Peabody Museum of Harvard University), but also
conducted extensive archeological excavations, which marked the
beginning of many years of investigation into what has become a
very rich area for the American archeologist.

The third exploratory agency was the Federal Government, whose
Bureau of American Ethnology sent out several expeditions to study,
collect, and report on the Pueblo Indians. Started by such collectors
as James Stevenson, the Bureau's Hopi collection grew tremendously as new material was uncovered in excavations conducted by
Fewkes, Hough, and later expeditions of other staff members.

The several scientific expeditions were adequately financed, and
spent freely in buying everything possible for their collections. While
some of these collections unfortunately have since been broken up
into small parts, they still remain as excellent nuclei for studying
Hopi material culture of the period.

The thorough studies made by these ethnologists enabled them to
gain a profound knowledge of Hopi culture, and in some cases individual scientists became so familiar with the ceremony that they
were able to point out errors in ritual made by the Hopi priests
(Stephen, 1936, p. 671) and impress upon the older men traditions
which were in danger of becoming lost. Their very real interest in
every phase of Hopi life, as well as their sympathetic attitude toward
religious matters, encouraged the Hopis not only in their determination to live their own lives, as against Governmental interference,
but particularly strengthened their resistance to the missionaries.

The relatively large quantities of ceremonial and domestic articles
which these various expeditions brought for Eastern display had
effects both good and bad. Not only did the Hopis learn to look at
their culture through other eyes, and therefore take more pains with
technical craftsmanship, but they also became aware of the commercial value of their manufactures. This was not entirely new, of course.
The Hopis had long traded artifacts with other Indian tribes; and
they were such excellent weavers that their textile output almost
completely dominated the Pueblo field, to the extent that many Río
Grande tribes abandoned their own looms in favor of the better-made

Hopi product. But articles up to this time had been made largely for practical use, ceremonial function, home decoration, or inter-tribal trade; now there began to be an important outside demand of an entirely new type.

It is not surprising, then, to see increased activity in the manufacture of the many articles which composed their material culture. When "genuine" articles were not available for expedition purchase, or were too badly worn for museum purposes, the collector often arranged with some Hopi to make a duplicate. This, of course, was entirely legitimate, since the new article was as authentically Indian as the worn-out specimen; but as a result many articles came to be made for other than their original, dedicated purposes, and in such instances esthetic appeal and salability were frequently emphasized more than might normally have been the case.

This was particularly true of the Kachina *tihü*. Since these were so colorful, and especially since they provided excellent means of becoming acquainted with a large portion of Hopi religious practice, they were in great demand by the several scientific expeditions. Voth, for example, collected well over a thousand; and Keam must have accumulated nearly the same amount; while Fewkes probably had upwards of 500. It is indicative of their place in Hopi life that this quantity was available to the collectors at this early period; it would certainly demonstrate that the tihü was not a recent innovation, even though many of those collected were made-to-order specimens.

Many of the conservative leaders bitterly resented the wholesale disposal of ceremonial objects. Most of the latter were obtained either from those few individuals who placed economic gain above religious loyalties, or from an equally small number of "Christian" Hopis who not only withdrew from their former religious life, but were encouraged by the missionaries to do all they could to destroy their culture. Some of these Christianized Hopis were traditional owners of ceremonial paraphernalia which they were quite happy to sell. When it became known that various religiously-important articles were on public view in Chicago and elsewhere, the conservative Hopis were outraged at the sacrilege.

It is not surprising, then, that the erstwhile generous and hospitable Hopis began to withdraw more to themselves, and in a short while they no longer offered the White scientists the degree of cooperation previously given.

1900 - 1925

Following the reports of the several expeditions to the Southwest, other scientific organizations began to take an interest in the Pueblo Indians, and as a result, we have an additional amount of written and collected material dealing with the Hopis. In addition to the excellent work of Voth and Fewkes, who continued to pioneer in interpreting Tusayan culture, collections were gathered by Culin, Spinden, Dorsey, and Hyde, among others. The material which had been gathered for the Columbian Exposition was placed on exhibit at the newly established "Columbian Field Museum," later the Field Museum of Natural History in Chicago.

These later collections are, in the main, excellent in themselves; but unfortunately they are not accompanied by the extensive written records which marked the earlier accumulations and made them so valuable. Actually some of these, even though gathered by scientists, are unaccompanied by data sufficient to enable the scholar to use them adequately; and have therefore even less value to the layman. One reason for this paucity of information may be that while the Indians were still willing to sell articles, they were much less inclined to supply information connected with their religious life.

The use by Indians of published material is an interesting factor in acculturation, and can be demonstrated in two remarkably similar instances. In 1665 there is a mention of an Indian coming to Pedro Manso de Valdés, asking to borrow his Bible, for he wanted to copy the illustrations contained therein (Hackett, 1937, p. 264). The effect of this type of illustration on Indian art is difficult to assay; but the other instance is more readily demonstrative of influence. When Mischa Titiev was living at Oraibi in 1933, preparing his study of that village, he engaged a Hopi to make several Kachina paintings for him. The Hopi, an excellent craftsman, turned out several fine specimens. One day, Dr. Titiev asked for a particular Kachina; the Hopi agreed and went away. Some time later he returned, carrying a sheaf of pictures, with the request that Dr. Titiev indicate which one he wanted. The pictures were colored illustrations clipped from the study by Fewkes (1903), made thirty years earlier! (In conversation with Mischa Titiev, 1951.)

Thus, the recorded word and picture had already been of benefit to the Hopi, as well as to the White, for many Kachinas were no longer known to the tribe. Without such a reference, it is almost certain that these forgotten beings would have joined the host of older Kachinas which have passed from memory. It would be interesting to know just how many copies of that volume are now in the villages providing source-material for the Hopis.[*]

However, it has undoubtedly also caused some innocent variations. I have examined the original illustrations from which the color plates were made (now stored in the library of the Bureau of American Ethnology), and find that not all of the colors were exactly

---

[*]A more recent addition to this repertory is Wright and Bahnimptewa (1973).

reproduced, owing no doubt to the method of printing used at the time. Since the Titiev incident indicates that the Hopis themselves have been using the volume as a reference, it would seem that not all color variants may be laid to Indian vagary. Thus even scientific efforts at recording factual information can be the cause of changes, variations, and errors in an original culture study.

THE ORAIBI SPLIT

Two other outstanding events during this period had much to do with the change developing in Hopi reactions to White civilization. The first was the result of the long feud at Oraibi, which came to a head in 1906. The inner conflicts, aggravated by tensions arising from missionary and Governmental interference, as mentioned in the previous section, finally resulted in a Hopi civil war. The village split up, and the Conservative faction established a new village, Hotevilla, on Third Mesa a short distance northwest of Oraibi. A short while later, a third village was established by disaffected members of the Conservative group at Hotevilla. This new village, Bakabi, was also built on Third Mesa, northeast of Hotevilla and Oraibi (see Fig. 3).

As a result of the activities of the Whites in this affair, especially the brutal Government action of separating families and unnecessarily imprisoning the very Hopi leaders who were trying to control the younger hot-heads, the Hopis retreated even further from their previous friendly attitude.

FEDERAL-INDIAN RELATIONS

The second and far more impressive effect was the increasingly concentrated effort, on the part of the Whites, to completely stamp out all semblance of Indian culture. This policy, although carried on throughout all Indian areas under Federal control, was felt particularly keenly in the Southwest, where the pre-European culture was still strongly maintained.

It is not within our province to go deeply into the matter of Federal Government-Indian relations, but the situation should be mentioned briefly, for it has a bearing upon our problem. Since its inception, the Indian Service had been forced by political pressure to fill its ranks with individuals who lacked knowledge, understanding, or interest in the Indian; the few in the Service who sincerely wanted to do a good job were overwhelmed by these incompetents, and thwarted by political fumbling and dishonesty.

There was no reaction or even interest aroused among the White citizenry when the Government essentially handed over the complete administration of Indian affairs to the missionary element. In due course, Senate policy came to accept nominations for the ten-man Board of Indian Commissioners from a Church committee, and these individuals naturally represented religious interests rather than the trained sociological, anthropological, or cultural point of view. As a direct result of this program, the problem of Indian administration grew to such shameful proportions that in 1928 a committee under Lewis H. Meriam was appointed to study the whole picture (Meriam, 1928).

By about 1910 the two forces of Church and State had joined in an Unholy Alliance which completely ignored the Constitution and prohibited by statute any Indian group from observing non-Christian religious activities. This reached its climax in several regulations of the Indian Bureau which were directly aimed at certain rites of the Indians, notably those of the Pueblo and Plains groups. As Cohen (1945, p. 175) remarks:

> Administrative control of Indian life, until recently, recognized no right of religious freedom.
>
> Administrators who identified civilization with a particular sect infringed the religious liberty of the Indians and interfered, on the ground of immorality, with many of the dances and other cherished customs of some of the tribes.

To illustrate just how far this attitude went, it will suffice merely to quote from an astounding directive issued by the Commissioner of Indian Affairs in 1923 (Circular No. 1665, in Cohen, 1945, pp. 175–176). This document defined the Sun Dance, and other dances and "so-called religious ceremonies" as Indian Offences, for which *corrective penalties* were provided. It continued:

> That the Indian dances be limited to one in each month in the daylight hours of one day in the midweek, and at one center in each district; the months of March and April, June, July, and August being excepted.
>
> *That none take part in the dances or be present who are under 50 years of age.*
>
> *That a careful propaganda be undertaken to educate public opinion against the dance.* (Italics mine.)

While the Sun Dance was specifically mentioned in the above, it should be realized that this directive went to all agencies, and resulted, as intended, in the flat prohibition of all native ceremonies, regardless of their harmless nature. Many Indians (both lay individuals and ceremonial leaders) were actually jailed for performing religious dances and ceremonials, and the only alternatives seemed to be for the native to give up his traditional customs or retreat into protective secrecy.

Obviously the latter course was the one which would be followed by those Indian groups who could possibly manage to do so. The isolated area of the Southwest was especially suitable for secret activity; there were few Government agents, and fewer missionary representatives, to pry into tribal affairs. There was the added advantage of the architecture of the Pueblo kiva, which aided in the efforts to keep out unwanted observers, so that more and more ceremonial practices left the *kisonvi* and went below ground to escape interference.

The primary purpose of the Government in its relationship with the Hopis has been summarized by Thompson and Joseph (1944, p. 31):

> ... to break up the traditional life of the Hopi and destroy the power of their "priests" and "chiefs," at the same time encouraging the Indians to develop White industries and skills. This attitude was reflected in most Government policies and contacts; as for instance, the persistent [unsuccessful] attempts on the part of the Federal Government to allot the Hopi lands in severalty (the first of which extended from 1892 to 1894 and the second from 1907 to 1910); the rule of compulsory attendance at schools, enforced by troops who compelled the people to give up their children during their formative years; and the encouragement of both Hopi and Navaho to increase their livestock as much as possible, regardless of range capacity. Moreover, when as a result of the growth of their herds the Navaho encroached on Hopi-occupied lands, the Government did nothing to protect the Hopi.

INDIAN SCHOOLS AND THEIR EFFECTS

An additional means used by the Government to break down Hopi culture was a program of deliberately discrediting Indian customs, language, and arts. In Indian schools this resulted in the Hopi child losing pride of race; in White society there was loss of whatever respect there might have been for this unique culture within our boundaries: and, worst of all, in legislative activities the Hopis were denied any sympathy for their plight which might otherwise have developed.

During this era (approximately 1875–1934), youngsters in Indian schools were forbidden to use their native tongue, and all other evidences of tradition were suppressed as much as possible. The result has been that a generation grew up which was largely prevented from using, learning, or appreciating anything of its own culture and traditional background. Of course, the village elders could and did instill some of the missing knowledge; but since the child was exposed to ridicule, censure, and criticism at school, the result was a travesty of American culture—the old had been largely lost, the new was not assimilated, and the middle ground had no tradition which might offer security to the bewildered cultural orphan.

Because the Indian child did not grow up learning to dance and participate in ceremonial activities, he naturally felt awkward and self-conscious. Without a bulwark of traditional knowledge and understanding for support, he had little motivation to participate in rituals which he did not fully understand. Having the criticism of his religion continually drummed in his ears by teachers, he felt resentful toward them, and yet his faith was strongly shaken—precisely what his White administrators desired.

As the Federal Government began to take over more of the education which had previously been administered in missionary schools, the emphasis on religion lessened somewhat (but did not entirely disappear), and secular studies were stressed more. Academic subjects such as history, geography, and science, further affected the situation of the young Hopi. Some of the material taught him in the White school was factually at wide variance with legendary accounts he had heard at home. He found that legendary accounts of Hopi origin via the *sípapü* did not agree with school-taught geological and anthropological beginnings, or with missionary stories of the Christian Genesis.

The typical youngster was bewildered—he had little faith in the new ways, yet his belief in the old culture had been disastrously undermined. The teachers at that time rarely knew anything about Indian moral or ethical values, and every effort was made to hold up the traditional Hopi concepts to ridicule; the result was that in most cases the Hopi youth lost his old values, but gained little to offset the loss. This "educational" program continued until the Collier administration.

It is true that a few Hopis were able to go through the school experiences unchanged, but they are in the minority. Others were completely dissuaded from the Pueblo world, and became, insofar as they possibly could, White citizens. And, much in the fashion of apostate-turned-zealot, some of these "fully-acculturated" Indians became the most severe critics (and often cultural traitors) of their own people. A typical example of this unfortunate characteristic is given in Thompson (1950, p. 145).

But by far the majority came out of the school period more antagonistic toward the Whites than before, frequently refusing to use English, although understanding it, and accepting only that portion of White life which suited them. This latter was usually the economic, material culture aspect; almost never did the religious teachings find willing converts, and some of the more useful factors, such as sanitation, hygiene, medical knowledge, and the like, were often rejected because of the manner in which they were presented, or due to Hopi inability to afford such luxuries.

The inevitable result was that the Pueblo people turned even more away from White involvement wherever possible. The Río Grande tribes recoiled the most violently—these pueblos do not permit outsiders to witness their masked ceremonies. This proscription applies not only to Whites but often extends to alien Indian visitors. Today, it is only at Zuñi and the Hopi villages that the outsider may witness the spectacular ceremonies with any sense of being welcome. And even in these cases, he sees only *tíkive*, or last-day phase; except for certain individual outsiders, the kiva ceremonials are rarely opened to other than village inhabitants. Pueblo withdrawal extended beyond just the religious, and today it remains a major problem in the successful resolving of political and social relations between Indian and White. In all fairness, it should be realized that this was not entirely a result of the inept Government-missionary joint action; it was the culmination of a long period of supression and persecution by the early Spanish and Mexican peoples, as well as by the later American immigrants—a cumulative resentment against four hundred years of experience in dealing with the White invaders.

Due to the above factors, during this period little interest was given to ethnological study of the Hopi, and there was small appreciation of their culture, except on the part of the few individuals who continued earlier scientific investigations. There is not, therefore, the great wealth of source material found during the period from 1900–1925 that characterizes the earlier period. Most of the published studies from 1910 to 1930 are fundamentally the results of field work carried on prior to 1910.

1925 - 1950

The repressive and restrictive policies outlined above were changed in 1933 with the appointment of John Collier as Indian Commissioner. He established a direct reversal of policy, with the aim now of teaching the Indian to appreciate his own ways, and of educating the White to understand the values of Indian culture and to assume the responsibilities of conquest. The whole philosophy was changed in order to orient education around Indian needs, rather than from the point of view of White ideas. Instead of trying to force the Indian into a mold, the attempt was now to assist him to adjust to and live in a world of different values but without loss of

everything he had previously found reliable. The effects of this new
policy insofar as the Hopis are concerned has been summarized in
Thompson (1950, pp. 149ff.).

Unfortunately, by the time Collier was able to put his policies into
effect, the reaction of the Indian in the Southwest had reached a
point where there was little trust of the White man. The reversal of
White educational policies seemed only an extension of the continual
chaos that the Indian had so frequently encountered in his dealings
with the Whites—one group would encourage him in his traditional
culture, whereas another group would vigorously oppose that culture, and seek in every way to destroy it.[*] The extremely inconsistent
attitude of the Whites so confused and disgusted the Indians that
their defensive avoidance and evasion had become a permanent shell
against the outside world. Not only did concealment and secrecy
continue, but mistrust and lack of faith in the White man diminished
very little.

Furthermore, Collier's policy did not meet with complete approval
by the Whites; it was strongly resisted by those who had long sought
to break up Reservation lands for personal profit, by the missionary
group, and also by many teachers and Indian Service employees who
sincerely believed in the older policy of eradicating Indian culture
and implanting White customs. Many teachers took very little interest in the problem one way or the other; they concerned themselves
with the day-to-day work, ignoring the long range goals. These latter
had seen so many changes in their careers that they no doubt felt
that "this too, shall pass away." But in justice, it should be said that
the majority of Indian School teachers are sincerely interested in the
future of their pupils, and are willing to try anything that might
offer the Indian youth a chance for the better life. (In this respect,
see also pp. 141–142, *infra*).

It should not be claimed that the Collier program was perfect;
many errors were made, and some of them were serious. But the
basic premise of attempting to work *with* the Indians, rather than
working *on* them, was a healthy change. Furthermore, the extension
of freedom in the matters of religion and social intercourse were but
the return to the Indian of rights long denied him but granted to
all other Americans.

---

[*]And the reversals continue. For comment on some of the recent changes in policy, see the
resolution adopted by the American Anthropological Association, appearing in *American
Anthropologist,* LIV, 1952, pp. 310-311.

VII.

The "Kachina Doll"

AMONG THE MORE COLORFUL ASPECTS of the Kachina Cult are the
small wooden "dolls," properly called *tihü*, which are carved from
cottonwood root to represent in stylized fashion a Kachina dancer.
These are carved by the men prior to Kachina ceremonies, usually
during the more leisurely winter months, and are then painted in the
traditional designs and decorated with feathers. They thus faithfully
portray the mask and costume of the particular Kachina represented.

On dance day, during one of the pauses in which gifts are distributed, the Kachina impersonators give the tihü to the children, who
take them home and keep them in the house (usually hung by a
string from the wall or rafter), thereby learning what each Kachina
looks like. As the children are told the stories of the Kachinas and
the legends of their origins, activities, powers, and appearances, they
become acquainted with the Cult through a system of painless education. Girls learn of the Kachinas at home, while the boys usually
become acquainted with them both at home and in the kivas.

The function of the tihü is frequently misunderstood; even a
thoughtful investigator like Bourke (1884, p. 131) made this observance:

> In Tegua [Hano] I bought several flat wooden gods or doll-
> babies. They are both. After doing duty as a god, the wooden
> image, upon giving signs of wear and tear, is handed over to
> the children to complete the work of destruction. These gods
> are nothing but coarse monstrosities, painted in high colours,
> generally green.

96   Bourke's unfamiliarity with Hopi practice, plus the evident respect given these dolls by the Indians, undoubtedly misled him, as it has many other writers on the Hopis.

The tihü is not an idol or god, nor is it worshipped in any sense of the word. Although they are not truly playthings, it is not "wrong" for a child to so regard them, and occasionally a Hopi youngster will be seen carrying a tihü around in much the same fashion as a White child carries her doll. Moreover, there is a close connection in the Hopi mind between the figurine and the Kachina personator, for the term *tihü* refers to the personator as well as to the carved wooden figurine.

Essentially, the tihü provides a means of education; it is a gift at dance-time; it is a decorative article for the home; it can be used as a toy, though not primarily so intended; but above all, it is a constant reminder of the Kachinas. This last function is especially important during the summer season when the Kachinas have "gone home" to the mountains and shrines where they dwell.

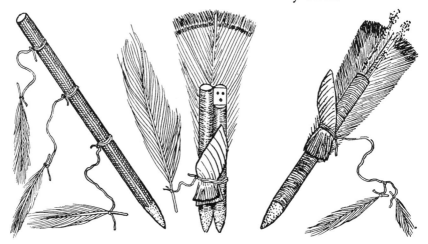

Figure 19. Types of Hopi *paho* (prayer-sticks).

Since the Kachina is a prayer messenger, the tihü is, in a sense, a duplicate of the Kachina, and the two are regarded in Hopi eyes as somewhat the same as a *paho*. The paho, or prayer-stick, is a short wooden rod (often two are used, in pairs), carved, painted, and decorated with feathers and corn husk (Fig. 19). It is usually made in preparation for ceremonies, and the type varies with the ritual. The paho is placed in shrines, on altars, and so on, wherever there is a need for a link with the gods, for it is believed to carry the wishes and desires of the makers. The sticks call the attention of the deity to the prayer; whenever the deity in question sees the paho, he looks for the attached prayer-feather, and there reads what is in the maker's heart (Stephen, 1936, p. 164).

It is important to bear in mind the similarity of the paho to the tihü, for just as both have a physical parallel (carved of cottonwood, painted, befeathered), there is likewise a certain degree of spiritual parallel in the minds of the Hopis regarding both. There is also a magical quality attached to the tihü: for example, a woman who wants a child is often given a tihü by a Kachina as a "phallic life-token" (Parsons, 1925, p. 51). Also, whereas the man owns the masks and ceremonial equipment, under Hopi common law these figurines belong to the woman, and are regarded as her "babies."

THE "KACHINA DOLL" IN OTHER PUEBLOS

While most of the Pueblos make various types of small wooden "dolls" of their Kachina impersonators, those of the Hopis have become most familiar to Whites. The Río Grande tribes do not carve theirs so realistically. They indicate only the masked head, leaving the body a plain cylinder. Mask details, such as nose, ears, feathers, and so on, are added; but the over-all appearance is crude in comparison to the more skillfully-made Hopi product.

It is worth noting that the Zuñi (who formerly made more of these figurines than they do today) most nearly duplicate the Hopi technique, with two important exceptions. The Zuñi tend to dress their statuettes in miniature costumes of cloth, leather, and wood, whereas the Hopi artist usually indicates these by painting them in (though in recent years the use of miniature costumes has also spread to the Hopis). Secondly, the Zuñi figurines are more slender, less stylized in concept, and are usually equipped with attached, movable arms. The Hopi carver almost never follows this practice—he customarily creates his tihü from a solid block of cottonwood, attaching only features such as nose, ears, and horns (*see* Plate XVI).

DEVELOPMENT OF THE TIHU

It is difficult to place any chronology on the development of the tihü, or of the several types in which they are more commonly found. Since they are carved from light wood, they are easily subject to destruction. Not being particularly sacred or revered, there is no tendency to place them in favored niches or shrines, nor are they buried with the dead. Hence, they are quite ephemeral—when the feathers and paint are lost and they become dilapidated, the tihü are either discarded or re-worked. To date, there have been very few specimens recovered from archeological excavations which might possibly be identified as prehistoric tihü (see p. 99).

Whether the whole idea of the carved wooden tihü originated with the Catholic saint statues is not yet clearly established; subsequent archeological work may bring more light to bear on this question. But whatever the actual origin, there would seem to be no doubt that the Catholic use of images, as well as the technique of church sculpture, may have exerted some influence on what came to be today's tihü. The degree of influence is less readily demonstrated, but it seems probable that these small statuettes either developed from, or were easily assimilated into, an earlier votive figure concept. With the introduction of the saint statuettes, a gradual evolution brought them to the state in which they were found in the 1880's. Subsequently, scientific and commercial demands resulted in the further elaboration characteristic of contemporary tihü.

Benavides (1916, p. 33) mentions that the early friars took great pains to teach the art of carving to the natives. While the clerics' primary purpose was to develop skills that would result in more artistic church decoration, this ability, once developed, could be expressed in any art form the Indian might choose. No small portion of the assigned task of these native carvers was the making of numerous statues of the various saints. An examination of any collection of New Mexican *santos* will readily demonstrate how one school of artists (in this case Mexican-Americans) developed a style of their own in this type of religious art. I believe that just as these carvers undertook to express their craftsmanship individually, so some Indian artists transferred their skills from Catholic art in wood to embellish or more fully develop the Indian ceremonial artifacts of wood.

The differences between the Hopi and Zuñi techniques in figurine-carving seem worthy of mention because they may represent a possible transition from the santo to the tihü, for the Zuñi article combines something of both. Many santos are costumed either realistically in cloth (as is the Zuñi figurine) or carved and painted in more realistic fashion than the Hopi tihü. Also, like the Zuñi figurine, the santos are characteristically equipped with movable arms and legs. The general figure proportions of the santo resemble the slender Zuñi figurine more than they do the chunkier Hopi carving. (For examples of santo art, *see* Wilder, 1943.)

There are many carved wooden fetishes and other articles of considerable age used in kiva ceremonies. Old-time Hopis say that these articles, and the art of tihü carving, is very ancient—many maintain that they brought these wooden objects with them up from the Underworld through the *sípapü*, relating legends in support of their claim. This is not offered as proof of age, but it is of interest in considering the origin of the tihü.

The earliest type of wooden tihü, in my opinion, is the flat, non-
sculptural *püchtihü,* usually about 6 to 8 inches long (Plate IX). This
is made from a single piece of cottonwood, smoothed down by rub-
bing on coarse stones or (in more recent times) by filing, with only
a slight amount of carving to indicate the break between head and
shoulders. Wooden ears, nose or horns are added as required, plus
a few feathers. The characteristic body painting is a series of three,
five, or seven vertical red lines, with shoulders and forearms painted
alternately in green and yellow. The arms are almost never carved,
being customarily indicated by painted lines; and kilt, legs, and feet
are not depicted. While a few that I have seen are cylindrical, the
great majority are made so that the cross-section is relatively flat. I
believe it was this type of carving which became more elaborate over
the years, especially with the increased demand for the more care-
fully-made tihü.

The earliest example known to me of what seems to be a prototypic püchtihü is the "effigy paho" excavated in 1887 by the Hemenway Expedition (Fig. 20). Discovered at Double Butte Cave, it
seems to show so many similarities to the later püchtihü that I am in
complete agreement with Haury (1945, pp. 198–200), who points out:

> ... one can recognize in this specimen the prototype of those
> [Kachina dolls] currently used ... The outstanding similarities
> are: the division of the face into ... halves, the diagonal body
> stripe, and the black-painted body. The headdress of the mod-
> ern kachina [doll] is considerably different than the simple pro-
> jection on the old example but this difference may be accredited
> to recent modifications. The persistence of symbolism over many
> centuries, however, may be indicated.
> ... The face treatment of the Double Butte effigy is unquestion-
> ably intended to represent a mask, a feature with which all
> kachina dolls are supplied ...

There are a few other points worthy of note concerning the possible relationship of the costuming of the effigy paho and contemporary practice. Black is commonly used as a body paint by many Kachinas; several others, notably the *Kachinmana,* wear the black
woven woman's dress (*kwasha*), which is traditionally edged with
two thin strips of red and green (Plate XI). The *kwasha* is worn
over one shoulder and under the opposite arm, leaving the shoulder
bare. Since the diagonal stripe of the effigy paho is painted red and
green, this may represent just such a costume. There is also the
thought that the diagonal may represent an early bandoleer. Frequently worn by Kachinas, these are usually of leather or yarn, and
I have seen a few examples of pre-1900 tihü with red and green yarn

100 bandoleers worn in just such a manner. The more common form today seems to be black and white yarn (Plate II); and the red and green twisted strings persist commonly as edging for certain masks, such as Añwüṣnasómtäqä (Plate VIII*a*).

Figure 20. "Effigy Paho" found at Double Butte cave (from Haury).

Figure 21. Early *Püchtihü. Polik Mana;* a common type, 1850–1900.

Figure 22. "Transition" *Tihü,* indicating possible links between the flat and in-the-round *Kachintihü.*

The date of this particular specimen is unfortunately not completely established. To quote Haury further (*op. cit.,* p. 200):

> While it must be pointed out again that the date of the Double Butte material is not secure, it is upon the strength of the analogy of this proto-kachina [doll] and the various forms of pahos with material known to be Pueblo that a Pueblo origin can be claimed for it. Since the Gila Basin has neither been occupied by Pueblo peoples within historic times nor before the Classic Period, there is then but one other ready explanation, namely, that this material dates from the Los Muertos-Casa Grande period of occupation in the thirteenth and fourteenth centuries.

And I might add one other suggestive parallel: the fact that one Hopi legend accounts for the origin of the Kachinas as coming from the Casa Grande area (*see* p. 10). In my opinion, the dove-tailing of these points is extremely suggestive, for it seemingly offers strong support for the accuracy of the legend and theory of migration.

Several factors seem to indicate that this may represent a very early style of today's sculptural figurine. There are extant numerous examples of early wooden charms, idols, or fetishes which bear, in one way or another, anthropomorphic designs. Most of these are quite clearly not reproductions of masked figures, although a few might be. It would be a most logical step, *if* the tihü can be regarded as having originated in these figures. It seems reasonable to assume that any such art medium would have had just such a simple origin— the dual skills of painting and carving would probably have required a longer time for development to a high degree, than were only one technique involved.

The transition from the earlier forms (if the Double Butte specimen is such) to the tihü as it was known by 1850 is not yet clear. I know of no extant specimens made during the years 1500–1850, nor are there any certain references to them in the literature of that period. Benavides (Hodge, Hammond, and Rey, 1945, p. 43) does remark that:

> ... from the house of only one old Indian sorcerer I once took out more than a thousand idols of wood, painted in the fashion of a game of nine pins, and I burned them in the public square.

Hodge (*ibid.*, p. 239) suggests that they were possibly Kachina dolls of wood. However, I believe that this, and similar Spanish comments on small wooden "idols," are actually references to the Pueblo *paho* which is made in tremendous numbers prior to most ceremonies. (Fig. 19.) They vary in size, but the style of painting, ornamenting with grasses and feathers, and, most importantly, the frequent inclusion of painted faces, would readily cause the Spanish to believe they were idols. The reference to nine pins is suggestive, for the European "pin" of the period was more nearly similar to the paho than the tihü; and finally, the quantity alone would seem to indicate that what Benavides burned was a batch of freshly-made pahos, rather than what would have been a truly huge output of "dolls."

Evidence of the existence of tihü in 1850 is supplied by a püchtihü collected in 1852 by Dr. P. G. S. Ten Broeck, and another collected in 1857 by Dr. Edward Palmer (U. S. National Museum). These are the oldest authentic examples I have yet been able to discover. Ten Broeck (Schoolcraft, 1860, IV, p. 82) saw several tihü "Hanging by strings from the rafters" which he believed were "little Aztec images made of wood or clay, and decorated with paint and

102 feathers, which the guide told [him] were 'saints'." This is the first mention of Kachintihü by an American I have yet found.

That the manufacture of tihüs was a common practice by the 1880's is demonstrated by Bourke (1884, p. 254):

> Another industry is the making of idols, which in scores and scores adorn or disfigure the living rooms. These are generally of wood.
>
> ...In another house...a row of wooden idols, fastened to one of the largest beams, and a supply of tortoise-shell and gourd rattles, masks, head-dresses, sashes, and other appurtenances of their dances (*op. cit.*, p. 298–299).

That these were not idols, but tihü, is proven by his description and mention of their use: even today the Hopis adorn the living rooms of their homes with these figurines, hanging them from the walls or rafters. Actual idols were never kept out in such public view; they were carefully housed in shrines away from the gaze of the uninitiated. But what is of much more interest is his phrase "scores and scores"—which would indicate that the art was certainly well developed.

I have been unable to locate any of the Bourke specimens, but his description plus the Ten Broeck and Palmer specimens, as well as other very early püchtihü in museum collections, would seem to suggest that the technique of making the flat type of figurine had existed for at least a generation or more, since they are not the crude results of a recently-developed art.

The fact that a majority of the older püchtihü in museums bear a mask design of a type shared in common by certain specific Kachinas may have a bearing on the origin of the tihü, or at least may indicate an influence prevalent during the mid-1800s. These similarly-masked Kachinas are Şálako, Şálako Mana, and Polik Mana (Fig. 21). There are, in Hopi ceremonialism, three types of Şálako performances. The first, called Sio Şálako, is not a true Kachina in the strict sense, and is a very close duplicate of the Zuñi *Shálako* performances; it employs the same elaborate framework to build the "body" of the Şálako up to a height of some twelve or fourteen feet. The second is a more typical Kachina dance, wherein the Şálako performer is masked and costumed without the framework, thus presenting a figure of normal human height, and is known as Şálako Kachina.

However, the third is a rite held in conjunction with the Pálülükoñ (Horned Water Serpent) ceremonies in February. These are not true Kachina ceremonies, albeit they are observed during the Kachina season. They seem more to be the "Snake Dance," so to speak, of the Kachina Cult, as opposed to the more accurately-termed Snake

Dance of the non-Kachina fraternities, which is held just about a half-year distant; and this rite seems to further the parallel activity between the Hopi world and the Kachina world.

But the point of interest to this discussion is that during the Pálülükoñ ceremonies, two small wooden marionettes are employed which are carefully carved and painted. These figurines, also called Ṣálako Mana, portray masked, costumed *mana* who symbolically grind corn during the ceremony, in front of a painted screen which conceals the manipulators.

Since a major portion of the püchtihü collected before 1890 known to me are Ṣálako-type designs, it raises the question as to whether or not there may have been a close connection between the development of the tihü and the carved marionettes. Whether the marionette grew out of the technique learned from carving the Kachina figurines—or vice versa, is an interesting but as yet unsettled speculation.

Furthermore, the recorded occasions of drought and pestilence which struck the Hopis in 1853 and 1854 and from 1864 to 1867 caused a large number of Hopis to flee to the near-by Zuñis, and a few to the Navajos. The *Shálako* is a major Zuñi ceremony, and by far their most impressive. It is not unlikely that the great quantity of Ṣálako-design tihü extant in the Hopi villages toward the close of the century is a direct reflection of this; there is a clearly demonstrable effect on Hopi pottery design which is traceable to this same sojourn.

One further word relative to early tihü development concerns the small clay figurines (*chüká tíhuta*). While there are a few references to them in the literature and some specimens exist in museum collections, they are not common. Many bear typical Kachina designs, while others seem intended as secular dolls; yet the shape and body markings suggest a possible similarity of function between the clay and wooden figurines. Stevenson (1883a, p. 388) comments on two such figurines, and (*ibid.*, pp. 395–396) illustrates several wooden tihü. He carefully distinguishes between the two, however—emphasizing that the clay dolls have no ceremonial significance. Two other *chüká tíhuta* are illustrated by Julian Scott (*in* Donaldson, 1893, p. 53) one of which (No. 3) is a quite remarkable specimen, for it is the most characteristically Kachina-like clay figurine I have yet seen.

Many of the published accounts mentioning these clay figures undoubtedly reflect the White viewer's misconception—a coating of clay paint on a wooden body might easily mislead the uninitiated. Whether or not the *first* tihü were made of clay, as some have suggested, is of course a possibility. However, I strongly doubt this;

the negative evidence of their absence from archeological excavations, plus the sheer preponderance in number of the wooden tihü as against the very few clay figurines supports this belief. And, since pottery is a woman's occupation, it seems unlikely men would invade this area—which would also account for their small number.

A study of the many large collections of tihü, in connection with known facts concerning their dating and circumstances of collection, seems to suggest the following theory of later development of the tihü: from the present evidence available, it seems that the type of tihü most familiar today, the stylized "typical" Kachina figurine, developed during the middle and late nineteenth century. The type of workmanship suggests that the rounded carving of the tihü was not a sudden novelty, invented by one man and then picked up immediately by others, but something which had been in process of evolution for some time, perhaps several generations. That it grew out of the püchtihü seems indisputable, for one unusual specimen (in the collection of the University Museum, Philadelphia, No. 38898) suggests the possible transition in technique from flat to round tihü (Fig. 22). The data accompanying the specimen indicates only that it was collected in 1900; but there is no way of knowing when it was made. It should be noted that the arms and shoulders of this tihü are painted in, not carved—whereas the balance of the figurine is round-carved in the more typical fashion. Further, the red striping, so characteristic of the püchtihü, is incorporated in the body painting—an added "transitional" feature.

The interest of White scientists in the tihü has apparently had the greatest effect on its development. With the large numbers collected during the later decades of the nineteenth century, the Hopis responded to the law of supply and demand by turning out greater numbers of the figurines.

In addition to the larger numbers of tihü being made, there was a very marked increase in the technical skill of the carvers. By 1900, the usual type of "doll" was more carefully painted, and usually well-carved, but retained the typical static proportion and form by which it has become well known. Sizes varied a great deal, and *Kachintihü* as large as two feet tall are not unknown.[*]

THE TIHU TODAY

Since 1900, a greater change has been noted. A very sophisticated style of carving has developed—many are carved in naturalistic poses, instead of the traditional conventionalization. Not only are they carved, painted, and feathered with extreme care, but whereas costumes were formerly painted on, now the figurines are often

---

[*]For two early types of "action" dolls, by A. C. Vroman in 1897–1902, see plates 32, in Webb, 1973; and 95 in Mahood, 1901.

dressed in miniature cloth, leather, and metal accoutrements (Plate
XV). In size they are usually ten or twelve inches tall, as in the past, although tihü as large as two feet in height are occasionally seen.

As a result of the increased demand for the small figurines, the regular carvers have been unable to turn out large enough quantities, and so other Indians have taken up the art. Many of the latter do not know the traditional designs well, or are careless in their decoration, so that inferior articles result. On the other hand, some Hopis who make tihü are opposed to selling the authentic article, and have turned to subtle escapes to ease the conscience and enjoy a bit of sardonic amusement. The tihü are very carefully carved as usual, but the painted designs (especially on the all-important mask) are often changed, mixed, or elaborated so there is only a semblance of accuracy. The ignorant purchaser, of course, is completely satisfied with the "genuine Indian made" product, so everyone is happy.

The demands of the tourist trade for cheap "knick-knack" souvenirs has resulted recently in the production of miniature tihü. These range from six inches down to two inches in height, are carelessly carved, and are painted with little concern for accuracy—and sold for as little as twenty-five cents. This emphasis on sales creates a strong resentment in the conservative Hopis, who object to having their religious figurines made objects of commercialization, even when inaccurately made.

Competition from alien craftsmen has also affected the carver. Prior to World War II, some dolls were made in Japan and shipped into the Southwest for tourist sale, although this never attained the importance that it did in the Northwest Coast Indian market, where Japanese-made souvenir "totem poles" nearly destroyed the market for the native product. A far more serious rival was the White man, who employed two techniques to defraud both Hopi and White. In the first method, a few men turned out small dolls (usually the six- and eight-inch sizes) in tremendous quantities by mass-production, doing much of the work on power lathes and painting them *en masse*. In the second (even more injurious since the tourist had no protection) the dolls would be turned out on lathes, much as before, but a few Indians would be hired to paint them, thereby giving token assurance to the purchaser that they were indeed "genuine Indian made."

Since both methods created an inordinately cheap article, the Hopi-made product was driven from the market, and souvenir outlets were flooded with spurious goods. Only those persons who could tell the difference between the two would buy the genuine, and sales were insufficient to support a regular production rate. Often the basic design of the spurious article is sufficiently accurate to enable the initiated to "identify" the doll, but secondary details are usually omitted or mixed up. Casual examination of a majority of the "Kachina dolls" on sale at most contemporary curio stores points up this fact strongly: very few are truly Hopi-made *Kachintihü* of traditional design—often in spite of advertising claims to the contrary.

A consideration of contemporary tihü carving should mention two Oraibi men who have become well known in that field. The first, Tewaquaptewa, the village chief who played a major role in the 1906 split, has been carving for about forty years. In this time he has developed so distinctive a style that his work is easily recognized. The dolls he turns out are sometimes carved in the characteristic *Kachintihü* proportions, and just as often are not; but the painted designs frequently have little similarity to any traditional mask designs (Plate XVI). Since his position as village chief has, until very recently, enabled him to establish a virtual monopoly, the contemporary Oraibi output thus largely represented the work and "interpretation" of one man. Whether or not this divergent technique is merely extreme Hopi reticence, a deliberate attempt to deceive, or artistic conceit, I cannot say; but it exists and should be recognized.

The second, Jimmy Kewanwytewa, a younger man, has been carving for perhaps twenty-five years. His work, too, is readily identified, yet does not sacrifice authenticity. Since he lives in Flagstaff the year round, the problem of competing with the chief of his own village apparently is not serious. It would seem that he has become deeply interested in the older types, and in trying to learn as much as possible about them, has perfected the art of tihü making. The fact that much of his work is done under the influence and encouragement of the Museum of Northern Arizona has undoubtedly had some effect upon this development. Jimmy has apparently been much more conscientious about retaining traditional accuracy in mask designs than many of his contemporaries; in my opinion his work represents the most technically-skillful Hopi tihü art (Plate XVa).

The work of these two Hopis contradicts the usual theory that the older men conserve tradition, while the younger diverge—but there are, it must be admitted, extenuating circumstances.

VIII.

Paraphernalia Changes

IN THE FOREGOING CHAPTERS I have attempted to touch briefly on the history of the Hopis' contact with the non-Indian world. Although not intended as a complete survey of the subject, it will suffice to give an idea of the length of time that the Hopis were exposed to alien cultures, and suggest something of the nature of the interrelationships.

The tracing of foreign elements in a culture can never be fully achieved, for too many are buried so deeply that they defy analysis. However, I shall try to examine the Kachina Cult as it appears today, in an effort to discern what changes, or types of changes, have resulted from the several Hopi-White contacts between 1540 and 1900, and the more intimate relationship from 1900 to date. Some changes will be quite obvious even in a casual survey; others will be less easily observed; and a few must be conjectures, supported by deductions or presumptions based upon the research underlying this study.

For convenience, I have divided these changes into two major categories: those relating to the material objects and physical accessories of the Cult, to be discussed in this chapter; and those which primarily affect the non-material aspects—the psychological, spiritual, or intellectual attitudes of the Hopis toward the Kachina Cult— which will be considered in Chapter IX.

These categories overlap to a certain degree. As discussed elsewhere, some new beings have been introduced through the acquisition of new things; new materials have been introduced into ritual use; and changes have been effected in the visual aspect of these ceremonies—which, in turn, have had their philosophical correlation.

To what extent the Hopis overlook the alien origin of many aspects of the Kachina ceremonials is difficult to determine. Undoubtedly many changes have been rationalized, and some have been tolerated as minor modifications. In discussing an obviously alien influence with the Hopis themselves, extreme tact is necessary; for in general they do not like to have their attention directed to evidences of alien invasion of their ceremonial world.

Certain changes are recognized by the Hopis, some of whom will admit these modifications as being of White derivation. The majority of the Hopis, however, unwilling to recognize non-Indian agencies, usually account for any departure from what can be termed "the traditional way" by claiming that it came from the Zuñis (or some other Indian group). This attitude of many of the Hopis toward White-derived innovations is such that care must be taken in crediting legendary accounts unaccompanied by sufficient supporting evidence. However, not a few of the developments for which they claim Indian origin are so palpably Euro-American introductions that they are appropriate for the present discussion.

Probably the most noticeable, and certainly the more easily demonstrable, White influences traceable in the Kachina Cult are those which have developed in the details of costuming the Kachina impersonators. (The most satisfactory detailed study of the materials and techniques of mask and costume manufacture is Roediger, 1941.)

The factors which have determined most of the changes in Kachina costuming have been brought about through the disappearance of natural resources and the introduction of varied technological materials and White artifacts. The following discussion does not pretend to cover all of the changes which have occurred in the past 400 years; but it is hoped that an adequate sampling is presented to indicate the nature and extremely wide range of those changes.

CHANGES IN EXCLUSIVELY RITUALISTIC OBJECTS

In this category fall those articles which are Indian-made and specifically designed for ceremonial use. They are rarely, if ever, employed for anything other than their ritual function.

The most outstanding example of White influence in this type of article can be seen in the Kachina mask (*kiiítii*) itself. Formerly masks were made of natural materials, such as grasses for the basket-type masks, and buckskin for leather masks. In recent years, the leather masks have been fashioned from saddle leather, and in many instances from felt hats (Fig. 23*b*). Stephen (1936, p. 167) observed the use of saddle leather was common as early as 1893, and Fewkes (1897, p. 263) noted that some masks he investigated in 1890 were constructed on felt-hat bases. This must have been fairly common

during this period, indeed, for at least half of the approximately 200
Hopi masks I have examined in museum collections had been made
on saddle-leather or felt-hat bases.

In the case of the more ancient and more sacred masks, such as
the *wöye* (clan ancestor) masks, it is difficult to say definitely whether they have undergone similar changes in basic materials, for this
cannot be judged accurately unless one can examine the inside of

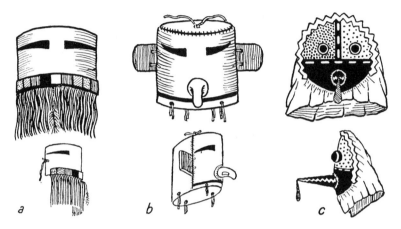

Figure 23. Types of Kachina masks:
  a. *Tíbuku* (maskette commonly worn by *Kachinmana*, and certain male
     Kachinas. See Pls. III, XI);
  b. *Küûtü* (standard helmet-type mask. See Pls. IV, X, XII);
  c. *Tühpóota tüvikü* (basket-type mask. See Pls. VI, VII).

the specimen. I have had the opportunity of doing this with only a
few of these masks, and in each the basic material was of native-
tanned buckskin.

The basket masks (*tühpóota tüvikü*) are covered with woven cotton cloth or buckskin, painted with specific designs which vary with
the Kachina represented (Fig. 23c). I have seen examples of this type
of mask (at the Museum of the American Indian), from as early as
1900, which were covered with commercial canvas in place of the
native material.

Various parts of the masks should also be mentioned in this category. The large ears (*nákabü*), which are usually of wood, were
formerly made of cottonwood, yucca, or pine; in recent times, slats
of "apple-box" wood have been used, and in one instance, a Kachina
mask, accurately made and painted, included *nákabü* made from
commercial Masonite board. This specimen was so atypical, however,

110   that I suspect it may have been made with an eye to salability (American Museum of Natural History, No. 50.2/5713). The horns worn by certain Kachinas were commonly made from split gourds, appropriately painted. In some instances, buffalo horns have been used, and at one dance I noted cow horns. Among other materials, I have even seen horns made from commercial wood and Masonite (American Museum of Natural History, No. 50.2/5717). Snouts (*móchobüh*) are commonly made in both curved and cylindrical forms. Those of the curved type (Plate IV and Fig. 23*b*) are made from gourds, or carved cottonwood, while the cylindrical ones (Plate X) are usually of wood. I have seen a *móchobüh* made from the cylindrical wooden core from a roll of wrapping paper.

A few masks use semi-circular visors (*wikya*) which are fastened to the forehead (Plate II). They are made customarily from woven twigs or a portion of basket-rim. One example which I examined had a visor of Masonite (American Museum of Natural History, No. 50.2/5713).

Certain Kachinas, notably Añwüṣnasómtäqä, wear cords of twisted red and green yarn which cross their masks and hang down the sides (Plate VIII*a*). Called *náluñ múzrükpü*, they are also found in other color combinations, such as red and dark blue, red and black, and red and yellow green. Earlier these were made from native cotton yarn; more recent examples utilize commercial yarn.

It is claimed that the black beards (*sowíchmi*) worn by many Kachinas were originally made from human hair. They are used in several lengths (Plates I, III, VIII). Today horsehair is used almost universally, and Stephen (1936, p. 542) notes this practice as early as 1892. This was undoubtedly one of the earliest innovations following the introduction of horses by the Whites.

There is another use for this material on masks. On some, such as Táṣap Kachina, there is a fringe across the forehead, which today is made from horsehair, dyed red (Plate IV). These forehead bands or bangs (*yúkvyükani*) are also commonly used on the maskettes (*tíbuku*) of the Kachina maidens (Plate XI and Fig. 23*a*).

An increasing number of impersonators are using horsehair today, for it has become more necessary because of the haircut required

Plate IX. The Typical Hopi Püchtihü
a. Tümáüyi Kachina (*rear, front, side*)—*White Chin Kachina.*
b. Malo Kachina—*A frequently-seen Kachina.*
c. Sio Hümis Kachina—*The "Zuñi Jémez Kachina" who is similar in many respects to the Hopi Hümis Kachina.*
d. Pálülükoñ Kachina—*The Water Serpent Kachina, now apparently extinct.*

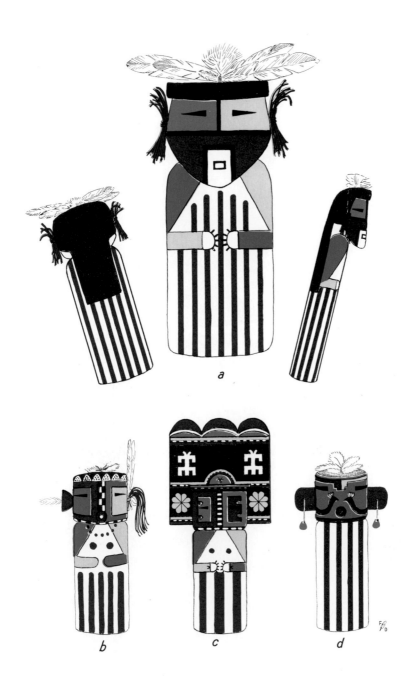

a

b   *c*   *d*

in Government schools and the military services. When human hair was so used in earlier times, it is improbable that alien hair (i.e., scalps) would have been used, for Hopi war customs and their Scalp Ceremony seem to preclude such usage. Today, the horsehair is treated in many ways: plain, dyed various colors, or "touched up" with spots of paint or tufts of cotton (Plate VIII*b*).

The ruff, or collar, usually worn by the various Kachinas, is almost always of evergreen branches or animal fur. There are, however, several beings who have cloth ruffs of various types (Plate XII). In some cases these ruffs have been made from commercial cloth, usually cotton.

A few masks employ flowers in their decoration; one may hazard a guess that in ancient times these were natural flowers. Later, two types of artificial flowers were common: *sinkwa*, and *hümíüyi şoyóhîmsi*, made from corn husks, folded and painted appropriately. In recent times I have seen these replaced by commercial artifical flowers, bought in the town shops (*see Píptüka* Kachina, Fig. 18).

The painting of the mask itself has undergone change. Originally vegetable dyes and earth pigments were used; but the greater ease and brilliant colors afforded by commercial paints have influenced this art; masks eventually came to be regularly painted with ordinary "showcard" or poster colors. Today, acrylic paints are almost universal.

Feather ornamentation on the masks is extremely important, both for beauty in design, and to indicate the relative importance of the particular Kachina. The feathers come from many birds, and in some cases are specific. Although parrots once ranged as far north as Oak Creek, just south of Flagstaff (Hammond and Rey, 1929, p. 183), and have been reported in the Sycamore Canyon area, also near Flagstaff, apparently they were killed off by about 1900. Mexico was a more common source for parrot and macaw feathers, via the tribes in southern Arizona (see Fig. 2). With the increasing difficulty of obtaining certain plumes, dyed feathers of domestic fowl have been introduced. This change was common as early as 1890, for Stephen (1936, p. 399) observed:

> ... The head plume (*na'kwa*) is of dyed pigeon, hen or other feathers, dyed by themselves [the Hopis] with aniline in imitation of parroquet or macaw ... This dyed feather plume, a marked innovation, is now common. In fact no parroquet feathers are any longer to be seen.

Plate X. Talávai Kachina

The "Dawn Kachina" who appears in pairs, touring the village early in the morning, and sings to the people.

I rather suspect that the feathers referred to in this instance were Hopi-obtained—i.e., not influenced by the Whites. In recent times these feathers are more commonly obtained from Whites: a favorite source is the millinery department of local variety or department stores, where they can be purchased already dyed. Also, white feathers are secured from butcher shops and poultry markets in neighboring Flagstaff and Winslow, and are then dyed by the Hopis.

Next in importance to the mask and its accessories are the costumes and costume decorations. Of those which fall in the "restricted" category, the predominant articles are ceremonial textiles. These are woven for dance use, and include such garments as the sash (*müchábñwün kwewa*), and the kilt (*kachinpítküna*); they are still made of cotton and embroidered in traditional designs. Commercial cloth is not used in these garments, although factory yarn is often employed in the embroidery and flannel is sometimes used in strips as decoration on the sash.

A few Kachinas, notably Táşap, wear a red bandoleer (*tóriki*) slung over one shoulder (Plates IV, X). In some costumes, these are traditionally prescribed to be made of buckskin, but in others the bandoleer is of cloth. Whether this cloth *tóriki* is a modification of an earlier rawhide or buckskin bandoleer is problematical. Today the cloth type is ordinarily made of commercial cotton cloth or flannel; the leather type apparently remains unchanged.

According to tradition, the small pouches in which various Kachinas carry sacred corn meal formerly were made of buckskin. As buckskin became more difficult to secure, these bags were sometimes made of native cotton. In recent years I have seen ordinary small-sized flour and sugar sacks so used.

Most Kachinas characteristically wear hanks of dark blue yarn on the wrist (*shakwaton máponi*) and at the knee (*shakwaton hokyashmi*). These were formerly of native cotton colored with vegetable dyes; in recent times this material has been supplanted by commercial yarn, either purchased already dyed, or else colored with commercial dyes by the Indian.

As a "source of supply," the White man has been used in another way; Fewkes was requested to bring back some sea shells when he went East. Turtle shells, for making the (*yöñóşona*) leg rattle, are becoming more scarce in the desert area, and James (1951) gives an account of sending a supply of turtles in response to a request.

The implications of the above changes are manifold. Even a cursory analysis demonstrates that numerous commercial materials have been used in making some of the most sacred parts of the costumes. It would be expected that the mask, which is regarded as the most

holy part of the costume, would be most resistant to innovations,
particularly to those of White manufacture. But as the examples
cited above suggest, apparently no part of the mask has escaped
substitution by similar White materials.

One obvious reason for the cosmopolitan attitude of the Hopis is
undoubtedly the pragmatic recognition that, with some articles, one
must either use White products or do without. Another, in all like-
lihood, is the measurement of convenience against the making of a
difficult or economically prohibitive trip to obtain the required article at its native source. Furthermore, there is apparently a similar
attitude on the part of the Hopi to that of the Christian: that it is
not so much the physical properties as the spiritual attitude and
ritual itself that determine the efficacy of the ceremony. This is
shown by the constant reiteration by the priests that all participants
must have pure hearts, and by the leader urging the people to think
straight, lest the holy power be weakened by lack of coöperative
concentration. It must be born in mind that Hopi spectators do not
just "watch"—they carry a continual obligation to mentally share
the physical efforts of the performers.

There is another similarity between Hopi and Christian religious
attitudes regarding the use of alien-produced articles. For example,
many objects used in Catholic liturgy are actually manufactured by
Jewish or Protestant firms; yet there is no objection to their use once
they have been consecrated (i.e., purified) by the priest. Likewise,
the Hopis will use for their own liturgical purposes articles made by
Whites, once they have been purified (i.e., consecrated) by the
priests.

This would explain the apparent unconcern of the Indian as to the
material which he incorporates into some of his ceremonials. However, there are certain qualifications of that relatively free acceptance: regardless of the maker, the Catholic requires that the bowl of
a chalice be gilded—the Indian likewise requires that the *paho*
be *finally* sharpened by stone, not steel knife-blades.

These changes have also occasioned philosophical adjustments in
Kachina activities. For example, the difficulty, due in great part to
White settlement, of securing bear or buffalo hides for costumes has
been met by the substitution of sheepskins; the fact that a "buffalo"
impersonator was actually wearing a sheepskin apparently has not
affected the Hopis' attitude toward the ceremony.[*]

However, it must be pointed out that the majority of readily observable elements of White culture accepted by the Kachina Cult
have been in the less important Kachinas. To a certain extent, it can

---

[*]Compare the philosophical attitude of the modern White woman, pretentiously attired in
mink-dyed rabbit fur!

be said that the greater the amount of White material culture used in a Kachina costume, the less ceremonially-important is that Kachina. The ancient *wöye* Kachinas, and Chief Kachinas (*moñkachina*), are not only costumed in their special masks, but usually retain more of the ancient costume elements, no matter how scarce, than do the social or more "popular" beings.

In making masks, undoubtedly the Hopis would prefer using materials that are completely Indian in origin, if they had any choice in the matter; but this is no longer possible, and they have, therefore, made the best of the situation in order to assure continuance of the ceremonial calendar.

DUAL-PURPOSE ARTICLES

This category would include those objects which are used both ritually and secularly. There is apparently no aura of holiness connected with them in their everyday function; but while being used as religious accessories they may take on something of the Kachina spirit, as does the impersonator wearing them.

Probably the most obvious infiltration of White influence is seen in the substitution for the native moccasins (*tochi*) of rubber-soled gymnasium shoes by the Táchüktî clowns—I have never seen the regular Kachinas wear any but the conventional red-brown or turquoise *tochi*. There is probably no part of the costume or daily dress of an Indian which seems so characteristically indicative of the degree of his assimilation into White culture as the moccasin. To see shoes and sneakers intruding into what is otherwise strongly Indian, is more of a shock than intrusions into details of mask-making where White influence is less obvious to the eye (although certainly more important philosophically).

Some Kachinas, such as Qöqöqlö Kachina, are not costumed in the traditional kilt; quite frequently the impersonators borrow clothing for these roles. Apparently in olden times Qöqöqlö Kachina appeared in any worn-out garments that could be gathered together, but today he often appears in cast-off American clothing. Or, as Titiev (1944, p. 214) has observed:

> The costumes were an odd mixture of shabby Hopi and American clothes, the only semblance of uniformity being a "collar" of cloth or fur.

Similarly, Nataşka Kachina no longer wears his former old-style Hopi clothes; his modern dress is usually ready-made shirt and trousers.

Pottery bowls used in the ceremonies are sometimes replaced by commercial dishes; and the gourd resonator (*tawişibvu*), which is (*shükyachi*) as it is rubbed along a notched stick (*rükünpi*) (Plate XI), has changed, as noted by Stephen (1936, p. 407) in 1893:

> Each maiden carried in her hands the kachina gourd fiddle, but instead of the gourd vessel . . . she had a small box as a substitute. (The five cent indigo box seems to be a favorite.) The other typical implements are still retained, viz: the notched stick and the sheep shoulder blade.

SCARCITY OF SUPPLY

Certain raw materials, or finished products, are so difficult to secure today (or have even become non-existent in the Hopi area) that the Indians have had to turn to articles or materials of White manufacture. For the most part, these have entered into Hopi acceptance as the result of two factors: the settlement of the land by the Whites with the consequent confinement of the Hopis to a limited area lacking these materials, and the destruction of the game and land resources which resulted from that settlement.

The most outstanding examples of this sort of change are the replacement of hand-woven textiles by store-bought cloth, ordinary trousers in place of the old-style buckskin breeches, broadcloth shirts for the Pueblo-style "poncho" shirt, store cotton for the native *Gossypium hopii*, and commercial calico or gingham. As both Hopi cotton and local game became more scarce, the Indians had to turn to other materials for their clothing, hence the increase in the use of commercial textiles.

Other scarcities developed when over-grazing or land settlement caused a serious decrease in the amount of shrubs and grasses. One result of this was greater difficulty in securing raw materials for vegetable dyes. While probably not the primary reason, it certainly was a factor in the introduction and extended use of aniline dyes, which as Parsons (1939, p. 1143) has noted, occurred early in the 1890's.

The scrota of some of the Spanish-introduced animals are occasionally used for rattles. With the gradual elimination of the buffalo, cow horns have been substituted for buffalo horns. Other uses of introduced cattle products include cowhide in place of deer or elk hide for dance moccasins, thongs, leather bandoleers, and other paraphernalia. Jeremiah Sullivan, in an unpublished MS on file at the Bureau of American Ethnology, notes (1887) the use of an ox-hide shield as a resonator during a Kachina dance.

Since the prehistoric trade routes have largely fallen into disuse, some of the articles obtained thereby are no longer commonly in evidence. While trading posts have tended to make many articles more easily available, they cannot stock everything the Hopis need; occasional lacks develop which would formerly have been supplied through intertribal barter. This is especially true of ceremonial objects for which the demand is irregular. If unobtainable in trading posts, some of these objects tend to lapse from regular Hopi use, and may in time completely vanish. The most notable of these fast-disappearing articles is the shell pendant which was formerly a common ornament. This *kaláhaiñüñünpi* is today occasionally replaced by a mirror or similar bright object, worn suspended from the neck by a cord. When available, these *kaláhaiñüñünpi* are obtained from curio stores. Among the things which Fewkes was requested to send back to the Hopis when he went East in 1893 was eight small conch shells. That this is not an unusual instance is revealed by the occasional discovery of clay imitation shells in archeological excavations; and as an added comment on Hopi reaction to scarcity, Fewkes (1892b, p. 64) mentions the artificial clay shells which the Indians made, and which were freely used in Kachina dances.

The effect of minor events can also have peculiar reactions in ceremonial life. Dorsey and Voth (1902, p. 95f.) mentions the difficulty caused at the initiation of a small Hopi boy, when it was found impossible to fasten the initiatory feather to his closely-cropped hair: it was finally necessary to hang it around his neck on a cord.

In view of the practical nature of the Hopis, these substitutions seem due to several causes:

In addition to the economic benefits of transportation and supply which White life has made available to the Hopis, there has come a problem which cannot be ignored. Along with the introduction of trade goods, has come an increasing dependence; for in point of actual fact, no longer can the Hopi do without some of these goods. Many of the present-day Kachina costumes and masks are dependent upon the materials or facilities of White culture for their very continuation.

It is perfectly true that the paraphernalia necessary to the Cult existed before the White man, and that native materials were then sufficient. But, the effect of the White man upon Hopi ecology has been such that no longer are there sufficient resources to supply the various needs. Bluntly, it is a question of either using something similar, though of foreign origin, or doing without. In most cases, switching to some other Hopi-made item is not practicable, since it is primarily a matter of raw-material supply.

It is quite probable that this will continue, and even increase; for as White settlement expands and Hopi population increases (as it has been doing the past decade) raw materials can only decline in

availability. What the result of this greater employment of White
materials will be, cannot now be estimated, but it is certain that it
will be noticeable in the Kachina Cult ritual.

BETTER FOR THE PURPOSE

Under this heading come those materials and objects of White
manufacture which are obviously, in Indian eyes, more suitable,
more efficient, or more appropriate for the purpose. For the most
part these are technological improvements on native objects. Some
of the innovations have become so completely a part of Hopi culture
as to result in the disappearance of the original; in other cases, there
may be a preference for one or the other, but both still exist side
by side.

A most outstanding example of this sort of change is the replacement of the old-time flint or stone knife (*yóishiva*) by a commercial
steel knife, or butcher knife. I have even seen a modern meat cleaver
used in one Kachina dance in this manner. Nataṣka Kachina, who
formerly carried an ancient black stone (flint or obsidian) knife, today has almost universally adopted a regular modern carpenter's
saw which he carries on his ceremonial trips around the village. Incidentally, the modern saw is known by the same name as the ancient flint weapon: *ṣiyara*.

However, this type of substitution is not completely practiced, for
one being, Hehea Kachina, still carries the ancient wooden hoe
(*wünawikya*) in his ceremony, although this has long been out-
moded as a farm tool by the more efficient iron hoe.

The ancient clay bells, which have been discovered at both Kawaika-a and Awátovi, were early replaced by cast metal bells of
copper or bronze (Fewkes, 1898a, p. 629). These latter have in turn
been replaced by brass and nickel-plated sleigh bells. The musical
instruments, particularly the hand-bells such as are carried by the
Talávai Kachinas, are today regular store-bought articles (Plate X).

With the introduction of new animals, especially sheep, cattle, and
horses, some changes took place almost immediately, since in several
instances the products made from these animals were either superior
to native materials, or else provided basic materials not previously
available to the Indian. Wool, for example, replaced cotton in much
of weaving, particularly in textiles for clothing. However, it is an
interesting fact that very little wool is used in Kachina costumes;
whether this indicates a subconscious reaction against Spanish materials, it is difficult to say; the fact remains that cotton is more widely used in this connection. The Hopis do not express any conscious
reaction against wool. It is certainly possible that in early times there

may have been a tabu against the use of wool in ceremonial costumes, particularly after Spanish oppression became onerous. However, this seeming preference is fast disappearing with the increasing use of commercial clothes for various costumes, as in the Qöqöqlö Kachina, mentioned above. It may be that the fact of wool material escapes conscious attention of the Hopis when the fabricated garment is taken over *in toto*.

Textiles improved to such a degree with the use of wool alone and in combination with cotton, that the prehistoric rabbit fur blankets were infrequently made, and are seen but rarely today. A few beings, such as Hehea, Ushü, and Kana-a Kachinas wear them, but they have disappeared from secular use, and are so rare that often even these Kachinas appear in sheepskins in place of the rabbit-fur blankets.

Sheep and ox hooves have replaced those of the deer and antelope for rattles, just as sheep scapulae have replaced their deer and antelope counterparts; and in those few Kachina costumes which employ the *chamímita* fringe of antelope hoof or shell "jinglers," recent observance has noted metal fringe jinglers made from tin cans. The native name for this metal fringe is *shiviva shilala*, "metal makes-it-clink."

The most striking innovation in Hopi art has certainly been the introduction of aniline dyes for textiles, and commercial pigments from which paints are made. These were in use as early as 1890, as has been mentioned. With the increased difficulty in securing plant and earth materials for pigments, it can readily be seen why the Hopis would turn to a steady supply, especially since the newer pigments were not only easy to obtain, but were ready for use, saving the tedious hours of grinding and preparing. Moreover, acrylic does not fade.

But even more important than the problem of supply was the wider range of colors obtainable, and the very brilliant hues which the commercial pigments provided. Less dramatic, but much more colorful than the softer vegetable dyes and earth pigments, the aniline dyes and "showcard color" which came into use developed quite a different basic color range in Hopi art.

In some instances, these modern colors are an advantage for the artist; in others, they are at best a mixed blessing. Their use often results in a clash of glaring colors; unfortunately, it is this garish color combination which many Whites have come to regard as "Indian art." And, since these colors soon came to be used in articles made for sale, the erroneous impression was only logical.

The native colored cotton strings have been replaced by commercial cordings, owing to their availability, attractive colorings, and greater strength. Native wool and cotton yarns have given way to commercial yarns for much the same reasons. Buckskin thongs for tying or fastening have given way in some instances to heavy twine, or even wire.

In the preparation of materials for Kachina ceremonies, some substitutions have also been noted. Stephen (1936, p. 894) notes the use of tin cans as early as 1891:

> ... He is making a large quantity of pigment for the hand prayer-sticks, he says. As he gets the surface of the slab well covered with the wet pigment he pours it off into a can and rubs down more. (These people are adopting tin cans, old coffee pots, wash pans and other modern abominations in their ceremony uses.)

The old-time yucca slats and hand-cut woods have been largely replaced by thin boards taken from the sides of boxes and crates, Masonite slabs, and other commercial woods. This is not a recent phenomenon, for I have examined examples of the flat dance batons (*mánayawi*) carried in various ceremonies, made from box slats around 1900 or earlier, whereon the original printing still showed through the overlying painted decoration (collection of the Cranbrook Institute of Science, No. 3868).

A final example of the substitution of a technically-superior article is the sword used by Cháveyo Kachina in place of the traditional club. This obviously superior weapon was probably adopted quite some time ago, for I have seen one such weapon used which was of the early Spanish type; and other examples seen were the cavalry sabers used by American troops late in the nineteenth century. That the philosophy guiding the Hopi selection was appropriate is shown by their realization that such an implement was more in keeping with the traditional menacing role of Cháveyo Kachina. I have unverified reports that the clowns have occasionally appeared armed with Army rifles. It may be that, in time, equipment from World War II will arm Warrior Kachina—perhaps with a Colt .45 automatic.

In summary, the changes sketched above as representing this category are essentially due to the Hopis' clear recognition of technical superiority of certain materials. From the point of view that "nothing is too good for the Kachinas," the substitutions seem wise and quite understandable. But in view of Hopi resistance to much of White culture, it may seem surprising that they would admit that superiority in religion. The explanation seems to be that the Hopis are practical-minded enough to accept these better materials, as long as their adoption does not disrupt the ritual or basic philosophy of the Kachina ceremonies.

There has been a tendency in certain Kachinas, notably the fancy-dress or *Kwivi* beings, to adopt certain materials or articles which have a very showy appearance. These have been added because they catch the Indian eye, or because of their inherent beauty, colorful quality, and dramatic appeal. Often their inclusion brings an incongruous note to the costuming, and detracts from the over-all dignity of the Kachina dancer. In some cases, however, the Hopis have been able to incorporate colorful materials of White manufacture with discrimination, and the result has been a very satisfactory blending of the two cultural expressions.

The articles which have been adopted because of their appeal to the eye are primarily dress goods: prints, gingham, calico, and other bright cotton fabrics. The use by Naván Kachina of velvet (or velveteen) and silk ribbons, obtained at the trading post or town store, is an excellent example of this. Naván Kachina apparently did not exist much before 1900, although the use of velvet and ribbons by other Kachinas had already become noticeable. In 1893 Stephen (1936, p. 324) noted:

> . . . a gradual increase of innovations; a strip of red flannel or other stuff from the stores, worn as a sash over right shoulder, instead of blue yarn; also one wears a piece of orange coloured print instead of a white kilt; and on the helmet masks are many ribbons.

This referred to Táṣap Kachina; even today many departures are seen in performances of this being. Since Táṣap is of Navajo origin, there is apparently a greater willingness to take liberties with tradition than with Ahül Kachina, or Eótoto Kachina, both of whom are quite old and regarded as very powerful.

Another innovation can frequently be seen in performances of Añákchina. This popular impersonator wears a long cotton string (*añáhaiíhpi*) from the top of the head, to which feathers are tied at intervals. To keep this string hanging straight down the back, some fairly heavy object is customarily used as a weight, and is called *átkyakabiadta*.

In ancient times, this may have been for the same purpose, or perhaps was a fetish or charm of stone or shell; whatever the reason, the variety of weights used today is amazing. I have seen used, in a single dance, everything from abalone shells, Navajo silver *naja* pendants, bolts, and metal ornaments, to mirrors, bracelets, and pocket watches. Stephen also noted (1936, p. 400): " . . . a bit of stone, bone, shell, fossil wood, a small bell, metal ornament, buckle, and I have seen a bit of American candy." Up to the present time, there has been no inclusion of war souvenirs or war trophies to my knowledge; but it will be no surprise if in time medals or uniform insignia appear in Kachina costumes.

Although referred to in another category, it seems appropriate to mention here the use of showcard, tempera, and other commercial pigments, which has become common. The brilliant colors obtainable with these materials has had quite an effect upon the over-all appearance of the costumes. Due both to convenience and the striking colors, they have become extremely popular, and have been responsible for many changes in Kachina color schemes. Perhaps the most noticeable is the increased use of turquoise. An examination of any collection of early masks or tihü will reveal an off-color green as the predominant base color, with a peculiar shade of yellow as secondary. These two, with red, are probably the colors most frequently used, and none can be called pure colors.

It was not possible to get a good turquoise color in early times with native raw materials, unless one went to the expensive length of using crushed turquoise itself. This was done, but not frequently, since the stone was too precious; the green obtainable from copper ores was commonly used.

Today this has changed: turquoise-colored commercial paints are readily obtainable, as well as brilliant yellows and strong, vibrant reds; the result is quite striking in comparison with older painted objects. Kachinas which were described as being painted in green in 1890 or 1900, are decorated in turquoise shades today; and, one suspects, the beauty of the newer shades has resulted in several Kachinas being changed from their original color to turquoise. In his series of color plates of Hopi Kachinas, Fewkes (1903, pp. 3–126) shows only five masks painted turquoise, although a majority of those masks colored green in his book are usually painted turquoise today.

The skillful use of feathers has been increasingly affected by the use of dyed plumes, which has tended to develop a greater elaboration in the ornamentation of mask and costume. Fortunately, as yet the tendency on the part of the Plains Indians to use brilliantly-dyed "fluffies" in their costuming has not been adopted by the Hopis; but with exposure to these influences via such "All-Indian" shows as are presented by the Chambers of Commerce of Flagstaff, Gallup, and other towns, it may be only a question of time before this and other costume techniques find their way into Kachina costuming.

THE ECONOMIC FACTOR

Some of the substitutions noted above are due not only to the preference of the Hopis for more attractive costuming, or difficulty of securing the needed articles, etc., as suggested; there is often an accompanying economic factor to be considered. It is obvious, for example, that some articles, though now scarce in the Hopi area, *could* be secured with persistent effort. However, this would take so much time and expense, it is much more economical to purchase a satisfactory substitute in the trading post. This situation is often the case in the matter of dyes, certain types of textiles, and some leather materials. It is often difficult, if not impossible, to discover whether the primary consideration in the substitution of aniline dyes, as a specific instance, was due to (1) an escape from the onerous task of preparing vegetable dyes, (2) the scarcity of certain shrubs used in the preparation, (3) the attraction of a wider range of more brilliant colors, (4) the economic saving in time over the small cost of a packet of dye, or (5) the recognition, in many cases, that the commercial dye was more efficient in giving a uniform color.

These reasons will all vary with the individual and the time involved. But each has its application some place in the whole picture of cultural change. Some substitutions seem almost irrational; as for example, the use of a cardboard box for storing feathers, in place of the customary cottonwood box. This would seem to have no point—the cardboard box is less durable, affords less protection to the fragile and valuable feathers, presents no particular attractiveness, and does not replace a hard-to-get material. The wooden box would not take more than a short time to make, and would long outlast and outserve the cardboard.

Another substitution equally perplexing is the use of heavy cardboard in place of yucca slats in making a *nakchi*. Were the substitution wooden slats, it would be quite understandable, for these are stronger and easier to use; but cardboard, vulnerable to wear and to moisture, has a much shorter life and must be replaced more often; it is also less secure on the head, for it tears easily. Although it is quite true that yucca is less common in the Hopi area today than formerly, a slight extra effort would result in a more serviceable material, and would agree with traditional prescription.

The reason for the above changes would seem to be either laziness, or economics. Perhaps the work necessary to prepare cottonwood or yucca for a box or *nakchi*, slight though it was, seemed overwhelming. More likely, the individual simply did not have time or opportunity to secure or prepare the materials, but in desperation grabbed at what was at hand—or else felt that his working time (economics) was spent more profitably on other things, and was unwilling to prepare anything more elaborate than was absolutely necessary.

There are a few articles of White manufacture which have been introduced into the Kachina Cult because of White pressure. These are almost completely due to the clash of two standards of modesty, and the Christian attitude toward sex. Originally, many of the Kachina dancers wore breech cloths, which were apparently the standard clothing for the men in early days. Today many of the younger Hopis participating in these particular dances wear regular commercial "shorts"—often *under* the breech cloth. This so-called modesty has been strongly supported by school officials, as well as by the missionary groups, so that there is an increasing sense of self-consciousness discernible at the public ceremonies.

A further indication of the forced alteration of costume is seen in several Kachinas, notably Qalavi, Kókoşori, and some of the Wáwaş Kachinas. These beings formerly appeared entirely nude, or with merely a woven belt around the waist. Their ceremonial roles differ, but the elements of germination and fertility are strong in each. The dual aspects of sex were neither avoided nor pruriently over-emphasized by the Hopis. The ritualistic portrayal of fertility and germination are a part of all cultures, and vary only in mode of expression, or degree of emphasis; and in the case of the Hopis, there is a major emphasis on this life-creating phenomenon. They, like all agricultural peoples, are extremely conscious of the forces of nature, and have endeavored to anticipate and dramatize her every expression. The Kachina Cult includes its share of both the physical elements of sex and the procreative demands of racial survival.

This tolerant balance was soon attacked by White moralists; and because of missionary pressure, Government *fiat*, and newly acquired modesty, many Hopis have been quite reluctant to participate in the more sexual roles. As a result, several of these Kachinas are less frequently seen today, and in those instances where they are performed, the personator wears either shorts or breech cloth.

The Kachina which is apparently the nearest equivalent to the physical aspects of sex is Kókopölö Kachina. This being was probably one of the several fertility beings in ancient times, and even today there is a strong fertility element in his activities, but the censure of Whites has greatly affected his costuming. Several authorities have suggested the probable connection between this Kachina and the ubiquitous little "humpbacked flute-player" seen in pictographs and petroglyphs throughout the Southwest.

In his publication illustrating Kachina costumes, Fewkes (1903, Pl. XXV) shows Kókopölö with, apparently, a natural penis; the contemporary personator usually appears wearing a large artificial phallus, commonly made from a gourd or carved of wood. He

124 dances around the *kisonvi,* occasionally pursuing a woman and simulating sexual intercourse with her. The women pretend to flee, but are actually eager for his embrace, since it is believed to assure fertility.

The same changes have been noted in the carved tihü of Kókopölö and a few of the other Kachinas who formerly appeared nude. Where these tihü were, prior to 1900, carved with small wooden penis (or vulva, in the case of the Kachinmana), today the tihü rarely indicates this organ*

These White-imposed changes of costume and activities are accompanied by conspicuous psychological reactions that may eventually have a great effect upon the Kachina Cult; however, these belong more appropriately in the next chapter, where they will be considered at length.

------

*But *see* page 155.

IX.

Outside Pressures

In the field of non-material influences occur those aspects of culture which are concerned with the intellectual attitudes, ideology, and spiritual concepts relating to the formation, development, and continuation of the Kachina Cult.

This phase of analysis is most difficult, for the student is faced with the problem of attempting to draw conclusions from the thought-processes of others. However, in the case of the Hopi Kachina Cult, certain definite patterns are readily discernible. Although it is impossible to draw conclusions from earlier attitudes, since no records exist concerning this phase of the Cult, some conclusions can be reached by comparing the observations of various investigators over the past half century.

Of the non-material influences, the most important is a consideration of such Kachinas as may have been inspired as a result of contact with White culture. As mentioned in Chapter II, there are several of these, quite obvious in name, costume, or function, as the seven examples listed below illustrate. Animal Kachinas dominate this particular list, but the animal concept is not a foreign thought; for there are many animals which are distinctively Hopi, such as deer, antelope, and mountain sheep.

Whether these Kachinas should be classified as material or non-material is open to argument. I include them here because of the basic philosophy of the Hopi toward a Kachina, which embraces a degree of control exerted over animals, the feeling of relationship established through the performance of animal Kachina ceremonies, and the place of animals in Hopi thought as reflected in legends and traditions concerning the Kachinas.

Kavayo Kachina. Deriving its name from the Spanish *caballo,* this Kachina could not have come into being until the Hopi knew of horses, which were introduced by the Spaniards. This Kachina has appeared only infrequently in the last fifty years.

Wakáṣ Kachina. The name of this being originated in the Spanish *vaca,* meaning cow. It is likewise a Kachina which dates from post-Columbian days, since cattle are known to have been introduced by the White man. It has appeared slightly more frequently than Kavayo Kachina in recent years.

Kanela Kachina. With a name obviously originating in the Spanish *carnero,* sheep, this is the third animal Kachina owing its creation to Spanish innovations. It is very rarely impersonated, and to my knowledge has not been performed in the past fifty years.

Kowako Kachina. Rooster, or Chicken, Kachina, has a non-Spanish name, but since the Hopi lacked these fowl in pre-Columbian times, the being is clearly White-derived. In Hopi, *kowako* means a fowl, and may refer to the sounds made by poultry; the etymology is obscure. The Kachina appears irregularly.

Tsili Kachina. The Hopi word *tsili* offers etymological evidence of Spanish derivation, and Whiting (1939, p. 88) has established the post-Spanish introduction of this plant. This Pepper Kachina occasionally appears as a Wáwaṣ Kachina.

Tawa Koyoñ Kachina. Colton (1949, p. 73) lists Tawa Koyung as a Peacock Kachina, introduced in 1936. I have no further data, nor have I ever seen it. The Peacock was unknown to the Hopis prior to 1540, although the name is Hopi-coined: *Tawa,* sun; *koyoño,* turkey.

Nüvak Kachina. Although snow was certainly nothing new to the Hopis, an etymological similarity has been suggested between the Spanish *nieve,* and Hopi *nüva* (also *neva*), meaning snow. The name, if not the Kachina, may have been Spanish-derived.

There are other beings similarly inspired from White innovations, but in some, their alien origin is less obvious.* Undoubtedy there

---

*For example, Chákwaina Kachina, reputedly derived from Estebán. *See* above p. 11.

Plate XI. Hümis Kachinmana

Many Kachinas are accompanied by maidens, representing sisters, sweethearts, or girl friends. Hümis *maiden wears a costume typical of many of these* Kachinmanas.

a

b

c

d

e

have been many which have come and gone within the 400 years that have elapsed since the Whites first came into Tusayan, but we can judge only by those of which we have record.

There is a possibility that some of these beings are actually older Kachinas remodelled, i.e., as older Kachinas died out, something of their concept and physical appearance may have been reworked into a being suggested by a newly-introduced White man's animal. I am inclined to doubt that this goes very far. The history of Cult flexibility has shown how readily impersonations can come and go, and it seems more likely that were the horse, cow, or sheep to replace an original "old time" animal Kachina, the impersonation of the older creature merely would be less frequent, and in time completely cease.

These old-time animals which have been continuously impersonated are rare. An example is the bison, or "buffalo," which, although no longer running wild, is still occasionally impersonated as Möşairü Kachina. It is interesting to note, however, that the *unmasked* Buffalo Dance—a social and not a Kachina ceremony—is given very frequently, both on and off the Reservation. I know of no prehistoric or early historic animal, now extinct, which is still recognizably retained in the Kachina roster.

While there is little concrete evidence to support the argument, it seems probable that Catholic hagiolatry has played a part in the secondary development of the Kachina Cult. There are parallels between the cults which may have been externally introduced: both include representations of the spirits of individuals who once lived on earth; the use of carved figures of those individuals; the use of ceremonial beings (Kachinas, Saints) as intermediaries to bless mortals, and to transmit prayers; the attributing of specific paraphernalia or costume to individual beings; the ritual aspersing by the *kachina'amû,* similar to the Catholic sprinkling; and flagellation, either for penitence (Catholic) or purification (Hopi). Also the various Saint's Day dances, so common in Catholic lands, show interesting features in this connection, as Parsons (1930, p. 586–587) has suggested:

> At the Saint's day dance at Jaltipán, Vera Cruz, about twenty men wear masks, wooden, painted red and green, one mask with

---

Plate XII. Wáwaş Kachina Masks
Racing Kachinas, who challenge spectators to race with them.
   a. Létotovi Kachina—*Dragonfly Kachina.*
   b. Kwitánonoa Kachina—*Dung-throwing Kachina.*
   c. Hümsona Kachina—*Hair-cutter Kachina.*
   d. Aya Kachina—*Rattle Kachina.*
   e. Kona Kachina—*Chipmunk Kachina.*

deer antlers on the forehead. Headdress of fowl features and macaw tail feathers with tufts of cotton at the tips. They carry crook sticks. Circle dance.

The Kachinas are not supposed to talk with the spectators; and if they do, their language is regarded as unintelligible to the lay Hopi: the *kachina'amû* must translate. The Catholic priest parallels this in his use of Latin; but in both cases, there are exceptions, and the everyday language is used in addressing the individual.

In my opinion, the most marked effect of Catholic hagiolatry is in the small wooden tihü. It is difficult to establish whether the actual origin of these can be attributed to the statues of the saints in the same way that the later New Mexican *santos* were developed. But it seems likely that the expansion of the tihü into a more sculptural and elaborated art form was greatly affected by the importation of figures of the Catholic saints by the priests, who realized that by the gradual introduction of similar religious features, Catholicism might in time replace the native practices. The effectiveness of this policy (and the peculiar resistance offered by the Hopi social organization to this tendency) is discussed at length by Hawley (1946, p. 407–415).

FORCIBLE SUPPRESSION AND THE KACHINA

The determined efforts which were made to stamp out Indian culture were tragically successful in some instances, and much has been lost that can never be entirely regained. The older men died off, and the younger were diverted by schooling and outside economic and social forces from learning the traditional rites. Thus it has become more and more difficult to obtain recruits for Kachina dances, for fulfilling ceremonial offices, and for handing on traditions. Some ceremonies have already died out because of lack of continuants, and others are threatened; but Pueblo clan organization contributes to this problem, since society or clan membership often establishes the tradition of ceremonial control of paraphernalia and ritual, and the lack of a properly related clan heir may result in the lapse of a particular ceremony. If no ritual transfer occurs, the ceremony becomes extinct within a very few generations, since there is no one to whom it may be passed.

Other recent changes have been occasioned by the attempts of political and religious groups to suppress native ceremonies in whole and in part, e.g. the attacks upon the sexual aspects of fertility and germination rituals, the undermining of the authority of the village chiefs (thereby affecting the ceremonial leaders' position in the tribe), and the interval during which ceremonies were prohibited by Indian Service officialdom.

Insistence by the Whites on adoption of a new way of life by the Hopis in the field of morals has placed an increasingly unhealthy emphasis upon sex. Whereas those rites which were accompanied by expressions of sexual activity were presumably once viewed naturally, today there is a tendency toward conscious obscenity, in an attempt to shock or insult White visitors. This unfortunate gesture has, of course, provided ammunition for those who would put an end to all native ceremonials.

One example of this changed attitude is manifested today in certain Kachina dances in which Kókopölö Kachina appears, with or without Kókopölö Mana, and performs in his usual manner. If White women are present among the spectators, almost invariably the impersonator will, sometime during the performance, go over to them, and either simulate intercourse, or otherwise attempt to embarrass them.

It is difficult to say to what degree White contact has affected the activities of Kókopölö Kachina. Certainly there seems to be a greater tendency to regard the impersonation as amusing and as giving opportunity to embarrass White spectators than to consider the fertility aspect. The increased consciousness of sex—certainly traceable to White contact—has not only affected the fundamental philosophy of Kókopölö (and, therefore, the basic reasons for his appearance in the Kachina cycle) but has had an even more marked influence upon his conduct. Today he still is seen occasionally in *kisonvi* dances, but more and more these several fertility beings are being gradually withdrawn into the security of the kiva, where they are less vulnerable to critical eyes.

Thus, this change in attitude toward Kókopölö, Mástop, and other fertility Kachinas, plus the wearing of clothing by formerly nude Kachinas, has had two noticeable effects. The inclusion of costume changes indicates an acquired sense of modesty which was never present before, and the apparent increase in physical sexuality as regards White spectators would seem to indicate consciousness of a phase of activity through which the Indian could "strike back," so to speak. The tendency to remove some of these more phallic personations to the kiva is but part of the tendency of the Hopis to avoid a serious clash wherever possible.

It is interesting to note here that although this clash with a dominant, disapproving culture has resulted in forced changes, the Cult organization as a whole has been able to accomodate itself to this adjustment and to continue its development.

However, the fact that Kachina ceremonies seem to be becoming increasingly secretive may be disastrous in the long run. The fear that esoteric information or artifacts may be sold (and thus dissipate their "power"), can well lead to a gradual tendency toward centralization of Kachina lore. In the past, all Hopis have been members of the Kachina society, and the men have had access to the ritual knowledge of the Cult. But this may eventually be considered unwise. As the elders continue to lose confidence in the ability, responsibility, and piety of the younger people, there will be increasing reluctance to trust such youths with the essential ritual knowledge, and there may be a decision to limit that knowledge to a small ceremonial group, as is the case with other Hopi ceremonies. Were this to develop, with "ritual owners" and heirs, the danger would immediately arise of the lapsing of a ceremony through the death of its "owner."

That this thought is no empty theorizing is illustrated by the following observation by Parsons (1939, p. 1159):

> No Wüwüchim initiation was held on First Mesa for at least eleven years, perhaps much longer, because Hani, Singers' chief, was too feeble to function, and Hani died without apprenticing his nephews. The initiation held in 1927 after Hani's death must have suffered some impairment.

It should be recalled that Wüwüchim is one of the primary ceremonials of the Hopi calendar. Therefore, if such an important ceremony could suffer such a lapse, no others would be immune.

Parsons (1939, p. 1160) goes on to discuss another aspect of secrecy in relation to the Cult, which is of importance to the present question:

> ... esotericism adds to the prestige of any group and so promotes membership. Secrets are a form of property, if they are nothing more than secrets from children or women, as kachina impersonation is or was secret. Persons who "know something" are persons of property in Pueblo opinion, and highly respectable. Many things of common knowledge, familiar flora, fauna, or minerals, if used in proprietary secret ways take on new desirable values. Common knowledge can change without loss, but esoteric knowledge must be conserved unchanged or risk a loss.

Economics and the Kachina Cult

The economic factors of White culture have made marked inroads upon Kachina ceremonies, perhaps most notably in the adjustment of the Hopi ceremonial calendar. Formerly Kachina dances were held whenever needed or desired; nowadays, they are usually held on Saturdays or Sundays so that "town Hopis" can get away from work to attend. (These Sunday performances are often misunderstood by Whites who attribute this coincidental timing to Christian

church influences.) Also, a feeling has developed among many Hopis
that the obligation of performing in Kachina ceremonies should not
interfere with school attendance or paid work; this often causes a
postponement of dances, or absence "from the ranks" of those participants who regarded attendance as inconvenient.

Since many Hopis work in Winslow, Flagstaff, and other neighboring towns, their participation is often difficult, and they may be prevented from meeting ceremonial obligations. This obligation to participate is very real to the Hopis, and they make every effort to
attend, both for religious and social reasons. This affects not only the
difficulty of obtaining recruits (since the town Hopis lack the time
for learning the necessary ritual and practicing the dances), but increased exposure to White customs and attitudes likewise levies a
toll upon the number of Hopis who retain their devout interest in
the Cult. The problem of making a living in a White wage-economy,
and the desire of many younger Hopis to move into the neighboring
towns, may exert even greater pressures in the future.

Although town life may be a beneficial economic influence by
providing means for making a living, it has very little to offer in the
broader field of life; few Hopis maintain their tranquillity long after
taking up town residence. Harshberger (1926, pp. 39–45) has discussed several of the influences resulting from changing economics
in Hopi life.

Many Hopi girls work as domestics in White towns, and gain
from this social experience an economic independence. This has
proven important, as it has tended somewhat to break down tribal
unity, for many of them meet non-Hopis and marry outside the
tribe, either with Navajos or men of other Pueblos. Those who marry
Hopi men often hope to remain in town instead of returning to the
harder life on the reservation. It is my impression that this reluctance
to return to the mesa villages is more prevalent among the Hopi
girls than the men.

Mention has already been made of the vacuum which results when
a woman who owns ceremonial knowledge or paraphernalia dies, or
becomes an apostate. If this disinclination to return to the villages
increases among the Hopi girls, or missionary efforts ever become at
all successful, Hopi ceremonial life and culture will undergo drastic
change.

The question of White economics has had its effect not only
among town Hopis, but also in the villages. Sale of Kachina paintings by Hopi artists, various artifacts bearing Kachina-mask designs,
or the tihü—all influence personal attitudes. The annual All-Indian
shows at Flagstaff and Gallup have introduced a factor never before
present in Hopi life—dancing for *personal* gain. Thus far, Kachina

dances are firmly proscribed for performances off the reservation; but this edict may fall some day, if the conservative group loses control.* If Kachina dances ever *are* presented for commercial gain, it will probably be via the entering wedge of a social Kachina dance, such as Kóhonino Kachina, Táşap Kachina, or some similar being.

The entry of commercialization has affected the attitude towards ceremonies on the reservation, as particularly exemplified by the "country fair" atmosphere at the First Mesa Snake Dance. Where formerly only a handful of Whites would be seen, now well up in the hundreds attend, sometimes outnumbering the native spectators —and there would be more, could the *kisonvi* hold the crowd. Craft articles are brought out for sale, and the general tone is anything but reverent. This is less apparent in the more conservative Second and Third Mesa villages, and on all three mesas the Kachina Dances so far remain freer from commercial inroads.

Appropriation of Kachina mask motifs by craftsmen in other arts, such as pottery, weaving, painting, and silver, tends to secularize and prostitute the Cult to a great degree, and may conceivably cause it to decline in preëminence in time.

Commercialization has seriously affected the religious culture of the Hopis, particularly since 1890. The sale of many articles of varying sacredness to scientific collectors has degenerated into tourist exploitation; and the manufacture for sale of some items, notably the tihü, has drastically affected the technique and appearance of the artifacts, as well as giving them a disproportionate importance. The artistic appearance and decoration of the tihü and of the impersonator have become more important in recent years as the Hopis have been able to obtain new materials for the purpose and have been made more self-conscious of the Cult by scientists and tourists.

Parsons (1939, p. 1142) has expressed the problem in this way:

> Pueblo arts are ritual arts, their motivation is religious. If this motivation lapses, the arts will lapse; for the only substitute motivation in sight is commercial gain. In commercial art the buyer controls, which means, when the artist belongs to another culture, a very rapid disintegration of traditional art forms.

The various Hopi art media have been markedly affected in recent years. While a few examples of old pottery with Kachina designs have been found, for the most part this type of decoration has been applied in more recent times. Most Hopi pottery is made at First

---

*This tabu seems recent, for I have photos of a Hopi group performing a Kwahu (Eagle) Kachina dance given in 1904 at Sherman Institute, California; the costumes and masks seem completely authentic. However, when some First Mesa youths proposed off-Reservation Kachina dances some years ago, for a commercial enterprise, they were emphatically vetoed by the council.

Mesa, particularly the better-grade ware; and First Mesa potters are
mostly Tewa people, living at Hano. It should also be remembered
that the revival of Hopi pottery was largely through the success of
Nampeyó, exploring among the Sikyatki ruins for prehistoric sherds.
These she would copy or adapt, developing in time a characteristic
art style which blossomed into a ceramic Renaissance as it was taken
over by her co-workers. [*]

In recent years, however, Hopi pottery art has developed many
new design styles, and among these, Kachina mask designs are very
noticeable. Fewkes (1898a, p. 659) mentions a few specimens as
being made in the 1890s:

> The large collections of so-called modern Hopi pottery in our
> museums is modified Tanoan ware, made in Tusayan. Most of
> the component specimens were made by Hano potters, who
> painted upon them figures of *katcinas*, a cult which they and
> their kindred introduced.

The inclusion of Kachina mask designs in basketry has been mentioned as early as 1879, when Stevenson (1883a, p. 393) collected a
few such plaques. Today these are much more numerous. To my
knowledge, no specimens of basketry have been excavated from prehistoric ruins which show any Kachina-like designs.

In the textile field, no prehistoric evidence of Kachina design has
yet been discovered. How far back the symbolic design on the
múchábñwiin kwewa (sash) goes in Hopi history, is not yet known;
but the design itself is commonly described as deriving from Wúyak-
küîta Kachina, and the mask symbolism is quite apparent. This same
design and other even more marked Kachina-like designs have been
seen on woven vests patterned on the American model. (One such
specimen is in the Cranbrook Institute of Science, No. 525.) And
finally, the large white robes with the brilliantly embroidered borders, called *tüiqi*, have undergone changes due to American influence.
Formerly the embroidered lozenges were decorated with floral or
geometric patterns. In recent years, these have been worked in with
aniline-dyed yarns, and more of them are seen with mask designs
decorating the interstices.

The art program in Oraibi High School has undergone a similar
development, particularly since 1937, when the talented Hopi artist,
Fred Kabotie, was appointed instructor in art. Under his direction,
old pottery and Kachina mask designs were adapted for use in several media. Woodwork (especially furniture) has been designed to

------

[*]A good illustrated description of the various styles of contemporary Hopi pottery can be
found in Underhill (1944, pp. 79–105), and an excellent account of the life of Nampeyó is
in Nequatewa (1943, pp. 40–42); and Collins (1970).

take advantage of these motifs; silverwork in a new technique, and mosaic work employing turquoise, jet, shell, and coral (similar to the Zuñi technique) features mask symbolism.

But it is in the field of decorative painting that the Kachina motif has been predominantly featured. Developed during the last thirty-five years, this medium has given rise to a whole generation of Hopi artists. Most of this work stems from the inspiration of Kenneth Chapman and Dorothy Dunn of Santa Fé, who encouraged the students in the Santa Fé Indian School to work out their own style in painting, instead of trying to copy the European style, so ill-suited to Indian art.

The natural artistic ability of the Hopis, and the tremendous wealth of ancient design which they can draw upon, resulted in a characteristic style of ceremonial painting. It has become representative of the whole Pueblo area, and is marked by flat areas of color, sharp linear outline, and little or no attempt at shading. The work is minutely detailed, with a crisp, clean appearance which, while static, is extremely delicate and "alive."

The subject matter of this graphic art varies with the several Pueblos, but in the Hopi area it is predominantly ceremonial, and Kachina ceremonies figure in three out of every four paintings. Undoubtedly one of the major reasons for this preoccupation with masked ceremonies is that the artists producing these paintings are all male. (In pottery and basketry, on the other hand, where objects are produced by women, geometric, floral, and abstract patterns predominate, with Kachina designs secondary.)

Modern commercial considerations have also affected Hopi art. Many of the fields of work discussed above are produced today primarily for sale (this is especially true of silver, pottery, and paintings), and a careful eye is kept on salability in their production. As a result, many items are turned out which cannot be called truly Hopi, even though made by Hopis.

The production of this type of goods is not necessarily indicative of a decline in cultural integrity, but there has been a noticeable, if gradual, change of emphasis in Kachina activity. Kachina ceremonies are still completely dominated by religious considerations, but there now seems to be a greater awareness of costuming and performance in the final-day dance. The manufacture of spurious tihü may result only in the deception of the purchaser; but if long carried on by Indians who themselves do not know more than a few Kachinas well, it can have a considerable effect on the Cult—particularly if these pseudo dolls are produced in the main by younger individuals, as is often the case today.

Plate XIII. Sio Kachina Dance

The typical regular dance in which the male dancers are accompanied by Kachinmanas. *Taken at Walpi in 1891.*

Courtesy Bureau of American Ethnology

Courtesy Bureau of American Ethnology

Plate XIV. Line of "Mixed Dancers"

A characteristic line of Individual Kachinas. Note the baskets of food in the foreground: corn, piki, fruit, and gifts. In the group can be seen Tukaü Kachina, Tükwinañ Kachina, Holi Kachina, Möṣairü Kachina, Ahote Kachina, plus several others too indistinct for identification. A pair of Táchíkti are also to be seen. Taken at Mishongnovi in 1891.

This commercialization and prostitution of the artistic element of the Kachina Cult has been very harmful, as it has diverted much worthwhile attention from the dramatic quality of the ceremonies to the less important tihü; this latter, while unique and colorful, is the least of the several characteristics which make the Kachina Cult such a remarkable expression of the art of religious pageantry.

Dependent upon the degree to which they relate to Hopi social organization, certain Indian Service activities in the field of Hopi economics could have a marked effect. If land ownership by individuals should become a standard pattern due to this program, it would radically affect the position of the male Hopi, since his lands are traditionally the property of his clan. In a matriarchal society, such as the Hopis', most of the traditional strength depends upon clan descent and organization, and the simple matter of private land-holding can well upset the two core strengths—clanship and matriarchy. Since both are represented in Kachina ritual, it cannot help being affected by a change in either.*

This consideration of economics and the Kachina Cult should not overlook one point which has a bearing on other facets of Hopi life. With the influx of students of Hopi culture as well as journalists and other curious White tourists, a thriving business has been built up in the supplying of ethnological information. The practice has been to employ an Indian, termed an "informant," who is paid by the hour, or day, to supply desired information. Needless to say, the value of this information is in direct ratio to the intelligence, coöperation, knowledge, or imagination of the informant.

It is impossible to estimate how many Hopis have worked as informants in the past; during the past fifty years, though, probably not over 50 have so served. Most Hopis do not willingly give out detailed information relative to ceremonial matters—some because they frankly do not know, but most because of normal reluctance to discuss private matters with strangers. Therefore, the securing of reliable informants is extremely difficult.

It follows that since most of the information gained through informants has come from perhaps as few as 50 members of the tribe, much of our knowledge of Hopi ritual is funneled through the interpretation of these few individuals, and must be considered in that light. We must guard against judging the group by the opinions or reactions of a very few of its members, many of whom may deliberately or unconsciously mislead.

---

*Dating from the enactment of the Allotment Act, this division of tribal lands in order to undermine tribal unity has long been a favorite weapon of those seeking to fully disenfranchise the Indian.

Another caution, already mentioned, must be emphasized: the amount of ritual knowledge varies tremendously. I would estimate that perhaps only one-fourth of the Hopis are truly "well-informed" as to the identities, costumes, and activities of the various Kachinas. Many will frankly admit this, but many more will volunteer offhand comments, trusting that the eagerness of their inquisitors will enable the informant to get by with such imaginary explanations.

Since this source of income is frequently available, it would seem that there would be many interested applicants. But this is not true, because of two major factors. The first, characteristic tribal reticence, has been mentioned above. The second is less frequently realized: the "monopoly" of certain individuals who have become almost professional informants. This exists in several villages, but is perhaps most marked in Oraibi, where Tewaquaptewa, the village chief, and Don Talayesva have been the chief informational sources for many years. This is not to condemn such a procedure, but merely to record the fact; for it must be borne in mind when trying to interpret, analyze, or explore Hopi customs, or that of any tribe, for that matter—particularly in the realm of native opinions, reactions, or explanations as to "why" a thing is so.

EDUCATION AND TECHNOLOGY

The effects of Government schools on the Hopis have already been discussed in a previous chapter; suffice it here to add consideration of one special aspect of that education. The technical courses offered in Government schools (such as Oraibi High School) are undeniably excellent for Hopi economic needs; however, it must also be admitted that they may strongly affect the Hopi system of the division of labor, and the ceremonial attitudes reflecting it. For example, the men are being taught commercial methods of preparing flour, and ceramics—both traditionally the work of the women.* Although twice attempted in the past, a flour mill has never been successful for any length of time in Tusayan. All corn meal is hand-ground by the women (usually with *hakomta* and *mada*). If this grinding work is taken over by the men, will those *mana* who grind meal during Kachina dances likewise be replaced by men with mechanical grinders?

It is axiomatic that any increase in technological skill decreases prayer, for the feeling of dependence upon the supernatural is in inverse ratio to man's ability to control his environment. One such

---

*Charles Loloma and his wife completed a course in ceramic arts at Alfred University in which part of their study concerned varying combinations of Hopi and White techniques. After a period of experimentation, Charles abandoned pottery, and has now become one of the most influential and creative silversmiths in the Southwest. Otellie independently pursues her career as teacher and artist in clay; her individualistic approach has earned her a wide audience.

example of the loss of ritual due to technological advance has been mentioned by White (1942) who points out that when the pueblo of Santa Ana acquired a dam and reservoir, ceremonial ritual concerned with rain-making decreased sharply. The Havasupai, who do not deposit prayer-sticks in their fields, as do the Hopis, make this shrewd observation: "We have a creek to irrigate with: the Hopi . . . have none and have to pray for rain all the time." (Spier (1928, p. 286).

In view of the tremendous importance of rain-bringing in the Hopi Kachina Cult (actually a primary function), the question arises as to its future, if wells or water pumps become numerous in the Hopi area. The passage of the Navajo-Hopi Rehabilitation Bill (1950) included plans for just such development; with regular irrigation, or water at the turn of a faucet, the basic needs may be so drastically altered that Hopi ceremonial attitudes may also change. One is irresistibly drawn to the conjecture, in due time, of a Cloud-Seeder Kachina, equipped with a buckskin sack of silver iodide crystals!

Other recent changes of this nature have had their derivative influences. Because of improved transportation and communication, and the means to travel on improved roads, each village and mesa learns more quickly what the others do; ideas spread more rapidly, and innovations are consciously or unconsciously absorbed into the local fabric.

The occasional presence of the White nurse, or Indian Service doctor, has apparently not had a marked effect upon the Kachina ritual, since curing is not a primary feature. Were curing more important, as in Navajo ceremonialism, it is probable that there would be a noticeable result.

The Effects of World War II

The last war has drastically affected the Kachina Cult, as well as Hopi life in general. With the return of many Hopis from military service (222 took active part in the war)[*] and other Hopis who worked in war plants and neighboring Arizona towns, new influences were soon felt. In the first place, Hopi psychology is not one which is easily accomodated in White civilization. There are different goals in each life-way, the ethical and moral values differ, and the ways of attaining success in either are at such variance that adjustment is difficult for the Hopis.

White culture regards competition as a healthy basis for proper development, while Hopi culture does not. The Hopi has found that coöperation—emphasis on the group rather than on the individual—

[*]Dow Carnal, Superintendent, Hopi Indian Agency, in correspondence with the writer, July 30, 1951.

has proved more efficient in promoting successful living in his environment. To the White, the individual is important; in the Hopi world, the common good is paramount, though there is no loss of individual dignity, since he has an established place in which he can attain a full measure of expression and achievement. The average White individual tends to compartmentalize his life, often making religion a "Sunday" matter; the Hopi cannot understand this attitude, for his religion is actually a 24-hour-a-day matter.

Many Hopis who went into military or town life returned with a bitter feeling toward the "outside world" and determined to have no more of it. They had been confronted with race prejudice; had discovered that, albeit drafted into military service, they were still regarded as second-class citizens; they were not allowed to vote; and frequently were denied equal status in law. More than that, though they had been trained in many trades while in military service, they found little opportunity to use these skills upon discharge, through no fault of their own.

Others, living in cities or towns, saw many material advantages in the luxuries, sanitary advantages, and comfortable living facilities, and naturally wanted these for themselves. Some veterans returned to the villages and immediately rebelled against the pressures exerted upon them by the village elders, who naturally expected to continue as the controlling factor in village life. When the younger men wanted to bring in innovations gained from Army or city life, the conservative elders often objected, with a resultant split between the two groups. Some items, such as the use of electricity and electrically-operated machinery, have long been debated in the several villages, and are still opposed in the more conservative towns. With the money they received in war-plant work or Service savings, some of the young men felt they would be doing their people a good service by bringing in such aids, and could not understand the strong opposition to their ideas.

The elders, who for the most part admitted the physical advantage of labor-saving machinery, saw only the long-range threat to their way of life, and opposed any let-down in a united front against further inroads of White practices, even if this meant a less luxurious life. They saw in the returning men not only the beneficial gifts of White life, such as well-made utensils, clothing, and other functional goods, but also some cultural degeneration, notably in the use of liquor. This latter had never been a problem in Hopi life, for the tribe is one of the few Indian groups which never developed a native intoxicant.

Thus the advantage of material gifts was far outweighed in the eyes of tribal statesmen, to whom material comfort was much less important than assuring the survival of Hopi culture in as pure form as possible. The veterans accused their elders of refusing to see that Hopi life had already been changed, and could not understand this tenacious clinging to old ways.

A second factor added to the growing tension. Since social, political, and religious control are largely one in Hopi life, any threat to the one was a threat to the whole. The young men, having returned from experiencing a certain degree of freedom, resented being told what to do, or having limitations placed on their activities. They likewise felt that, having seen something of the White world, they should have a voice in guiding Hopi destinies. This was completely at variance with Indian philosophy that "children should be seen and not heard." Needless to say, the veterans did not regard themselves as children, and bitterly quarreled with their leaders over the matter. The latter saw in this quarrel a threat to their own position, and likewise felt that the willingness of the veterans to embrace White material culture could only result in a complete degeneration of Hopi life.

This struggle of the elders versus younger Indians just returned from the outside world is not peculiar to the Hopi villages. Two Río Grande pueblos, San Ildefonso and Isleta, are currently threatened with serious cleavages over the same general problem,* and it has already been shown how Oraibi was affected by internal dissension. Whether the current Hopi situation will have such serious consequences is impossible to say. As yet, the Hopi discord has not reached the violent stage, but it does seriously threaten tribal unity and peace. Thompson (1950) has attempted to consider this whole problem in detail in a recent publication.

The basic problem in all of these questions of split loyalties and growing skepticism of religious matters is a key one for the Kachina Cult. In the first place, there is the simple matter of obtaining sufficient novices to fulfill the ceremonial roles and participate in the dances. A second difficulty is the frustration and apathy resulting from the clash of the several culture factors. Many of the younger men cannot reconcile the various teachings and no longer believe the traditional accounts, yet are unwilling to accept the White world.

This confusion in the minds of the younger generation and skepticism toward traditional teachings, resulted in a growing refusal to respect the village elders and thus lessened the effective control of the elders in the tribe. This has had a serious effect upon the authority of the latter—and when the elders lose control in any traditional

---

*For an excellent study *in re* this problem of Río Grande internal strife, *see* French (1948) and Whitman (1947).

culture, that culture, as such, is doomed. As the old men became increasingly fearful for the perpetuation of Hopi life, they were inclined to assert their seniority, trying to compel the youths to fulfill their ceremonial responsibilities. The result has been an increase in contention.

The effect of this on the Kachina Cult has been somewhat different from that of earlier controversies. When the problem of White contacts first began to be noticed, the Hopis in general presented a more unified front; those apostate Indians who sided with missionary and Government forces were clearly recognized as no longer members of the group. (In fact, these apostates were regarded by their relatives as being dead, and were frequently termed so, never to be mentioned again as living people. Needless to say, they were not expected to become Kachina!) Thus their influence, particularly as regards Hopi reaction, was important only insofar as they "gave away" Hopi secrets.

This was not true in later dissensions, particularly in the assault of the younger men upon the Hopi gerontocracy; for here was a situation in which both sides were completely Hopi, and wanted to remain so, but differed in the type of culture which they desired to foster. Since Hopi culture is primarily based upon the theory of gerontocracy, a drastic change in that field can only result in a cultural change equally drastic. And since much of the basic Kachina Cult theory depends for its strength upon the *Wüwüyom,* or old men, and their traditional teachings, this modification can only result in considerably affecting the Cult.

Another result which has already become noticeable, is the reaction by many of the youths whose ideas have been rebuffed by the Elder Statesmen: they have refused to participate in Kachina activities (as well as some other religious ceremonies) and thus have made it still more difficult to secure recruits.

Out of this discord comes an important point previously made evident by the Oraibi schism and the subsequent Hotevilla-Bakabi split, and emphasized more recently by the division of Moenkopi: the Hopi people have been able to overcome successfully the threats against their cultural integrity from Spanish, Mexican, American, Catholic, and Protestant interference—but the danger of Hopi versus Hopi is once again the gravest problem facing the tribe.

The full effects of World War II on the Kachina Cult are still much too close for intelligent evaluation. In other rites, there has been a revival of the old War Ceremonies, Purification Ritual, and the like, common in the days of intertribal warfare. In Kachina activity, there has been the introduction of many material objects, as a

continuation of the long gradual process of absorbing American culture; but to my knowledge there have been no major changes in
philosophy, nor the introduction of any Kachinas as a result of the
war. However, considering Hopi adaptability, it may even be that
in time Hilili, the Warrior Kachina, will undergo a change and
emerge as G.I. Kachina, the American Warrior!

INDIAN BUREAU ACTIVITIES

Hopi tribal unity may be subjected to further strain due to recent
Indian Bureau policies. During World War II, a part of the Mojave
and Chemehuevi lands on the Colorado River Indian Reservation
(Fig. 1) was set aside as a concentration camp, in which a large number of Japanese-Americans were temporarily "relocated." With war's
end, the camp, with its emergency buildings, was turned back to the
Indian Service. Since the Chemehuevi and Mojave living there did
not actually need all of their alloted area, it was decided to try to
accomodate some of the Navajos and Hopis from Arizona, and thus
relieve their over-crowded reservations.

This was done on a purely voluntary basis; first, with a large group
of Navajos, joined shortly afterwards by 24 Hopi families. This
experiment is too new to allow adequate analysis as yet, but so far,
slightly over half of the Hopis who first emigrated from the villages
have stayed; the balance became homesick and returned. Some
others have since joined the Hopis, saying they will stay permanent-
ly; at the time of writing there were 36 Hopi families settled there.

What effect this move will eventually have is difficult to say. Many
of these Hopis are Christian, and therefore their departure has not
had a marked effect upon village ceremonial life. Whether they have
taken any remnants of traditional ritual with them has not as yet
been made clear.

Efforts to undo the work of the Collier era continue, and in the
last two years (1950 to 1952) have become particularly pronounced
with administrative changes in Indian Service personnel. The opposition forces are several, and each has a particular goal, some of
which are good, some evil.

The two most vocal groups are the opponents of the *laissez faire*
attitude towards Indian traditional life, and the neighboring Whites
who see in the large reservation areas potential sources for exploitation. The first group, usually sincere, is often seconded by those Indian Service workers who also opposed the Collier program from its
inception; both believe that the only way to achieve Indian acculturation into White civilization is to go "full steam ahead" and eradicate Indian culture without compromise. The second group (less
altruistic in their motives) includes settlers, ranchers, municipal

142   governments, or state administrations who view the lands as sources for taxation, grazing, timber, or mineral profit.

In fairness, it must be admitted that many of the Whites who wish to destroy Indian culture honestly think their way is best for the Indian; they argue that the change is inevitable, and cannot temporize with anything short of "overnight" action. All of these forces are influential with the many lay groups who, knowing little of the problems of Indian-White relations, earnestly desire to do what they can to help the Indian to adjust. Unfortunately, they also often drive ahead in an effort to mold the Indian into a White pattern without any thought as to what will happen after that forced molding has taken place. All too frequently the Indian problem is confused with the whole American minority issue, and Indian-Oriental-Negro matters are indiscriminately lumped together as though a common solution could be found.

The political power of the Indian in the past has been almost completely absent.* However, with the recent Court decisions which finally gave voting rights to the Indians of Arizona and New Mexico, their political voice may become more articulate.

Even more serious in this matter of the breakdown of a culture is the fact that as yet no effective substitute for the traditional Hopi way of life exists. Therefore, as the traditional system is completely upset by the inroads of White civilization, the result may be chaos. The tendency so far has been for the White culture to pull the younger Hopis away from their mesa homes without affording them means to meet the problems of a new environment, and without strengthening the home area against the shock of the resulting vacuum. (The ramifications of this problem are discussed at length by Thompson, 1950, pp. 173ff.)

SOME RESULTS OF THESE INFLUENCES

The effects of skepticism, disunity, confusion, and economic demands which prevent participation cannot help but affect the attitude of the Hopis towards their own masked ceremonials. There is greater difficulty in securing novices and dancers, particularly those who will be completely devout participants. Certain Kachinas, especially the fertility beings, are in very real danger of lapsing or of undergoing great changes in costume or activity.

While it is difficult to establish accurately the degree, it is nevertheless quite apparent that there is more of the social atmosphere of self-gratification surrounding Kachina dances today than was the

---

*Although Congress granted full citizenship in 1924, several states denied Amerind franchise on grounds of "wardship." Full citizenship was gained only after litigation culminating in a State Supreme Court decision in 1952.

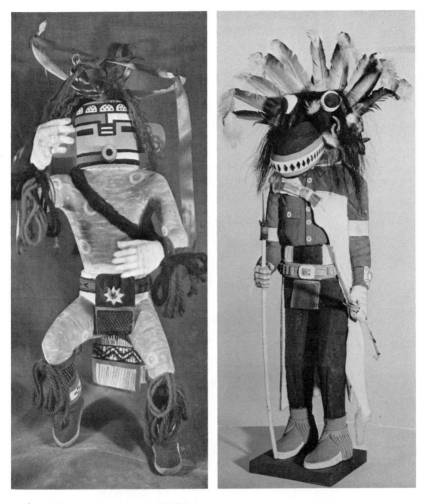

Plate XV   Contemporary Tihü

    a. Qáö Kachina, *by Jimmy Kewanwytewa. Characteristic of the*
    excellent work of this Hopi, this Corn Kachina demonstrates
    the great amount of action and sculptural qualities typical of
    contemporary tihü *carving.*
                      Courtesy Museum of Northern Arizona

    b. Nataşka Kachina. *While less sculptural, and perhaps less so-*
    phisticated, this tihü *shows the tremendous amount of detail*
    often included in recent years. In this specimen, all costume
    details are carved and painted.
                      Courtesy Denver Art Museum

Plate XVI. Tihü by Tewaquaptewa

This doll is characteristic of the individual style developed by the Village Chief of Oraibi.

case previously. Undoubtedly there is much religious reverence and
respect still present, especially in the feelings of the older people;
but it seems to me that the increasing numbers of White spectators,
especially the female tourist in her shorts and halter (a display obscene in itself to Hopi eyes), the visitors' scattering of candy wrap-
pers and poking into Hopi homes, cannot fail to destroy some of
this sentiment, however fervent.

The older Hopi men frequently complain (as do most older men
in any civilization) about the lack of interest or respect shown toward their teachings. They maintain that younger men who have
gone away to school return to the villages lacking in feeling for the
ancient ways, with little inclination to participate in Kachina ceremonies.

A LOOK TO THE FUTURE

In spite of the foregoing rather gloomy observations, and the last
half-century of opposition, persecution, controversy, and internal
dissent, it is worthy of comment that the Kachina Cult continues in
its traditional cycle. There are recusants, true, but for the most part
these are the few converted Hopis, or the younger men discussed
above, and the majority of the tribe tries to ignore them. To outward
appearances, the lessening of fervor of the participants is not great,
but there has been an increasing inward tension because of the
defections.

This tension is not only due to the bickering that goes on, but
also to the firm belief that Kachina ceremonies are ineffective unless
there is a collective good-will atmosphere in the village. More practically, there is the conscious realization that if the apostates persist,
or their numbers increase, the various Hopi ceremonies are doomed.
Without apprentices, the complicated ceremonial structure cannot
be handed on. It may be that the Kachina Cult will disappear from
the American scene; but if so, this will not be soon, for by far the
larger number of Hopis participate in it with complete enthusiasm.
If the time should ever come when the final *Nimán* is danced, it will
not be until Hopi culture is no longer a vital force.

As a matter of fact, it seems probable that the Cult will continue;
for history has shown that even in the years when it was most vigorously attacked, it persevered. It is a dynamic, not static, religious expression, and its unique flexibility has much to do with its ability
to survive. At present there seems to be something of a revival of
interest in Kachina dancing, as has happened so frequently in times
past.

Therefore, it seems well to review briefly the apparent reasons
for the tenacity and current Renaissance of these ceremonies. In the

first place, there was the natural resentment against the prohibition of ceremonies; when the Government ban was lifted, greater activity resulted. Secondly, the interest of White artists and ethnologists created in the Hopis an awakened appreciation of the Kachina ceremonials, particularly in the pageantry inherent in the dances.

Thirdly, as many Hopis came to realize just how much they had forgotten of their own religion, plus the fact that some of the ancient ceremonies (notably Yáyatû, Póboştü and Momchit) had actually become completely extinct, they became interested in trying to regenerate the one Cult to which they all belonged. A fourth reason would seem to be that participation in the masked ceremonies does not involve such exacting demands as do some of the other ritual activities. This fact of less rigid requirements is particularly attractive to younger Hopis, who are frequently reluctant to take active part in Hopi ceremonial life.

Another cause for this Renaissance is that the broad scope of the Kachina ceremonies meets more of the spiritual needs of the Hopis than do the other, more specialized, rites. This is especially desirable today, when so many factors new to Hopi life have been introduced. The position of the Hopis as a relatively ignored minority, indifferently attended to by the Indian Service, has no small effect. Nash (1937, p. 377f.) has demonstrated that nativistic cults invariably arise among deprived groups who resent their secondary role but are helpless to remedy their plight.

Of considerable importance to this long record of continuity is the inherent stubbornness so characteristic of the Hopis. Several examples of this have already been mentioned; it will suffice here to point to the several times in the past when the ceremonial life of this people has waxed and waned under exterior pressures. Each time this happened, there were a goodly number who kept the old ways going until opportunity for regular observances presented itself. Usually the retainers were priests, or ceremonially important individuals, but often they may have been devout laymen.

The fact that all Hopis are included within the structure of the Kachina Cult is doubtless responsible for strengthening its activity. And finally, an important point is that there is not so much of the single-clan-control element in the Kachina organization as in the other societies. Thus, the death of a ceremonially important individual, or the extinction of a clan through the death of its female members, does not mean the termination of this all-clan ritual, as has obtained with certain other ceremonies which have in recent years been lost because no living member of the group knows the complex ritual.

And this Renaissance, if such it be, is good. There are too many fine things in the Kachina ceremonials to allow the Cult to disappear. The continual exhortation to unity, pure thinking, coöperation; the colorful qualities of the drama, costuming, and dancing; the concern with children and their education; and the happiness basic to Kachina belief—all of these are very real values, and can contribute much to both Indian and White. Although the Kachina Cult is certainly not a factor of major importance to Whites (most of whom have never heard of it), it is nevertheless one of the most colorful segments of American Culture, and its dissolution would not only be a tragedy for the Hopis, but a very real loss to those Whites who concern themselves with a deeper understanding of other people's lives. In an era of growing concern for minority groups, interests in the values of others, and tolerance of differing viewpoints, the responsibility for such a loss will rest largely upon White shoulders.

This is an important factor, for the Hopis are not a dying tribe. Their population is increasing, and their potential gifts are many. Unless wisely guided, (and not prematurely forced) toward a strong, integrated culture, well-adjusted to White life, the alternative will be a body of Indians who have lost their old traditional culture, who live in a White world yet are not White, and who as a result have become marginal people—one more of those tribes who traded a continent for second-class membership in an alien civilization.

10.

Thirty Years Later

IN THE YEARS SINCE the publication of the preceding pages, the Kachinas seem to have thrived more than I had earlier anticipated. Where once the future for their survival seemed gloomy, it is heartwarming to realize the degree to which the ceremonies have retained their ancient importance. While they continue to change, it is not in ways that threaten their integrity in Hopi life. The innovations still tend to occur primarily in the realm of maternal culture, and pose no threat to the intrinsic values of the ceremonies. Indeed, following a brief decline after World War II, there has been a dramatic resurgence of interest and respect for the importance of the Kachina as a fundamental strength within the tribe. Although there are those Hopi people who no longer accept the religious qualities of the Kachina world, they have not denied the social importance which can be so readily perceived. In fact, this appreciation of what it means to be a Hopi spreads into other aspects of regard for traditional customs, and it is this awareness that provides much of the glue holding together the whole Hopi world—and of this, the Kachina remains a major element.

The mundane world to which the Kachinas return annually has changed radically. The Hopi people now live completely in a cash economy, dominated by White financial and political interests. They report to a wholly different calendar, dictated by the five-day, 9-to-5 routine, working primarily for federal, state, or local governments, reservations industries, or in clerical or labor capacities in neighboring small businesses. Farming has decreased in acreage, since with a cash economy, it is easier to buy corn at the store than

148   grow it. In 1882, approximately 5,000 acres were regularly worked; today, this number has declined to about 3,000 acres (Bradfield, 1972). But the proportion of working people is not high; as on all Indian reservations, unemployment remains the major problem; in 1983, 33 percent of the employable adults seeking work were unemployed (BIA statistics, January 1983). This is the crux of the fear that haunts many conservative Hopis: if farming is abandoned, for whatever reason, what will happen when the money runs out (that is, if there is no cash income job)? It is this fear of dependence upon an outside world over which there is no control that causes many Hopis to reject the easy life, so-called, of modern dollar economy; and it affects their willingness to accept other aspects of that same culture.

Some surprising adjustments of traditional practice include the recent construction of a kiva with commercial cement building blocks, the introduction of wooden flooring in a kiva, and the paving of a kiva floor—further demonstration of Hopi pragmatic blindness to problems demanding new solutions, even though this may clash with tradition.

The Revitalization Movement, which has become such a controversial part of Hopi life in the past three decades, continues to fractionalize the Hopi, although the aging of two of its major protagonists has somewhat blunted the force of this disruptive schism. The lack of tribal unity remains the greatest political weakness, and that this is serious can be seen in the recent split of Moenkopi village into Upper Moenkopi and Lower Moenkopi, harkening back to the Oraibi breakup in 1960 (Clemmer, 1978; Nagata, 1970).

The dispute over the position of the Tribal Council has not abated, and remains difficult of solution. The matter of representation from the several villages, the role of the *Kikmongwi* (village chief), and full Hopi participation, also threaten fractionalization— and all of this is compounded by federal pressure. No longer can the Hopi villagers retreat from the outside world; a way must be found to solve the dilemma, and the undeniable fact is that the Tribal Council is still the only agency that can deal with the *Bahana* with anything like a Hopi voice.

With the aggravation of tribal antagonism between the Hopi and Navajo due primarily to the District 6 controversy (*see* p. 2), fewer Navajo visitors are to be seen in the villages, or in attendance at such events as Kachina dances.° The number of Anglo visitors has increased, of course—on occasion, busses pull up to disgorge groups

---

°The recent court decision in *Healing v. Jones, 1983*, deciding against the Hopi claim to their own land area, has been a bitter blow to the search for an equitable settlement of the conflict.

of visitors, balanced, if not in numbers, by private airplanes landing on the nearby airstrip to unload tourists coming to witness the liturgy. And a far more serious threat to Hopi culture will be the proposed Turquoise Trail, planned to extend from Kayenta to Shungopovi, which will inevitably serve as a throughway from Farmington to Winslow or Flagstaff, bringing in greater numbers of visitors than ever before.

When the hippie invasion was at its crest, a tremendous wave of justifiable resentment swept through the Hopi and Navajo country. The new breed of intruders, unkempt, often physically dirty, and lazy, imposed tremendously upon native traditions and the hospitality of the people. Frequently being high on drugs or liquor, they invaded their homes uninvited, gobbled food without payment, and in general took advantage of the traditional openness of the villagers.* This, of course only exacerbated the feelings of the Hopis, long-suffering from the incursions of the day-to-day tourist, and it resulted in further efforts to banish outsiders from the ceremonies. Attendance has long been a problem because of the physical limitations of the *kisonvi*. The Snake Dance, in particular, is a major attration to tourists, who regard it solely as an exotic experience. The dance area simply cannot hold the number of spectators seeking admission; furthermore, while the desert floor offers ample parking space, the tendency is for them to crowd their cars into the restricted area atop the mesas.* Irregularly, the Snake Dance has been closed to non-Hopis, depending upon the immediate circumstances. But thus far, there has been no proscription against attendance at Kachina dances, in recognition of the traditional regard for joint good feelings of participant and spectator alike. uniting in spiritual cooperation for the common good. However, it must be admitted that the 1982 Shálako performances at Shungopovi dramatically demonstrated the problem of too many people in too little space: the performers in their towering headdresses and elaborate costumes simply could not make their way through the crowd, and sheer human numbers detracted grievously from the profound impact and dignity of the ceremony. Such incidents clearly indicate why the Hopi people feel the way they do, and why they object so

---

*This was not new; in the 1930s, a long-haired Anglo youth wandered into the Navajo-Hopi region and insinuated himself uninvited into the Indians' lives to an intolerable degree, leaving a wake of resentment and confusion in his path.

*A further indication of the lack of consideration for the importance of the Kachinas to the Hopis was demonstrated in Phoenix a few years ago, when a White youth dressed up in a homemade Hümis Kachina costume, complete with mask and headdress, and paraded through the downtown streets. One can imagine the feelings of devout Catholics in New York City, for example, were a Hopi youth to stride down Fifth Avenue arrayed in a bishop's outfit, with miter and crosier.

violently to events such as the annual Smoki Pageant in Prescott, Arizona, in which a number of White men dress up in pseudo-Hopi costumes and perform their version of the Snake Dance as part of a local tourist attraction.

Although perhaps not directly related, but apparently inescapable in the face of social pressures, the problem of liquor on the reservation has become serious. Once unknown in the villages, it was taken as a matter of faith that "Hopis just don't drink." This is no longer true, and drunkenness is now a major social problem; I was quite surprised at a recent Kachina ceremony to see a young Hopi staggering along the mesa, quite incapable of handling his liquor. This sad situation cannot be wholly blamed upon the revocation of the federal restrictions against liquor on reservations, although the repeal has made purchasing liquor easier and less expensive.

As for the Kachina religion, there is no longer any question as to its ancient origin. The existence of masked beings in prehistoric times is now generally accepted. While further discoveries relating to the theme continue to be made in archeological exploration, and contributory evidence such as additional petroglyphic sites is noted, these are essentially supportive in nature, and it can be confidently said that masked performances were in full bloom well before 1500 A.D. It will never be possible to establish their specific origin, although a close relationship with pre-Columbian Mexican rituals seems certain. We simply do not know the precise avenue of contact.

With the dances themselves, larger numbers of performers are taking part; on one occasion in 1982, well over 100 various Kachinas were involved—I was astonished, but delighted, to see this, and to recall the time when there were fewer than 25 dancers in a line. It is undeniable that there is more of a social air than formerly, when the religious aspect predominated; the Hopi people seem less reverent, and sometimes equal the White spectators in displaying an apparent indifference to the splendor of the rituals.

Off-reservation presentation has become noticeable in the last quarter century, with groups of masked dancers taking part in staged shows (see p. 132). A relatively mild departure was the portrayal of a "Kachina dance" in Winslow, with traditional costumes, but using pseudo-Kachina "Mickey Mouse" character masks: However, in 1968 in New York and other eastern cities, a troupe of Hopi performers presented quite real Snake Dances and masked Hilili Kachina dances on stage. While this was organized and promoted by a White "friend of the Hopis," it nevertheless was in remarkably accurate detail.

There are more social activities during the Kachina dance season than occur the balance of the year, and this is in part a reason for the warm welcome felt at their return. The deep interrelationship of Hopi culture within itself—the complex interweaving of ceremonial activities beyond just the Kachina ritual—has continued the strength of Hopi religious and social fiber. But a price has been exacted from modern economic routine: at one time, "everyone" belonged to one or more societies; today, there are a fair number of adult Hopis who have never gone through Kachina initiation, and it is not unknown to have a middle-aged man initiated into the Wüwüchim. Earleir, this would have taken place almost automatically while he was a young boy.

The need for a "correct" appearance is still a problem for the dancer who has his hair cut. Following the return of many young men from military service in World War II and Korea, wearing the mandated hair cut, commercial mannequin's hair falls became common purchases from commercial display houses. The inclusion of various manufactured knick-knacks on costumes, as weights, decorations, or ornament, continues, and in much the same proportion as formerly. Many dancers use lipstick under their masks for facial painting, and other ready-prepared paint pigments are incorporated into regular use. While textiles seem to have maintained their traditional role—it is still rare to see a Kachina in commercial costuming, except for the clowns—the proportion of handmade materials is obviously slowly yielding to the more easily obtained machine-made substances. And wristwatches occasionally replace bowguards!

The demands of outside employment and White social pressures continue to control performance schedules. Kachina initiations are now more abbreviated, since many Hopis cannot take time away from work to go through the prolonged full-scale ritual. Dances are held less frequently and almost universally on weekends to accommodate work schedule demands. Many of the ceremonies are simply too expensive—people cannot afford to sponsor them as freely as when the cost was largely in crops or craft work, rather than job-earned dollars. Time taken to grind cornmeal on a *hakomta* is no longer as available, and much of the meal is bought at the commercial mill.

In the resurgence of Kachina ritual, there have been a few new individuals introduced, but most of the innovations have been in the revival of older ones. This has been a fascinating development, since some are Kachinas never seen by younger people today. Another dramatic renewal has been that of the great Shálako ceremony, one of the most colorful American Indian rituals. This had been performed on an irregular basis in the past, but following the most recent presentation, in 1982, it will apparently now be sponsored on a regular four-year interval, bearing further witness to the determination of the people to prevent further relapses of treasured observances.

Attendance at the ceremonials has changed markedly. The purely social aspects of the dances have increased, although this is of course nothing new; there has always been much social interchange at the Kachina performances. However, it is more distinct today, and certainly extends to the Hopi people themselves. Many, who feel that they are "modern Christians," while loathe to abandon this colorful part of their heritage, subtly reveal the strains of their apostasy: witness the casual attitude expressed by these Hopi viewers, who explain that they are there only to have fun, claiming evasively that "I don't really believe in them any more."

But of all the outside influences, in my opinion the most profound has been the increased interest by the White art world. This is evidenced by the dramatic change in museum displays, in which objects are regarded as art rather then ethnography, and by art museums' acceptance of them as valid esthetic expressions. Furthermore, the remarkably expanded interest of collectors and dealers in the visual qualities of the Kachina arts has also served to raise the level of respect and active concern. This intensification has also had its effect upon the Hopis themselves, of course.

With this increased interest have come some changes within the White art world. Any given museum exhibit today of contemporary ethnic arts will extend a welcome to Kachina carving as sculpture, and it will be treated accordingly. Although it is true that the flat-color paintings of single Kachinas as subjects are done less often today, many artists abstract mask designs or draw from the dances in their compositions. But it is in the *kachintihü* that the increased interest has been the most dramatic. Now regarded universally as *objets d'art*, they are treated as fine sculpture, and they have earned a quite different place in Hopi life as well.

The increased demand has resulted in a flood of dolls on the market, and the number of carvers has exploded to meet that need. A census of Hopi carvers would probably reveal that almost every adult male has produced *tihü* for sale at one time or another, and a surprisingly large number make a comfortable living at the art.*

There are a fairly large number of recognized master carvers who have gained wide recognition in the art world for the quality of their sculpture; their work is eagerly sought after by collectors, who willingly pay high prices. Each has a recognizable style and almost invariably signs his work, since individual attribution is important to the purchasers.

---

*Erik Bromberg, a major wholesaler of Kachina dolls, estimates that approximately 400 carvers are active full-time today (personal communication, 1984).

The increased awareness of Indian art in general, and interest in the Kachina doll in particular, have affected the economics of the art as well as its development. Although "old dolls" readily hold their own in the contemporary art market—some dolls, made before 1900, have brought as much as $15,000—even the elaborate contemporary dolls by well-known artists sell regularly for $1,000, and in singular instances for as much as $5,000 or even $10,000. When sums such as these became commonplace in the market, the influence is explosive and unpredictable.

Several of the more extensive early collections, of which the best known were those of Sen. Barry Goldwater and film actor John Wayne, have been incorporated into museums and in turn have widened public familiarity with *Kachintihü*, while others have been broken up and sold piecemeal. But new collections continue to take their places, and while there is no census of collectors available, at least a dozen very large-scale aggregations are in private hands, supplemented by several hundred smaller collections scattered throughout the country.

This increased attention has simply been an extension of the interest earlier expressed in the carved dolls (*see* pp. 104ff). While much of the on-going growth of *tihü* art was still in the more traditional forms, the "action doll" continued to be in favor, and in time has become not only more elaborate, but today is the standard by which the art is judged. The costuming has actually changed less than the degree of carving detail and pose—meticulous detail in carving; dramatic, lifelike postures; and finely cut features. Costume detail is not new, of course; one finds many examples of tiny woven textiles and accessories before 1900, and this has continued to the present. But now such elaboration is almost universal, with carved and painted miniature body parts, costume, mask, and accessories all created with astonishing skill. Indeed, one of the interesting differences in this devotion to detail is that the mask, by which the Kachina was formerly identified and therefore the most important part of the doll, is today less significant; the pose, costuming, and the accessories have become the desiderata.*

In the 1970s, legislation culminating in the Endangered Species Act of 1973 made it impossible for the Hopis to use the feathers of migratory birds for decorative purposes. Since certain feathers are traditionally mandatory for specific Kachinas, this caused a great problem for carvers in seeking substitutes. In most instances, the dyed feathers of domestic ducks, chickens, or geese are used; other-

---

*However, collector appetite has also induced several Hopi carvers to revive the rigid old-style *tihü*—not as deceptions, but simply to satisfy the demand for this now-rare type.

wise, carved wooden feathers are painted realistically. Some ignore the traditional feathering and add the feathers of any bird they can obtain. Little by little this has subtly altered the appearance of many Beings.

Another alteration, again not new but now more prevalent, is the use of accessories obtained from model and hobby shops, in which small cast or manufactured articles are incorporated into the figurines. Those Kachinas which carry hand bells, for example, no longer display a carved or painted wooden bell; instead, tiny cast brass "schoolbells" are frequently seen in the hands of such individuals as Tálavai Kachina (see Plate X); a tiny cast rubber turtle was seen attached to the lower leg of a *tihü* to fulfill the need for a turtle-shell rattle. Plastic, fiber, or rubber Christmas tree branches are used for collar ruffs, or held in the hands; and the inclusion of turquoise-colored trade glass beads to suggest turquoise necklaces is almost universal. In short, this is demonstrably a mature art form in which innovations become the lifeblood of survival.

If the Endangered Species Act has drastically affected the manufacture of *tihü*, no less serious is the increasing scarcity of cottonwood. Most carvers still prefer this tree, not only for traditional reasons, but because it is easier to carve than harder woods, is a local product, and gives the desired visual texture. But cottonwood trees are dying out in the Southwest, with the lowering of the water table and the damming of streams. One can no longer rely upon the large quantities of old trees, which were formerly common along the rivers or washes; the carver has to travel farther and farther from home for a source of supply. The shortage is so acute that a few Indians have become professional cottonwood gatherers, traveling long distances in pickup trucks, returning with wood which is retailed to the carvers for as much as $25 to $35 per foot for prime lengths. This is no small business—by one count, over 10,000 Kachina dolls are turned out annually. (Erik Bromberg, personal communication, 1984).

Although women assisted in the production of dolls for many years, it was never a common practice. It is true that some *tihü* were the results of a family enterprise, with women and children preparing various parts of the doll or its accessories, but the basic work was by the men. Today, several women have become widely recognized as full-time doll carvers and enjoy a good income from their art. A few specialize in the making of certain accessories, weaving costumes, or painting detail, but many perform the whole task. A more frequent role is that of making the miniature dolls that have become so popular. This is a fairly recent phenomenon; although small dolls were made in the 1920s and 1930s, they were not com-

mon. Nor were they as diminutive as the contemporary product:
most were in the 2-to-4-inch range. Today, it is not uncommon to
obtain miniatures as small as 1 inch in height, complete with costume and accessories. Even groups of these gathered together,
placed upon small wooden slabs, are to be found in galleries and
curio stores. Part of the reason for this customer-oriented production
is the fascination with the miniature and the challenge it presents
to the carver. Perhaps another factor is the move from houses into
apartments, whereby the consumer still desires the Kachina doll,
but lacks the space for a large collection. These tiny figures provide
a solution.

As a corollary, huge carved wooden figures also continue to be
made in increasing numbers, although they are less common than
the miniatures. Usually the older examples were recognized as
exotica, and regarded as freaks by the Hopis. On occasion, they
might be passed off to the gullible collector as "sacred kiva figures"
and sold at inflated prices; but they were never common. Those
made today are far more carefully carved and painted, and they
are often supplied with a glass display case. Most are around 18 to
20 inches in height, although some are as large as 3 or 4 feet (*see*
p. 104).

Another notable phenomenon, which is related to collector interest, is the anatomical detail which has become part of the art. The
major attention paid to the human form in the traditional *tihü* was
usually confined to carefully carved hands or feet. The recent
examples of fine anatomical detail include well-modeled figurines
with subtle musculature, realistic body proportions and form, and
even detailed breasts on the few "women" Kachinas (that is,
Kókopölö Mana). These modeled bodies are not necessarily phallic
or erotic; while Kókopölö carvings do indicate genitals, and are
often posed in provocative postures, the body structure of these
anatomical figurines is simply carefully rendered detail by skilled
sculptors. It must be emphasized that the new types of action figures
can no longer be regarded simply as Kachina dolls; they have become costumed sculpture or *genre* figures. The degree or detail,
precise proportions, and lifelike activities portrayed in the round
now ensures an entrée into the world of sculpture for objects once
seen as merely folk carving.

Concomitant to this development has been the creation of small
figurines cast in bronze, silver, lead, or other metals. These are sometimes decorated with colored pigments, but usually they are left
uncolored. A few Hopi artists have emphasized the sculptural
quality of their work by carving cottonwood *tihü* in meticulous detail but leaving them unpainted. Some are full-figured Kachina

subjects, while others are one-piece compositions showing a partial masked figure growing out of a log base, for example, or perhaps simply a head and shoulders emerging from a flat wooden surface. Here again, one is impressed by the sculptural quality of the composition rather than the colors by which one previously identified the Kachina.

A certain degree of stylization remains in Kachina carving today, but it is expressed primarily in the selection of subjects. There seem to be a limited number of types that are carved over and over, reflecting the carver's interest in certain favored beings, or the popularity of a given group in the market. This changes from time to time, as do all fads, of course; many of these beings are actually not Kachinas at all—Buffalo, Snake, and Butterfly Dancers, or Clowns, for example—but they are so popular with collectors that some carvers produce almost nothing else. This degree of specialization means that it would be very difficult today to obtain a complete set of the Kachina figures representing the most commonly performed beings; one might accumulate 100 types or so, but it would be slow going from there on.

Kachintihü are carved to order, as in earlier days, but the current tendency is becoming a presentation of "scenes" or "action groups." These are selections of three or four Kachinas mounted on a single wooden slab, replicating a dance scene. Furthermore, since dolls are no longer suspended from the roof beams in the traditional manner, they are almost universally mounted on small, flat wooden bases, commonly a cross-section of a cottonwood branch, so that they can be displayed vertically in the home. They are no longer used primarily for religious or educational purposes, save in a few Hopi homes; they are almost invariably created for, and used in, home display or decoration.

The high market value has inevitably introduced some adverse results. One, unfortunately, is a very high incidence of theft. While this was never absent from the reservation, the amount of religious material stolen from tribal and private owners has increased markedly. Ancient masks and sacred paraphernalia, regarded as the property of particular kivas or clans, have been stolen from kiva repositories and sold to dealers or collectors; individually owned masks and religious objects have also suffered such depredation. Some of these have been recovered, but many have not, since the purchaser frequently does not know of the theft. Occasionally masks or altar art are recognized, especially when displayed in museums; and when these can be demonstrated as stolen property, they are usually returned to their rightful owners. Sadly, much of this thievery is by Hopi apostates.

Another problem is the repainting of old, faded dolls, which are presented as genuine antiques. Some are actually faked "antiques," and much of this forgery is engineered by non-Hopis, White or Indian. Furthermore, the fact that Hopi artists cannot supply the market demand has attracted non-Hopi carvers. This shortage in the past was filled largely by White or Oriental carvers; now, the sources are Navajo, a few Indians from other tribes, plus a growing number of Anglo and Hispanic entrepreneurs.* And this is no small matter: it is safe to say that well over one-half of the contemporary Hopi Kachina dolls in the typical Indian curio store are not made by Hopis. While some are well made, most are inaccurate, and these travesties are problems to collectors, an affront to Hopi carvers, and a threat to the integrity of the *kachintihü*. While the term "American Indian art" can be used loosely, as it often is, it seems unquestionable that a Hopi Kachina doll should be made by a Hopi Indian. Surprisingly, aside from private grumbling, few Hopis have made this misrepresentation a major matter, and rare is the White consumer (or, for that matter, the curio store owner) who knows the difference.

Other fraudulent products includes plaster cast dolls, which were common in the 1930s but died out during the war; these have returned, as have the lathe-turned doll. But a more startling innovation, at least to me, is the recent production of a line of small clay figurines, approximately 8 inches in height, cast in molds, painted, and fired to bisque ware. They are advertised as "collectibles;" sold at a high price (for what they really are), and are suggested as being a good art investment. The idea seems to be that, if the project is successful, one can purchase a "complete Kachina doll collection" over a period of time. The originals from which the molds are made are created by two of the better Hopi carvers. While it is difficult to condemn such participation in free enterprise, since the Kachina doll long ago entered the commercial world, it is equally difficult to welcome such aberrant products. They cannot be sold as Kachina dolls, or fine art, or anything other than meretricious curiosities. It will be interesting to see what success they have.

These derivative forms introduce a problem common to many fields of art. We—the writer included—tend to regard traditional art forms as an unvarying trait with rigidly prescribed parameters. We seek the "correct type," or "authentic designs," in the feeling that traditional art somehow ought not to deviate from an established norm, which is often established by outside dicta. This

---

*The insatiable demand has also prompted a few Navajo carvers to invent Kachina dolls patterned after Navajo *Yei* designs.

158 rigidity, of course, limits any degree of creativity, imaginative exploration, individual whim, or healthy experiment. The goal of esthetic purity, while admirable, contains the seeds of its own destruction, just as do any of the reproductive forms of art, particularly in the field of graphics. The solution is not easy, and if this book has demonstrated anything, it is that the Hopis are a conservative, traditional people who have managed to maintain perhaps the oldest "original" way of life in the New World against overwhelming odds—and yet who are likewise innovative, imaginative artists continually experiencing dramatic social, economic, political, and ecological challenges. The manner in which they have adjusted to those confrontations is remarkable.

The pressures exerted have indeed taken a certain toll—a loss of the freedom of isolated growth; the indignity of being encircled by often hostile forces, confining them to a far smaller region than they formerly roamed; a lifeway subject to outside control; and the inability to direct their own future.

But I believe that the ebb and flow of Kachina vitality—to select only one very minute aspect of native cultural adjustment—brings into focus a singular quality of Hopi psychology: it seems evident that the Kachina has provided the Hopis with a buffer against that outside world whenever confronted by forces that cannot be controlled—internal as well as external. It seems that every generation or so has had to resort to internal means of strength in coming to terms with the outside world. In this, the Hopis are certainly not alone, for the threat of cultural extinction has been experienced by every American Indian group.[*] The difference is that the Hopis have developed a socioreligious response which has proven uniquely effective in answering the need.

It cannot now be proven, but such limited evidence as exists suggests that the dramatic intensity of Kachina activity has been most evident during periods of conflict. It appears that most of the Kachina beings active today were created during the last half of the nineteenth century, and it is quite surprising that new Kachinas have not emerged out of the recent era of Hopi-White conflict.

The differences cited in this chapter demonstrate how many innovations, subtle changes in practice, and material or substantive adjustments have been incorporated into the ritual and have merged into the ceremonies without destroying the integrity of the Kachina religion and its values, which remain important to the Hopis. It seems obvious that they have discovered the binding effects of

------

[*]The most dramatic effort was the Ghost Dance of the Northern Plains Indians, which ended tragically in 1890 with the Wounded Knee massacre.

ritual, while enjoying its pleasures. The changes that have occurred are essentially external, in materialistic terms, and have only mildly affected the fundamental concepts of Hopi religious beliefs. These beliefs provide a social value, a visual delight, and an emotional power with a creative force unlike that of almost any other cultural expression in the country, which the Hopis have maintained—and which has supported the Hopis—for many centuries.

There is no longer any doubt about the prehistoric origin of the Kachina, although much remains to be learned concerning the degree of outside influences that have affected its development. Along with it attaining major recognition in the art world, it has also established a value in the non-Hopi world that in turn accrues to the people. The Kachina has dipped high and low over the many centuries in history, but he dances on, and I am confident that he will continue to bring beauty and strength for many centuries to come.

In closing, it is interesting to observe that this revival and resurgence seems to parallel a movement in contemporary White society, whereby one sees an increased degree of conservatism, a "strong return to religion," and a rejection of many of the material aspects of modern life. In no small part, these trends are undoubtedly due to many of the same factors: a fear of the unknown; a lack of faith in leadership; a strong desire for a better society; and a dissatisfaction with conditions which one cannot change, but to which there appears no attainable solution. In such unsettling circumstances, some people see in religion a blindfold or a cushion. The Hopis have provided one avenue toward a more tranquil life that works partially for them, but they realize it is not the entire answer. Unfortunately, for both Hopi and White, the outside world will not go away; adjustments and solutions must be actively worked out, not passively hoped for.

Historical Summary
HOPI-WHITE CONTACTS, 1540-1850

IN AN EFFORT to indicate the actual degree of isolation enjoyed by the Hopis, I have attempted to list the known contacts of Whites with the Hopis, as drawn from historical records. Many additional items (such as maps, early publications which include mention of the Hopis, and some of the directives given to Spanish governors concerning the Hopis in their charge), although they do not represent actual *physical* contacts with the Hopis, do indicate the extent to which the White world knew of these people in early days.

No claim has been made, on the basis of this record, that all contacts were of equal influence; many were only "in passing." However brief, even these had the effect of keeping the Hopis ever-conscious of an alien culture, and may also have been instrumental from time to time by leaving behind miscellaneous material culture articles.

In compiling this list, I have drawn from a wide variety of sources, but wish especially to acknowledge my indebtedness to the pioneer work of Katharine Bartlett, whose fine papers on Hopi History (Bartlett, 1934, 1936) have long given service, and to Colton (1930), Hargrave (1935), and Brew (1949). Since this list is intended as preliminary to a more complete history of the Hopis, I would appreciate any corrections or additions.

1539   Marcos de Niza, in his *Relación*, made the first-known reference to the Hopi area, which he called "Totonteac."

1540   A small party sent by Coronado were the first Whites known to have entered the villages, known to them as "Tusayan."

1540   Melchior Diaz mentioned "Totonteac," which he heard of while in Sonora.

1540   Fernando Alarcón wrote briefly of "Totontoac" in his account of his voyage up the Colorado.

1542 The Ulpius globe, in delineating "Tontoneac," was the first graphic placement of the Hopi area.

1565 Francisco de Ibarra and Baltasar de Obregón attempted to go to Tusayan and Cíbola; they got no farther north than Sonora, Mexico.

1566 The *Karte* of Zalterius, more accurate than Ulpius' globe, definitely located "Tuchano."

1569 Gerardus Mercator, in the first of a long series of influential maps, indicated "Tuchano."

1581 The Chamuscado-Rodríguez expedition reached Zuñi, but was prevented from going on to Tusayan.

1583 Antonio de Espejo visited the villages and explored the surrounding area in search of legendary mines.

1589 Hakluyt spoke of the "Mohotze" in his *Principal Navigations*, and published a map of "Tuchano"—probably the first popular mention of the Hopis in English.

1598 Juan de Oñate took formal "possession" of the Hopis for the crown, and also searched for mines in the area.

1598 Fray Andrés Corchado, and perhaps Juan Claros, were assigned the Hopis; there is no evidence that either man personally visited the villages.

1598 Cornelius Wytfliet began his series of well-known maps, and included "Totonteac."

1599 Two Hopis, captured in a Spanish raid on Acoma, were punished by having their right hands amputated.

1602 Viceroy Monterey wrote of the five villages of the "Cummoaquí."

1602 Vicente Zaldívar, in defense of his work with Oñate, wrote of having been in the Hopi villages earlier.

1604 Oñate passed through the villages enroute to California, seeking the legendary "South Sea."

1605 Oñate returned from his South Sea expedition via Tusayan.

1608 Another famous early cartographer, Judocus Hondius, located "Tuchano" on his series of maps.

1614 Capt. Jerónimo Márquez and 25 men were recorded as having been in the villages.

1615 Fray Juan de Torquemada, in his *Monarchia Indiana*, described the "Caçina." This is the earliest published use of the term that I have yet discovered.

1621 The Zuñis and Hopis were specifically exempted from paying tribute to support the Santa Fé garrison.

1621 In his *Mikrókosmos*, a map well known in England, Peter Heylyn detailed the Hopi area.

1625 Purchas' *Pilgrimes* further established the Hopis in English minds by mapping the "Pueblos de Moqui."

1628 Antonio de Peinado was detailed as resident *fray* and instructed to establish a mission—perhaps the first to actually work in Tusayan.

1629 Considerable mention was made of the Hopis in the *Relación* of Gerónimo de Zárate-Salmerón.

1629 Three friars, Francisco Porras, Cristóbal de la Concepción, and Andrés Gutiérrez, arrived in Awátovi to establish the mission of San Bernardo de Aguátubi.

1630 Fray Alonso de Benavides, in his *Memorial*, claimed the 10,000 Hopis were being converted rapidly. A record exists listing the following missions at this time as:

> Awátovi—San Bernardo
> Shungopovi—San Bartolomé, *visita* at Mishongnovi
> Oraibi—San Francisco, *visita* at Walpi

Sometime between 1629 and 1633 Francisco de Buenaventura went to work in Tusayan; a fifth cleric also must have entered, for in 1640 Fray Bartolomé Romero was listed as having been in the Hopi country for ten years.

1631 Viceroy Marqués de Cerralvo decreed supplies and equipment for the purpose of furthering religious work among the Hopis.

1633 Fray Porras was poisoned at Awátovi.

1634 Fray Benavides' *Propaganda Memorial*, a redaction of his earlier *Memorial*, included considerable mention of the Hopis.

1640 Francisco Antonio de la Rosa Figueroa, in an account of the work of Benavides, mentioned his activity in Tusayan.

1641 A friary was mentioned as being in existence at Shungopovi.

1650 Oppression caused resentment among the Pueblos, and Taos organized a revolt; the refusal of the Hopis to join caused the uprising to be given up.

1653 Fray Alonso de Posada was recorded as being at Awátovi until 1655.

1655 Fray Salvador de Guerra, reported as *guardián* at Shungopovi [?], was accused of having poured turpentine on some Hopis and having set fire to them for possessing "idols."

1659 As a result of drought and resulting crop failure, grain was distributed to the famine-stricken villages of Oraibi and Shungopovi.

1659 López de Mendizábal became Governor, and to undermine the clergy, encouraged the holding of Kachina dances.

1661   Governor Diego de Peñalosa Briceño visited the Zuñi, and probably the Hopi villages sometime during his four-year term.

1661   A signature CARLOS ARNAIS 1661, carved on the rock wall of Inscription House, north of the Hopi villages, is suggestive of a possible Spanish visitor at that time.

1662   Fray Jacinto de Mompeán was recorded as being at Awátovi.

1663   A report was sent to Mexico City concerning the status of Hopi missions.

1663   Fray José de Espeleta was recorded as being in service in the villages until the time of the Pueblo Revolt, when he was slain.

1664   Fray Bartolomé Márquez listed those missions active in the Hopi villages:
> Oraibi
> Aguátubi, *visita* at Gualpi
> Shungopovi, *visita* at Mishongnovi

1664   The long trial of ex-Governor Bernardo López de Mendizábal, unfinished, ended with his death in jail. One major charge had been his encouragement of the revival of *catzina* dancing among the Indians.

1665   Governor Peñalosa y Briceño was credited with having settled the *Cruzados* [Yavapais] and *Coninas* [Havasupais] in two large pueblos in Tusayan.

1666   Mission "San Miguel de Oraibi" was listed as being active.

1667   Fray Domingo Cardoso listed friars active at Oraibi, Shungopovi, and Mishongnovi, and asked for an additional friar for the latter pueblo.

1672   Fray José de Trujillo was listed as friar at Oraibi.

1680   The Pueblo Revolt forced the Spanish out of the Southwest. Following the Revolt, many Río Grande people fled to the Hopis.

1680   A mission "San Francisco de Oraibi" was listed in a document of this date.

1680–1741   The Revolt also marked the beginning of a period of competition between the Franciscans and Jesuits for possession of Tusayan.

1692   Diego de Vargas, reconquering Nuevo México, entered Tusayan and obtained promises of allegiance.

1693   A brief uprising against De Vargas occurred among the pueblos, especially Jémez; the Hopis felt no effect other than the reception of additional refugees.

1696   A more serious Tewa uprising further swelled the Hopi population.

1697   Fray Eusebio Kino twice sent messages to the "Moquinos," in anticipation of a visit to Tusayan.

1697 Fray Augustín de Vetancurt listed the various Hopi missions,
the fate of their clerics, and the general church situation.

1699 The Hopis were recorded as voluntarily offering to rebuild the destroyed churches, and rejoin Christianity. Presumably as a result, Fray Francisco Alvarez obtained permission from the *Custodio* to go to Tusayan; but was ordered to return by Governor Cubero.

1699– Fray Kino sent another message to the Hopis, planning on
1700 visiting them, but without result. He anticipated reaching Tusayan by way of the Colorado River.

1700 The Hopis sent three envoys to Santa Fé to forestall the entry of a military force, and requested the Governor to send missionaries. Three were sent, who preached for six hours, but found the Hopis still recalcitrant; they petitioned Governor Cubero to send a garrison to Awátovi to protect the Christian Hopis at that village.

1700 Fray Juan de Garaycoechea, after reopening the mission at Halona [near Zuñi], went to Tusayan and baptized 73. He reported the natives as friendly.

1700 The Hopis sent 20 ambassadors to Santa Fé to propose a treaty of peace with the Spanish. The main term was that each nation would retain its own religion; the Spanish refused.

1700 Awátovi was destroyed by Hopi warriors from other villages.

1700 Fray Kino planned to visit the Hopis, but was prevented by unsettled conditions.

1701 Governor Cubero headed a punitive expedition to Tusayan; after killing a few natives, he returned without achieving any real conquest.

1702 The Hopis were accused of inciting the Zuñis to rebellion; Governor Cubero dispatched Juan de Uribarri to Zuñi to investigate.

1704 The rumors of revolt continued, and again the Hopis were found to be at the bottom of the movement.

1705 Fray Kino demonstrated his awareness of the Hopi area by accurately mapping the "Moqui."

1706 The Hopis attacked the Christian Zuñis. In retaliation, Governor Cuervo y Valdés dispatched two expeditions which accomplished little beyond nuisance destruction of crops.

1706 The first fur trappers were reported in the Rocky Mountains. They were French, and shortly became known throughout the area, even to the Gila River.

1707– José Chacón became Governor; regarding the treatment of
1712 the Hopis as too harsh, he embarked on a more conciliatory program, without success.

1713– Governor Flores Mogollón, frustrated by Hopi resistance, held
1715 five war councils. During this period, several groups of Hopis visited Santa Fé, promising loyalty; the Governor later learned they were merely traders using this device as protection.

1713 Two Zuñis who were given a permit to visit the Hopis to trade reported that the Hopis were peaceful.

1713 An inquiry was held at Santa Fé into the attack and destruction of Awátovi; testimonials and documents were recorded.

1715 Fray Campos, a Jesuit, suggested to the Viceroy that the Hopis be given to his Order to proselytize.

1716 Building a very optimistic picture, Fray Luís Velarde supported the efforts of Campos in behalf of the Jesuit cause.

1716 An elaborate expedition, headed by Governor Félix Martínez, failed to conquer Tusayan, and was forced to return to Santa Fé.

1718 Governor Antonio Valverde y Cosío invited the Hano-Tewa refugees to return to their former homes, guaranteeing sanctuary.

1719 The King granted the Jesuits full rights to add Tusayan to Sonora.

1719– Governor Valverde toured his province, visited Tusayan, and
1720 reported on conditions among the Hopis.

1720 Instructions were issued to the Governor at Santa Fé to keep out the French traders "at all cost." Since, apparently, several parties had been seen, the result was increased activity along the northern boundaries of Nuevo México.

1722 A clerical *Parecer* is on record which discussed the destruction of Awátovi.

1723 Juan de Torquemada listed the missions active in Nuevo México and included a brief consideration of the Hopi villages.

1724 Frailes Antonio Miranda and Francisco Irasábal went to Oraibi to preach, but enjoyed no success.

1724– Don Pedro de Rivera toured Nuevo México as *visitor;* al-
1726 though he claimed to have visited all parts of the province, he did not specifically mention having been in Tusayan.

1725 The Viceroy authorized a change of jurisdiction over Tusayan in favor of the Jesuit order.

1726 Jesuit support by the King was guaranteed by a royal *cédula* conditionally approving their authority.

1727 Rivera advised Viceroy Casafuerte to establish a *presidio* which should include Tusayan. The pressure of Utes, Apaches, and Comanches on the northern borders was increasing.

1730 The Viceroy reported that any attempt to conquer the Hopis would be impractical.

1730   The Jesuits started a legal suit to further their efforts in Nuevo
México; they blamed the Franciscans for many failures, especially for their inability to convert the Hopis.

1730– Fray Francisco de Archundi and José Valverde visited the
1731   Hopis. They preached in the villages with no success.

1731   A priest was recorded as having sacrificed his life in an attempted *entrada* into the Hopi villages.

1731   Viceroy Casafuerte was commanded by the King to compile a statement of distances between California and the Hopis.

1732   Fray Francisco Techungui brought back five Tewa Indians to Isleta from Tusayan.

1736   Pedro de Rivera discussed the "Moquinos" in his *Diario*.

1738   Governor Enrique de Olavide reported that he had visited all the pueblos.

1739   Several French traders visited Santa Fé; they inquired with interest about the Painted Desert—evidence that they or their forerunners knew of (or had visited) that area.

1741   Orders were issued for three Jesuits to work among the Hopis, replacing the Franciscans then there. This *cédula* assigned the Hopis to the Jesuits and cancelled the Franciscan franchise.

1742   A spurt of activity by the Franciscans resulted. Exaggerated claims of converts were sent to the King—although no missions actually were re-established, and many of the Hopi "converts" were Navajos.

1742   Fray Carlos Delgado and Pedro Ignacio de Pino went to Tusayan and brought back 441 "Hopis," who were settled at Isleta. They could have brought more, they said, had Governor Mendoza co-operated more fully.

1742   In his famous *Historia de la Conquista*, Mota Padilla commented on "Tonteaca."

1743   Fray Delgado attempted to re-enter Tusayan to repeat his success, but was prevented by the Governor.

1743   Fray Keller, a Jesuit, tried to go to the Hopi villages but was waylaid by the Apaches.

1743– Frailes Delgado and José Trigo went to Tusayan, where they
1744   claimed to have converted 5,000 souls (!) [These were not Hopis—a later communiqué from Trigo revealed that they were Navajos.]

1744   Fray Delgado was listed as having gone to the Hopi country to bring back the bodies of the martyrs of the Pueblo Revolt.

1744   Another Jesuit, Father Sedelmayr, traveled as far north as Bill Williams Fork, seeking entry to Tusayan. This is the last Jesuit effort to get to the Hopi villages.

1744 Fray Miguel Menchero comments on the Hopis in his *Declaración.*

1745 Fray Delgado, with Juan José Toledo and José Yrigoyen, went to Tusayan where they had no success; Delgado reported that there were 10,846 Hopis at that time.

1745 The Jesuit *Provincial*, Cristóbal de Escobar y Llamas, in effect declined the Hopi field in a letter to the Viceroy.

1745 As a result of the Delgado success, plus Escobar y Llamas' letter, the King rescinded his *cédula*, and returned the Hopis to the Franciscans.

1746 A further communiqué from Delgado detailed his work in Tusayan, in company with Toledo and Yrigoyen.

1747 Fray Menchero was ordered by the Viceroy to resettle the pueblo of Sandía with "Hopi Indians"; undoubtedly these were not true Hopis, but expatriate fugitives and their descendants.

1747 The Viceroy ordered an expedition to Zuñi, where the Hopis sent their chiefs to intercept him and prevent his entry. Interest in California made the reconquest of Tusayan imperative to Spain.

1748 Governor Codallos y Rabal granted a tract of land at Sandía for settling Christianized Hopis; Menchero finally settled 350.

1748 José Villaseñor commented at length on the "Moquinas."

1749 Fray Menchero declared that the Hopis had come to him at Sandía three times, asking his help.

1750 Governor Vélez Cachupín wrote to the Viceroy, mentioning that the Comanches were causing trouble by attacking the Navajos, Zuñis, and Hopis.

1754 Five Havasupais and their chief, enroute to Santa Fé to request Spanish sovereignty, were killed by the Hopis to prevent them from bringing the Whites into Tusayan.

1754 A record of the Hopi population listed five villages, with only 8,000 people.

1755 Fray Rodríguez de la Torre visited the villages, preached, but was effectively opposed by the priests and chiefs.

1757 Miguel Venegas located and discussed the "Maqui" in his *History of California.*

1760 Fray Juan Sanz de Lezaún recorded a complete description of the Hopis in his *Comentario.*

1766 The Marqués de Rubí made a tour throughout the province as an inspector for the Viceroy.

1770 Fray Francisco Garcés mentioned finding Hopi textiles among the Gileño Pimas.

1774   Gov. Francisco Crespo commented upon the quality of the Hopi weaving he encountered in the *Jalchedune* [Halchedoma] country; this convinced him of the feasibility of opening a route to Tusayan.

1774   As part of his instructions, De Anza was directed to go to California; thence, on his way back, to find a route to Nuevo México and the Hopi villages.

1774   Fray Garcés tried to get to Tusayan, but failed. He mentioned finding Hopi weaving among the Mojave, Pápago, and Yávapai.

1775   Fray Escalante was ordered by Governor Mendinueta to find out about the Hopis, and a possible California-Sonora route. He visited Tusayan, listing seven villages and 7,494 Hopis.

1776   Fray Garcés entered Oraibi, but was completely rebuffed. He mentioned "Muqui concabe" [Moenkopi].

1776   Escalante again passed through Tusayan on his return from California.

1776   Viceroy Bucareli wrote to Arriaga in support of the plan to open the route to the Hopis.

1776   Lieutenant-Colonel Antonio Bonilla advised the use of force on the Hopis; they no longer feared Spanish arms.

1777   The Great Drought began.

1779   Because of the drought, many Christianized and orthodox Hopis were reported living at Zuñi. Some went to Sandía with more to follow.

1779   Viceroy Croix wrote to De Anza, advising the use of peaceful means, and suggested the assignment of El Sabinal as a home for the starving Hopis. He warned of a possible Hopi-Apache alliance unless the Spanish acted wisely.

1779–   Fray Andrés García was dispatched to rescue the Hopis from
1780   raiding Navajos; 77 returned with him, and 73 came later.

1780   Governor de Anza visited the villages and recorded that there were only 798 Hopis left (!). He was able to bring back only 30 families, although others asserted they might come later.

1780   A report asserted that most Hopis were living with the Havasupais due to the famine.

1781   Galindo Navarro, Assessor-General, advised the continuance of Anza's policy, stating that it had already resulted in 200 Hopis leaving Tusayan to settle in the Río Grande area.

1781   A serious outbreak of smallpox hit the villages; De Anza offered help. But as the drought broke, his golden opportunity was gone.

1781   Croix reported to the King that the Hopis continued inexorable.

1782 Fray Jean Augustín Morfi discussed general conditions in Nuevo Mexico—mentioning that the inhabitants of the Río Grande area were much worse off than the Hopis, albeit the latter were *still* independent.

1786 In his *Instructions*, Bernardo de Gálvez specifically requested information concerning the condition of the Hopis.

1787 Fray Francisco Paloú mentioned the "Moxi" in his *Relación*.

1792 The *Crónica Seráfica* of Arricivita mentioned the "Macueques."

1799 José Cortez mentioned the Hopis and listed seven villages.

1804 Baron von Humboldt's map included the Hopi area, showing four villages.

1810 Zebulon Pike mapped the *Internal Provinces of New Spain*, and included the Hopis. He listed four villages. This is the earliest U. S.-published map showing the Hopis which I have yet found.

1811 Humboldt devoted several pages of his *Political Essay* to Hopi life.

1812 Pedro Bautista Pino noted that Navajo lived among the Moqui.

1815– American fur-trappers began to enter the Nuevo México
1821 area, presaging a later expansion.

1818 John Pinkerton's 1816 *Atlas* [London] was published in Philadelphia. This is the first atlas showing the Hopi area published in the U. S.

1818– Because of Navajo raids and increasing Navajo settlement
1819 adjacent to the villages, the Hopis sent a delegation to Governor Melgares, asking Spanish help.

1821– American fur-trappers were recorded as being common in the
1823 Southwest as far as Río Norte.

1821 Mexican Independence ended Spanish sovereignty over the Hopi. As far as is known, no Mexican authorities visited the Hopis.

1824– Fur-trappers covered the Southwest so completely that the
1826 once-numerous beaver became rare.

1826 James O. Pattie visited the Hopi, and apparently was the first "American" to do so.

1826– With the disappearance of the beaver, the fur-trappers left
1832 the Southwest, to go westward into California.

1827 Richard Campbell and 35 men went from Zuñi to San Diego. He said he knew the route via the Hopi villages was shorter, but not suitable for wagon travel.

1827 Bill Williams, famous guide, was apparently in the villages sometime during the year.

1828   George C. Yount, a fur-trapper, was the first American to
        leave detailed description of Hopi life.
1830   Antonio Armijo traveled from Santa Fé to California, connect-
        ing with the "route the Moqui use in trading with the
        Mojaves."
1831   William Wolfskill, and perhaps Ewing Young, passed through
        the Hopi villages.
1833–   Joseph R. Walker was in the villages for several days some-
1834   time during this period; he wrote a short account of his ex-
        periences while there.
1834   A party of American fur-trappers raided Hopi truck gardens
        and killed a score of Indians who opposed the raid.
1840–   At least two expeditions were recorded as having gone to the
1845   Hopi country to locate quicksilver mines long known there.
1840   A party of Americans, including four women, were mentioned
        as having been in the villages while en route west.
1842   A brief description of the "Munchies" was written by Sage.
1844   Josiah Gregg mentioned the Hopis, their language and cul-
        ture, and stated there were 1,000–1,500 of them living in
        seven villages.
1845   Capt. Charles Wilkes wrote of the "Monkey Indians."
1846   During the Mexican War, Colonel Doniphan was sent to re-
        move the Navajo threat; while he specifically mentioned the
        Hopis in his considerations, he did not visit the villages.
1846   Governor Charles Bent visited the villages, and recorded the
        first American census of the Hopis [2,450].
1846   Captain A. R. Johnston indicated the "Miqui" on his map.
1847   Pritchard wrote a short account of "Monquoi" Indians.
1847   George F. Ruxton spent some time with the Hopis, and wrote
        of their life.
1848   Albert Gallatin located the "Moqui" on his map of U. S.
        Indian Tribes.
1848   E. G. Squier wrote several articles dealing with Hopi life,
        mapped their locality, and apparently knew a great deal about
        them, for his time.
1849   James Calhoun, Indian Agent, mentioned the Hopis in his re-
        port to Indian Commissioner Medill.
1849   Commissioner Wilson, of the General Land Office, indirectly
        mentioned the Hopis in his instructions to agents.
1849   Lt. James H. Simpson presented a portrait of "Chief Che-ki-
        wat-tewa;" this is the first Hopi portrait published.
1850   Antoine Leroux, the famous Southwestern guide, visited the
        villages, and recorded a population estimate of 6,700 Hopis.

172　1850　George A. McCall reported on the Hopis, giving their population (evidently based on Bent's census).

1850　James Calhoun, Indian Commissioner, recorded that seven Hopis visited him at Santa Fé, requesting his assistance.

❂　❂　❂

I have elected to bring this chronological listing to a close at mid-century, since for the purposes of this book a year-by-year list of the next hundred years would be superfluous. With 1850, the last real isolation of the Hopis ended; from that date on, I have been able to establish definite records of White contacts with the Hopis for every year to the present. The so-called isolation of The Peaceful People had come full circle, and was no longer an effective shelter protecting them from the abrasive force that was inexorably closing in upon their old way of life.

Hopi Glossary

GLOSSARY OF HOPI WORDS USED IN THE TEXT

KEY TO PRONUNCIATION: Excepting as noted below, Hopi consonants are as in English; all vowels follow Continental pronunciation. Unless marked, accent is antepenult. Hopi has distinct dialects with marked differences in some of the villages; this Glossary is not intended as a linguistically-perfect reproduction of Hopi sounds—it is intended to permit reasonably accurate pronunciation by English-speaking persons. To facilitate that pronunciation, the following arbitrary symbols are employed:

These sounds are not common to English:

ä   A very weak *a*, similar to English *a* in *at*.

b   Hopis differ only slightly between *b*, and *p*. Many pronounce the same word two ways: *Poli, Boli* (butterfly); *Bahana, Pahana* (White man).

ch   Always as in English *church*.

f   Similar to English; many speakers, however, sound it more like English *v* or even *p*.

h   A slight expulsion of air; as in English when used as an initial letter.

î   Short *i*, close to English *i* in *it*.

ñ   *Not as Spanish ñ;* peculiar to Hopi, it is similar to *ng* as in English *singing*. The *g* is harder, however, often as though the word were *sing-ging*. Nasalized *n* plus *g*.

ö   Short *o*, similar to French *eu* in *fleur*.

p   Usually as English, but see *b* above.

q   An arbitrary symbol to indicate the peculiar Hopi variety of *k*. There is no English sound like it—it is closest to a soft, swallowed *k* sounded far back in the throat.

ş   An arbitrary symbol to indicate a variety of Hopi *s*. (In older texts, especially Fewkes, this was indicated by *c*. I substitute *ş* to give a closer resemblance to the English sound; e.g.: *Tacab* to many readers would be pronounced as *Takab*.) A combined *s* and *sh*, which is more markedly *s* with some speakers, and *sh* with others.

ü   Similar to German *ü* in *über*, or *für*.

û   Short *u*, often accompanied by a noticeable expelling of breath, almost like *uh!* when at the end of a word.

v   Similar to English *v*, but see *f* above.

Álosaka. The "Two Horn" God, equated with Múi'yiñwû, *q.v.*

añáhaiihpi. Cotton string worn down back of head by Añákchina. Any small article may be tied to the end.

átkyakabiadta. Terminal "sinker"; weight or object at end of *añáhaiihpi.*

Awátovi. "Place of the Bow." Extinct village on Antelope Mesa, destroyed *circa* 1700 A.D.

aya. Gourd rattle, carried by dancers.

Bahana [also *Pahana*]. Hopi name for Americans.

Bakabi [Báa-ka-bi] "Place of the Reeds." Third Mesa village, founded as a result of the Oraibi-Hotevilla split. Population *ca.* 175.

Chaákmoñwî. Crier Chief who announces the various coming events in the village. Very similar to the New England town crier.

chamímita. Rattle fringe on bottom of kilt, etc. Formerly of shells, now made of antelope or sheep hoofs.

Chüchübtî. Antelope-Snake Rites, held in late August, alternately with Flute Ceremonies. *Chü'a* = Snake; *Chüb* = Antelope.

chüká tíhuta. Small clay figurines, often bearing Kachina-mask designs, as distinguished from the more characteristic wooden *tihü.*

Cíbola. Early Spanish name for the Zuñi area. It did not include Tusayan.

hakomta. Corn grinder; large stone upon which corn is ground. Spanish: *metate.* See *mada.*

Hano [also called *Tewa*]. First Mesa village, founded *circa* 1700 by Tewa emigrants from the Río Grande valley. Population *ca.* 300.

honáni. Badger.

hónaû. Bear.

Honányümü. Badger clan; Badger clan people.

Hotevilla [Hóht'vi-la]. "Skinned Back." Third Mesa village established in 1906 by Conservatives ejected from Oraibi. Now the largest Hopi village. Population *ca.* 650.

hümiüyi soyóhîmsi. Artificial flowers (all kinds), made of corn husks.

hürünkwa. Warrior feathers, worn in a bundle on top of the head or mask.

Kachina. 1. A spirit being. 2. The masked impersonator. 3. Occasionally, the unmasked impersonator.

kachina'amû. Kachina father. The leader during Kachina dances who acts as father to the dancers, encouraging them, etc.

Kachinmana. Maid who accompanies certain Kachinas. Actually a male dancer dressed in women's clothing.

kachinpítküna. White kilt with embroidered end; the standard dance kilt.

Kachintihü. Specifically a Kachina doll, as differentiated from any other carved figurine. See *tihü.*

kaláhainiadta. Cluster of sheep scapulae, used as a rattle. Also often called *wüwüyom aya* (old men's rattle), although its use is not restricted to them.

kaláhainüñünpi. Old-time shell pendant, worn around the neck.

Kawaika-a [also *Kawaiokuh*]. "River People's Place." Extinct village on Antelope Mesa, near Awátovi. Possibly destroyed prior to Spanish entry.

Kiakóchomovi [also *Kikóchmovi*; *Kyakátsmovi*]. "Hill of Ruins Place." Village at the foot of First Mesa, founded following the break-up of Oraibi. Commonly called *New Oraibi*, or *Lower Oraibi*. Population *ca.* 600.

kísonvi. Plaza dance area, usually in the center of the village.

kiva. 1. Under-ground chamber in which most religious rites are performed. 2. Secularly, a room in which the men do much of their craftwork, etc. 3. "Men's club," where males may retire for any social purpose.

Koko. The Zuñi masked being, similar to the Hopi *Kachina*.

Kókoshi. A Zuñi *Koko* very similar to the Hopi *Añákchina*.

kowako. 1. Fowl. 2. Chicken.

koyoño. Turkey.

Kuaua [Ku-á-ua or Ku-wá-wa]. "Evergreen." Extinct village north of Albuquerque, New Mexico. Inhabited *circa* 1300–1600 A.D.

kücha. White (adj.).

küchá ómau tüvikü. Literally, "white cloud mask." Cotton layer placed over face of dead at burial.

küitü. 1. The head. 2. Regular helmet-type mask.

kwáchkyabû. White cotton robe or blanket. Part of the groom's gift to the bride.

kwasha. Regular old-style woman's black woolen gown.

Kwátaka. An ancient mythical creature, half-bird and half-man.

Kwivi. A class of Kachinas. "Proud" Kachinas, so called for their ornate costuming.

mada [also *mata*]. Stone corn grinder, held in hand. Spanish: *mano*. See *hakomta*.

mana. 1. An unmarried woman; maiden. 2. The "female" dancer who accompanies the Kachinas, more properly called *Kachinmana*.

mánayawi. Ceremonial baton of wood, carried by *mana*.

Maraû. 1. Woman's Society. 2. Women's Ceremony, usually in September.

Mishongnovi [Müshóñ'novi]. "Risen-up Place." Second Mesa village. Population *ca.* 300.

moadta. 1. Mouth. 2. Nose or snout of the mask.

móchobüh. Cylinder-type snout, or beak, on mask; usually made of wood.

Moenkopi [Mü'enkapi]. "Place of Running Water." Village forty miles west of Oraibi, established at Moenkopi Wash on the foundations of an earlier village. Population *ca.* 400.

Momchit. Warrior Society, now practically extinct.

moñkachina. Literally, "chief kachina." One recognized as being chief among fellow Kachinas. Ex: Şoyál, Eótoto.

Moqui. Early name applied to Hopis. An attempt to imitate their own word *Mó-kwee*, which was an ancient name for the tribe.

müchábñwün kwewa. Embroidered sash worn by a majority of Kachinas.

176   *Müi'yinwû.* The God of Growth and Germination, equated with Álo$a$ka, *q.v.*

naja [Navajo]. Crescent-shaped pendant of silver, worn with "squash-blossom" necklace.

nákabü. 1. Ear. 2. Ear, usually of wood, attached to mask.

nakchi [also *naktchi, naktci*]. 1. Headdress. 2. Upright flat board attached to many masks, commonly called *tablita.* Ex: Hümis Kachina, Butterfly Dance.

na'kwa. Head plume; large feather on mask or headdress.

náluñ múzrükpü. Cord of twisted yarn worn on masks, as in Añwü$n$asómtäqä.

ñatyüñpi. Long staff carried by many Kachinas.

Nayénezganî. Literally, "Slayer of Enemy Gods." One of the Navajo Yei. Brother of Thōbādzhîstshîni, *q.v.*

Nimán. Final major Kachina rite. The "Going Home" of the Kachinas to their traditional homes, usually in late June or early July.

ñülükpi. Wooden crook staff, or wand, carried by some Kachinas.

nüva. Snow.

Oáqöl. 1. Woman's Society. 2. Women's Ceremony, usually held in October.

Oraibi [O-ryé-bi]. "Place of the Orai rock." Third Mesa village, oldest of the presently-inhabited towns. Population *ca.* 200.

paho. Prayer-stick. Made of cottonwood, usually about six inches long, and decorated with feathers, corn husk, and paint. There are many types.

Pálülükoñ. Literally Water Serpent. Water Serpent Ceremony, not to be confused with Snake Dance Ceremony.

Payupki [Pa-yüp-ki]. "River People house"? (Apparently named for Río Grande refugees who settled there following 1680 Revolt). An extinct Second Mesa village, inhabited *circa* 1690–1742.

piki. Hopi bread. Corn mush rolled out in very thin sheets and baked.

piva. Hopi tobacco (*Nicotiana attenuata*).

Póbostü. "Eye Seeker" Society. Now extinct.

porópta'nakchi. Net skull cap worn by Warrior Society, War God, etc.

Powamû. First rites of the Kachina Cult; usually in February. Initiation into Kachina Cult at this time.

püchkohü. Rabbit stick; the Hopi non-returning boomerang.

püchtihü. The earlier, flat type of wooden figurine.

Pü'ükoñhoya. One of the Two Little War Gods; twin of Palüñgahoya.

qöqöntinumya. The Kachina Parade. A Kachina performance minus singing or dancing.

rükünpi. Notched stick, used with resonator. See: *tawísibvu; shükyachi.*

$a$kwa. Green, or blue.

santo. A small carved wooden representation of a Catholic saint or holy person. The art is peculiar to the 18th and 19th Centuries in New Mexico.

shakwaton hokyashmi. Blue yarn worn at knee by dancers.

shakwaton máponi. Blue yarn worn around wrist of dancers.

Shipaulovi [Și-paú-lo-vi]. "Mosquito." On Second Mesa; smallest of the villages. Population *ca.* 150.

shiviva shilala. Metal "jingler" fringe on kilts. Usually made of tin.

shükyachi. Sheep scapula. Used as part of a musical instrument. See: *tawișibvu; rükünpi.*

Shungopovi [Shuñópovi]. "Place by the spring where tall reeds grow." On Second Mesa; according to legends the original Shungopovi was the first Hopi village. Population *ca.* 425.

shürüadta. Fan-shaped feather ornament attached at the back of masks.

Sichomovi [Tsichómovi]. "Flower Mound Place." First Mesa village; a "suburb" of Walpi. Population *ca.* 325.

Sikyatki. "Yellow House." Extinct village adjacent to First Mesa, inhabited *circa* 1350–1540.

sinkwa. Artificial squash blossom, usually made of corn husk.

sípapü. 1. Mythical opening from whence came all people, out of the Underworld into the present. 2. The "center" of the village, marked by a flat stone—regarded as the place the Kachinas come out of when returning to dance. 3. "Emergence" hole found in all kiva floors.

șiyara. 1. Ancient flint weapon, or obsidian knife. 2. Modern saw (as carried by Natașka).

Șótüq'nañwû. The Sky God; sometimes called "Heart of the Sky" God. Similar to the Christian God.

sowíchmi. Beard worn by a Kachina, usually of horsehair.

Șoyál. 1. The Kachina which officiates at the Winter Solstice ceremonies. 2. The fraternity in charge of those ceremonies.

Soyala. The Hopi Winter Solstice ceremonies ushering in the Kachina cycle; designed to induce the sun to start on its northward journey.

Soyálüña. 1. The "coming out" or mimic emergence through the *sípapü.* A critical act during Soyala, symbolic of the Hopi Genesis. 2. The "coming out" of the Kachinas at Soyala.

tablita. See *nakchi.*

Táchükti. "Ball-Head." The Hopi clown group, commonly called "Mudheads" from their peculiar mask. Similar to the Zuñi *Koyemsi;* usually known by that name, even in the Hopi area.

tawa. Sun.

tawișibvu. Gourd resonator. See *rükünpi; shükyachi.*

Thôbádzhístshíni. Literally, "Born-from-Water;" one of the Navajo Yei. Brother of Nayénezganî, *q.v.*

tíbuku. Abbreviated maskette; a leather mask which fits in front of the face, as differentiated from the "over-the-head" *küitü* type mask.

178   *Tihü.* 1. The carved figurine or "Kachina Doll." 2. The Kachina personator. 3. A doll, See: *Kachintihü.*

tíkive. 1. The dance on the final day of a ceremony. 2. The actual "dance day" when public performance, or dance, is given. Usually in the *kísonvi.*

tochi. Buckskin moccasin.

tóriki. Bandoleer, worn over shoulder.

tsilí. Chili pepper.

tühpóota tüvikü. Basket type, circular or "disk" mask. Worn by Tawa, Ahül, Wüpamo, etc.

tüiqi. White blanket or robe with elaborate embroidered edge.

Tusayan. Early Spanish name for the area then occupied by the Hopis.

Walpi. "The Place of the Gap." Village at tip of First Mesa; probably the best-known Hopi village, and one which has been exposed to more White influence than the others. Population *ca.* 200.

Wáwaṣ. A class of Kachinas. The Racing Kachinas, who challenge spectators to races during masked ceremonies.

wikiup. An Algonkin term applied by Whites to the brush-thatched hut used by the southern Arizona tribes, especially Apache.

wikya. 1. Twig or basket visor for many masks. 2. A wooden hoe; see *wünawikya.*

wöye [ancestor]. 1. The ancients of a clan. 2. One's ancestors. 3. Any ancient or ancestral being. 4. An ancient mask.

wünawikya. 1. Old-time wooden hoe. 2. Wooden weeding tool. Now used only ceremonially, especially by Hehea Kachina.

wüqti. A married woman. The old woman who accompanies certain Kachinas is called *Kachinwüqti.*

Wüwüchim. 1. A Society. 2. Tribal initiation ceremonies, usually held in November. One of the most important rites.

wüwüyom ["wise old men."] 1. Old men of the tribe. 2. Ancient Wise Men.

wüwüyom aya. Old men's rattle—synonym for *kaláhainiadta* rattle.

xacal [also *jacal*]. Hut dwelling, common in Southern Arizona, primarily used by the Yaquis, etc. A Spanish term, not used by Hopis.

Yáyatû. Hopi clown society, now extinct.

Yei. Navajo masked beings, somewhat similar to Hopi Kachinas, but regarded by the Navajo as gods rather than 'in-between' spirits.

Yeibitchai [Navajo]. The Navajo masked dance, similar to Hopi Kachina dances, in which the Yei appear.

yóishiva. Ancient flint or stone knife.

yöñóṣona. 1. A turtle. 2. Turtle-shell leg rattle worn by most Kachinas.

yúkvyükani. Bangs over forehead, of red or black horsehair.

Selected Bibliography

THE LITERATURE dealing with the Hopi Indians is so extensive that I have not attempted to include all books dealing with their culture, nor even with the Kachina Cult itself. Rather, I have listed only those works actually consulted in the preparation of this book, or which should be of value to the reader particularly interested in further study of the subject.

AITON, ARTHUR S.
    1939. Coronado's muster roll. Amer. Hist. Rev., vol. 44, pp. 556–570.
        A transcription of the original Spanish text. It has cleared up several long-standing misconceptions concerning equipment, numbers, and nationality of the Coronado Expedition, 1540–1542.

ANDERSON, FRANK G.
    1955. The Pueblo Kachina cult; a historical introduction. Southwest. Jl. Anthro., vol. 10, pp. 404–419.
        Primarily a consideration of Zuni archeology, but includes Hopi data as well, presenting a survey of the historical origins and development of the Kachina. A summarized version of the author's dissertation.

BAHNIMPTEWA, CLIFF
    1971. Dancing Kachinas; a Hopi artist's documentary. Phoenix: Heard Museum, 35 pp., illus.
        Catalog of an exhibition at the museum of 48 paintings, reproduced in color, with commentary.

BAHTI, TOM
    1970. Southwestern Indian ceremonials. Flagstaff: KC Publs., 64 pp., illus.
        A well-written summary involving all tribes, with data on the Hopi, including observations on the Kachina dances.

BANCROFT, HUBERT HOWE [actually written by H. L. Oak]
    1889. History of Arizona and New Mexico, 1530–1888. San Francisco: The

History Company, Publishers, 829 pp., maps.
    A classic volume, summarizing all that was known of the history of the area
to date of printing, utilizing original sources. Indispensable to any historical study
of the early Southwest.

BANDELIER, ADOLPH F.
  1890. Final report of investigations among the Indians of the Southwestern
      United States, carried on mainly in the years 1880 to 1885. Part I.
      Cambridge: Archaeological Institute of America. Papers, American
      Series, vol. 3, 323 pp., illus.
      A valuable historical summary of the ethnography of the Southwest in the
      XVI-XVII Centuries comprises the first half of this volume; the sketch of Indian
      conditions in the 1880s completes the book, and is of especial value for present-
      day comparisons.

BANDELIER, ADOLPH F., and EDGAR L. HEWETT
  1937. Indians of the Rio Grande Valley. Albuquerque: University of New
      Mexico, 274 pp., illus.
      A good summary, particularly useful for the *Documentary History* section, by
      Bandelier.

BARNES, WILL C.
  1935. Arizona place names. Tucson: University of Arizona, General Bulletin
      no. 2, 503 pp.
      A valuable encyclopedia of nomenclature and a mine of information on the
      early days of Arizona.

BARTLETT, KATHARINE
  1934. Spanish contacts with the Hopi, 1540–1823. Flagstaff: Mus. N. Ariz.,
      Museum Notes, vol. 6, pp. 1–12.
      A discussion of the various expeditions which entered Tusayan and their
      reception.
  1936. Hopi history, No. 2. The Navajo wars, 1823–1870. Flagstaff: Mus. N.
      Ariz., Museum Notes, vol. 8, pp. 33–37.
      A continuation of the above, but primarily concerned with Hopi-Navajo rela-
      tions, and with the entry of the first American Whites.
  1940. How Don Pedro de Tovar discovered the Hopi and Don García López
      de Cárdenas saw the Grand Canyon, with notes upon their probable
      route. Plateau, vol 12, pp. 37–45, map.
      Based upon Castañeda's account, in Winship (1896). The author has carefully
      retraced the routes of the two parties, and presents a detailed mileage table,
      accompanied by an excellent map.

BEAGLEHOLE, ERNEST
  1937. Notes on Hopi economic life. Yale University Publ. in Anthropol. no.
      15, 88 pp.
      A good study of a much-neglected phase of Indian life. Included with it is a
      brief discussion of Hopi foods by Pearl Beaglehole, particularly good for the
      recipes listed.

BEAGLEHOLE, ERNEST, and PEARL BEAGLEHOLE
  1935. Hopi of the Second Mesa. Amer. Anthropol. Assoc., Memoir no. 44,
      65 pp.
      A general study, and one of the few ethnographies dealing with the Hopis of
      this mesa. Excellent for use in comparing the villages of the three mesas.

BEALS, RALPH L.
  1932. Masks in the Southwest. Amer. Anthropol., vol. 34, pp. 166–169.
      Concerns masked ceremonies at the time of the Spanish *entrada*, citing docu-
      mentary sources and Yaqui-Mayo customs.
  1943. Relations between Meso America and the Southwest. III Mesa Re-
      donda. México, D.F.: Sociedad Mexicana de Antropología, pp.

A paper presented at the *Mesa Redonda* symposium, concerning inter-tribal movements and trade between the several peoples of the region.

BENAVIDES, ALONZO DE
1916. Memorial de 1630. [Translated by Mrs. E. E. Ayer] Chicago: The Lakeside Press, privately printed, 309 pp.
The first translation in English of one of the more important Spanish documents on the Southwest. A later volume, by Hodge *et al.*, (q.v.), includes more information, and was based on Benavides' own revision.

BENT, CHARLES
1850. Report on Moqui. *In* U. S. H. R. Exec. Doc. 17, 31st Congr. 1st Sess., pp. 191–194.
The first attempt at a Federal survey of the Hopis. Includes useful materials on Hopi-White relations at mid-century.

BLOOM, LANSING B.
1931. A campaign against the Moqui pueblos. N. Mex. Hist. Rev., vol. 6, pp. 158–226.
Report of the abortive expedition of Gov. Phelix Martínez in 1716 to reduce the Moqui villages. Includes Vetancurt's roster of Hopi missions.

BOURKE, JOHN GREGORY
1884. The Snake-dance of the Moquis of Arizona. London: Sampson Low, Marston, Searle, & Rivington, 371 pp., illus.
The earliest attempt by a well-qualified observer to give a full ethnographic account of this ceremony, and still invaluable for contemporary details of Kachina activities and Hopi life in general.

BOYD, E.
1946. Saints and saint-makers of New Mexico, Santa Fé: Laboratory of Anthropology, 139 pp., illus.
A well-illustrated volume discussing the history of *santo* art.

BRADFIELD, MAITLAND
1972. Changing patterns of Hopi agriculture. London: Royal Institute of Anthropology, Occasional Papers #30.

BRADLEY, GLENN D.
1920. The story of the Santa Fe. Boston: Richard D. Badger, 288 pp., illus.
Primarily a history of the Atchison, Topeka and Santa Fe railroad; however, it includes interesting sidelights on the history of the area, and the Old Santa Fé Trail.

BRAND, DONALD D.
1938. Aboriginal trade routes for sea shells in the Southwest. Assoc. Pacif. Coast Geogr. Yearbook, vol. 4, pp. 3–10, map.
Considers other trade articles as well, and includes a useful map of these routes.

BREW, JOHN O.
1943. On the Pueblo IV and on the Katcina-Tlaloc Relations. III Mesa Redonda. México, D.F.: Sociedad Mexicana de Antropología, pp. 241–245.
A brief paper detailing suggested parallels between the mask designs on certain Kachinas, and the goggle-eyed Tlaloc depiction, the early Mexican rain god.

1946. Archaeology of Alkali Ridge, Southeastern Utah. Papers of the Peabody Mus. Amer. Archaeol., Ethnol., Harvard Univ., vol. 21, 346 pp., illus.
An excellent archeological report on an important excavation, fully illustrated.

Of particular value is the material on pp. 15–105, which constitutes in succinct form, an unusually well-written general résumé of Southwestern archeology.

1949. *see* Montgomery, Smith, and Brew, 1949.

BRODY, JEROME J.
1977. Mimbres painted pottery. Albuquerque: University of New Mexico Press, 276 pp., illus.
The best contemporary summary of Mimbreño art, with 180 excellent illustrations, and an extensive text.

BUNZEL, RUTH L.
1932. Zuñi Katcinas. Bur. Amer. Ethnol. Ann. Rept. 47, pp. 837–1086, illus.
An exhaustive study which also includes information on masked ceremonies in the Río Grande and Hopi areas. Unfortunately, the illustrations are poor for ethnological purposes.

CASO, ALFONSO
1929. El uso de las máscaras entre los antiguos mexicanos. Mexican Folkways [México, D. F.], vol. 5, pp. 111–113, illus.
A brief discussion, based upon examples taken from the Aztec *Codex* illustrations.

CASTAÑEDA, PEDRO DE [*see* Winship, George]

CLEMMER, RICHARD O.
1978. Continuities of Hopi cultural change. Ramona, Calif.: Acoma Books, 90 pp.
A brief, but profound survey of recent developments in the Hopi villages, with emphasis upon the impact of outside forces with traditional Hopi lifeways, and a very perceptive review of the Resistance Movement.

CODY, BERTHA P.
1939. Kachina Dolls. The Masterkey, vol. 13, pp. 35–40.
A brief popular account concerned with the *tihü*, including words to a Kachina song.

COHEN, FELIX S. (ed.)
1945. Handbook of Federal Indian law. Wash: G. P. O., 662 pp., maps.
A very useable summary of Federal law as applied to Indians, accompanied by analytical commentary, and case examples.

COLLINS, JOHN F.
1974. Nampeyo, Hopi potter. Fullerton: Muckenthaler Cultural Center, 52 pp., illus.
Catalog of an exhibition, with excellent text and illustrations of her work.

COLTON, HAROLD S.
1930. A brief survey of the early expeditions into northern Arizona. Flagstaff: Mus. N. Ariz., Museum Notes, vol. 2, no. 9, pp. 1–4.
1941. Prehistoric trade in the Southwest. Sci. Monthly, vol. 52, pp. 308–319, map.
Discusses the various trade routes, and the influences of introduced articles and ideas on various peoples. By an outstanding authority.
1947a. What is a Kachina? Plateau, vol. 19, pp. 40–47.
Includes a listing of some 250 Kachinas. *See also* Colton, 1949, *infra*.
1947b. Hopi deities. Plateau, vol. 20, pp. 10–16.
An explanation of the differences between Hopi concepts of Kachinas and gods.
1959. Hopi Kachina dolls. Albuquerque: University of New Mexico Press, 144 pp., illus.
The major book-length study of the subject. Expands the list of Kachinas in his 1947a aritcle (*supra*); summarizes much of the information in Fewkes and Stephen, and adds new material.

COLTON, HAROLD S., and FRANK BAXTER
1932. Days in the Painted Desert and San Francisco Mountains. Flagstaff: Mus. N. Arizona, Bull. no. 2, 113 pp., illus.
An excellent guide to Northeastern Arizona, with historical background information and maps of the area.

COSGROVE, C. B.
1947. Caves of the upper Gila and Hueco areas in New Mexico and Texas. Papers of the Peabody Mus. Amer. Archaeol., Ethnol., Harvard Univ., vol. 24, no. 2, 182 pp., illus.
A voluminously-illustrated report summarizing a series of important excavations in a wide area of eastern New Mexico and western Texas.

COSGROVE H. S., and C. B.
1932. The Swarts ruin: a typical Mimbres site in Southwestern New Mexico. Papers of the Peabody Mus. Amer. Archaeol., Ethnol., Harvard Univ., vol. 15, 178 pp., illus.
A very fine report of the excavation of a remarkable Mimbres site. It is of especial value because of the large number of carefully-drawn illustrations of Mimbreño pottery designs.

COVARRUBIAS, MIGUEL
1929. Notas sobre máscaras mexicanas. Mexican Folkways [México, D. F.], vol. 5, pp. 114–116, illus.
Primarily concerned with masks as works of art.

DAVIS, SHELTON O., and ROBERT O. MATHEWS (eds.)
1978. The social impact of energy development on Indians in the Far West. Cambridge: Harvard University; Anthropology Resource Center.
An evaluation of the effects on Hopi (and other neighboring tribes) cultural lifeways, due to the exploitation of subsurface minerals by outside forces.

DIPESO, CHARLES C.
1950. Painted stone slabs of Point of Pines, Arizona. Amer. Antqty., vol. 16, pp. 57–63, illus.
Report of the excavations of two flat stones, painted with masked designs, found in a prehistoric ruin.

DOCKSTADER, FREDERICK J.
1944. Christmas—Hopi style. Cranbrook Inst. Sci. News Letter, vol. 14, pp. 38–43, illus.
Comparisons of Hopi Kachina ceremonies with Christian Christmas customs.

DONALDSON, THOMAS
1893. Moqui Pueblo Indians of Arizona and Pueblo Indians of New Mexico. Extra Census Bulletin. Wash: U. S. Census Printing Off., 136 pp., illus.
An extremely useful compendium of information concerning the historical background, contemporary conditions, and culture of the Pueblo people. An "appendix" to the 1890 census, with extra-censory perception in many of its observations.

DORSEY, GEORGE A., and H. R. VOTH
1901. The Oraibi Soyáy ceremony. Chicago: Field Columbian Mus. Anthropol. Series, vol. 3, no. 1, 59 pp., illus.
A thorough study of this ritual as observed at First Mesa. Since there have been tremendous ceremonial changes at Oraibi due to the 1906 split, the material is uniquely valuable.
1902. The Mishongnovi ceremonies of the Snake and Antelope Fraternities. Chicago: Field Columbian Mus., Anthropol. Ser., vol. 3, no. 3, 104 pp., illus.
One of the best studies of the Snake ceremonies, and invaluable for comparisons with accounts of other years, and at other villages.

184   DUTTON, BERTHA P.
1957. Indian artistry in wood and other media. El Palacio, vol. 64, pp. 3–28, illus.
    A well-written account, with interesting illustrations, of a new exhibit installed in the Hall of Ethnology.
1962. Sun Father's Way; the kiva murals of Kuaua. Albuquerque: University of New Mexico Press, 287 pp., illus.
    Comprehensive study of the prehistoric murals found in the area of Coronado State Monument, New Mexico. Many are illustrated in full color, showing masked beings.

EARLE, EDWIN, and EDWARD A. KENNARD
1938. Hopi Kachinas. New York; J. J. Augustin, 40 pp., illus.
    The most readable book on the subject, beautifully illustrated with excellent color plates of Kachina dancers painted by a White artist.

EGGAN, DOROTHY
1943. The general problem of Hopi adjustment. Amer. Anthropol., vol. 45, pp. 357–373.
    A penetrating analysis which considers many phases of Hopi life, including the relation of the individual to the Kachina Cult. It should not be overlooked by anyone hoping to understand Hopi personality more fully.

EGGAN, FRED (ed.)
1937. Social anthropology of North American tribes. Chicago: University of Chicago Press, 456 pp.
    A symposium dealing with the theme of social organization among a half-dozen widely-scattered tribes. See Nash, 1937.
1950. Social organization of the western Pueblos. Chicago: University of Chicago Press, 373 pp.
    A scholarly treatment by a specialist; indispensable to any understanding of Hopi-Zuñi social structure, and helpful for neighboring areas.

ELLIS, FLORENCE M.
1975. A pantheon of Kachinas. New Mexico magazine, vol. 53, pp. 13–28, illus.
    A well-illustrated article, with useful commentary on both Hopi and Zuni masked dancers.

ERICKSON, JON F.
1977. Kachinas: an evolving art form? Heard Museum, 112 pp., illus.
    A beautifully illustrated catalog of an exhibition surveying the development of *tihü* styles, based upon the collections of the Museum.

ESPINOSA, J. MANUEL
1942. Crusaders of the Río Grande. Chicago: Institute of Jesuit History, 410 pp., illus.
    A thorough treatment of the work of the *Conquistadores* of the Río Grande area; especially considers the activities of Diego de Vargas.

FERM, VERGILIUS (ed.)
1950. Forgotten religions. New York: The Philosophical Library, 392 pp.
    A symposium; the several articles discuss various lapsed or little-known religious systems of the world. See Titiev, 1950.

FEWKES, JESSE WALTER
1892a. A few Tusayan pictographs. Amer. Anthropol., o.s. vol. 5, pp. 9–26, illus.
    An interesting early attempt to relate pictographs to ceremonial and artistic figures.
1892b. A journal of American Ethnology and Archaeology. vol. 2, Boston: Houghton Mifflin, 193 pp., illus.

Largely the results of Fewkes's work with the Hemenway Expedition. Some very excellent material included in it is impossible to duplicate today.

1893. A-wá-to-bi: An archeological verification of a Tusayan legend. Amer. Anthropol., o.s. vol. 6, pp. 363–375, illus.
    The earliest article calling attention to the archeological and historical significance of Awátovi. Fewkes stresses the internal strife of the villages, and gives legendary accounts of the destruction of Awátovi.

1894. Dolls of the Tusayan Indians. Internatl. Archiv für Ethnog., [Leiden], vol. 7, pp. 45–74, illus.
    The first scientific study of the Kachina tihü. Valuable for the excellent color plates, and for the opportunity it affords for tracing changes in artistic style.

1896a. The prehistoric culture of Tusayan. Amer. Anthropol., o.s. vol. 9, pp. 151–174.
    Especially concerned with the village of Sikyatki, its history and destruction, but also discusses the other Hopi villages.

1896b. Preliminary account of an expedition to the cliff villages of the Red Rock Country, and the Tusayan ruins of Sikyatki and Awatobi, Arizona, in 1895. Smiths. Inst. Ann Rept. for 1895, pp. 557–588, illus.
    A general summary of Fewkes' work at Awátovi and in neighboring areas. See also Fewkes 1898a, infra.

1896c. The Tusayan ritual: A study of the influence of environment on aboriginal cults. Smiths. Inst. Ann. Rept. for 1895, pp. 683–700, illus.
    An early effort at relating Hopi ceremonialism to its environment.

1897. Tusayan Katcinas. Bur. Ethnol., Ann. Rept. 15, pp. 245–313, illus.
    Fewkes' first lengthy, detailed study of the Kachina Cult; it was preliminary to his later (1903) work, and is of secondary importance to that volume.

1898a. Archaeological expedition to Arizona in 1895. Bur. Amer. Ethnol. Ann. Rept. 17, pt. 2, pp. 519–742, illus.
    Final report of his Awátovi-Sikyatki work. Many excellent illustrations in color.

1898b. The growth of the Hopi ritual. Jour. Amer. Folklore, vol. 11, pp. 173–194, illus.
    A good ethno-historical study tracing the development of Hopi ceremonies, and discussing the origin of the Kachina Cult.

1901. An interpretation of Katcina worship. Jour. Amer. Folklore, vol. 14, pp. 81–94.
    One of the earliest attempts to consider the reasons for the development of Kachina ritual.

1902. Sky-God personations in Hopi worship. Jour. Amer. Folklore, vol. 15, pp. 14–32, illus.
    A suggested correlation of certain Kachinas with the Hopi God of the Sky. Although Fewkes was ignorant of the mural designs later discovered at Awátovi, many of his observations in this article have proven correct.

1903. Hopi Katcinas, drawn by native artists. Bur. Amer. Ethnol. Ann. Rept. 21, pp. 3–126, illus.
    A thorough investigation of the Hopi Kachina Cult illustrated by some 225 colored drawings. Fewkes' best-known work on the Hopis and, in spite of some errors, still the best study of Kachinas so far published. A classic volume on the subject.

1904. Two summers' work in pueblo ruins. Bur. Amer. Ethnol., Ann. Rept. 22, pt. 1, pp. 1–196, illus.
    A summary report on Fewkes' work in the Hopi Jeddito valley area. Valuable especially for the illustrative material.

1920. Sun worship of the Hopi Indians. Smiths. Inst. Ann. Rept. for 1918, pp. 493–526, illus.
    Especially good for the description and illustrations of a little-known ritual.

1922. Ancestor worship of the Hopi Indians. Smiths. Inst. Ann. Rept. for

1921, pp. 485–506, illus.
    Presents his thesis for the existence of ancestor worship in the Kachina Cult and other Hopi ceremonials. Well-illustrated (many of the drawings are taken from his 1903 volume).

1924. The use of idols in Hopi worship. Smiths. Inst. Ann. Rept. for 1922, pp. 377–397, illus.
    While this article deals primarily with other, non-masked, ceremonies, it is important for its possible bearing on the development of the *tihü*.

1925a. Designs on prehistoric pottery from the Mimbres Valley, New Mexico. Smiths. Inst. Misc. Coll., vol. 74, no. 6, pp. 1–47, illus.

1925b. Additional designs on prehistoric Mimbres pottery. Smiths. Inst. Misc. Coll., vol. 76, no. 8, pp. 1–46, illus.
    These two publications comprise one of the best collections of Mimbreño designs available. Excellent for a study of design.

1927. The Katcina altars in Hopi worship. Smiths. Inst. Ann. Rept. for 1926, pp. 469–486, illus.
    Especially useful for the several illustrations, some colored, of altars. Compares ceremonies of the several villages.

FRENCH, DAVID J.

1948. Factionalism in Isleta Pueblo. New York: J. J. Augustin, [for] Amer. Ethnol. Soc., Monogr. 14, 48 pp.
    A study of the causes of internal strife within a Río Grande village. Of interest to this book because of its parallel to the Oraibi schism at the turn of the century.

HACK, JOHN T.

1942. The changing physical environment of the Hopi Indians of Arizona. Papers of the Peabody Mus. Amer. Archaeol., Ethnol., Harvard Univ., vol. 35, no. 1, 85 pp., illus.
    The best single study of the Hopi environment and its influences on Hopi culture.

HACKETT, CHARLES WILSON (ed.)

1916. Otermín's attempt to reconquer New Mexico, 1681–1682. Old Santa Fé [Santa Fé, N. Mex.], vol. 3, no. 9, pp. 44–84.
    Drawn from original sources; treated at greater length in Hackett, 1942, *infra*.

1937. Historical documents relating to New Mexico, Nueva Vizcaya, and approaches thereto, to 1773. Wash: Carnegie Inst. of Washington, 3 vol., 532 pp.
    An invaluable collection of materials relating to early Pueblo history; many references to the Kachina ceremonies may be found therein.

1942. Revolt of the Pueblo Indians of New Mexico and Otermín's attempted reconquest, 1680–1682. 2 vols. Albuquerque: University of New Mexico Press.
    The classic account of the Pueblo Revolt. This includes translations of the documentary material relating to the Revolt, and exhaustive critical commentary.

HALLENBECK, CLEVE

1949. Journey of Fray Marcos de Niza. Dallas: The University Press, 115 pp.
    Concludes that Fray Marcos was concerned less with truth than with politics in the report he submitted to Viceroy Mendoza in 1539.

HAMMOND, GEORGE P.

1927. Don Juan de Oñate and the founding of New Mexico. Santa Fé: El Palacio Press, 228 pp., illus.

HAMMOND, GEORGE P. and AGAPITO REY (ed. and trans.)

1927. The Rodríguez expedition to New Mexico, 1581–1582. N. Mex. Hist. Rev., vol. 2, pp. 239–268; 334–362.
    Account of the ill-fated second Spanish entry into the United States area.

1928. Obregón's history of XVIth Century explorations in western America.
Los Angeles: Wetzel Publ. Co., 351 pp.
A translation of one of the earliest histories of the Southwest, with excellent
annotations.
1929. Expedition into New Mexico made by Antonio de Espejo, 1582–1583.
Los Angeles: Quivira Society, 143 pp.
Essentially a translation, with notes, of the diary of Diego Pérez de Luxán,
chronicler and *compañero* of Espejo.

HARGRAVE, LYNDON L.
1935. The Jeddito Valley and the first Pueblo towns in Arizona to be visited
by Europeans. Flagstaff: Mus. N. Ariz., Museum Notes, vol. 8, no. 4,
map.
A thorough discussion of the history of the several settlements in the Jeddito
area, and a description of their archeological excavation.

HARSHBERGER, JOHN W.
1926. Changes in the habits of the Hopi Indians, Arizona.. Bull. of the
Geogr. Soc. of Phila., vol. 24, pp. 39–45, illus.
A brief summary of innovations in Hopi life, especially in the field of economics and ethnobotany.

HARVEY, BYRON III
1970. Ritual in Pueblo art; Hopi life in Hopi painting. New York: Mus.
Amer. Indian, Contrib. 24, 81 pp., illus.
A collection of 185 paintings depicting various themes in Hopi life, with an
extensive text.

HAURY, EMIL W.
1945. The excavation of Los Muertos and neighboring ruins in the Salt River
Valley, southern Arizona. Papers of the Peabody Mus. Amer. Archaeol.,
Ethnol., Harvard University, vol. 24, no. 1, 223 pp., illus.
Based upon the unpublished reports of the Hemenway Expedition into this area
in 1889. Well-written and accompanied by excellent illustrations.

HAWLEY, FLORENCE
1946. The role of Pueblo social organization in the dissemination of Catholicism. Amer. Anthropol., vol. 48, pp. 407–415.
Suggests one reason why Catholicism succeeded in the Río Grande area, yet
failed among the Hopi-Zuñi people: one area followed patrilineal social structure, whereas the other was matrilineal.

HEWETT, EDGAR LEE
1938a. Pajarito plateau and its ancient people. Albuquerque: University of
New Mexico Press, 191 pp., illus.
A general survey of the archeology of the area; especially valuable for this
study is Appendix I, *Pajaritan Pictography.*
1938b. Pre-Hispanic frescoes in the Rio Grande valley. Santa Fé: Papers of
the School of Amer. Research, pp. 1–14, illus.
Contains several illustrations of the murals at Kuaua.

HIBBEN, FRANK C.
1975. Kiva art of the Anasazi at Pottery Mound. Las Vegas: KC Publications, 145 pp., illus.
A report on the murals recovered from a Pueblo ruin in northwestern New
Mexico, with full-color illustrations.

HODGE, FREDERICK W.
1895. The first discovered city of Cibola. Amer. Anthropol., o.s., vol. 8, pp.
142–152.
Considers the question of whether Hawikuh or K'iakima was the first village
seen by Estebán and Marcos de Niza. His "on the scene" studies favor Hawikuh.

188　　1937. History of Hawikuh. Los Angeles: The Southwest Museum, 155 pp., illus.
In this exceedingly thorough study, Hodge presents a tremendous amount of evidence to support his identification of Hawikuh as the village wherein Estebán was slain, and the one which Marcos de Niza saw from a safe distance.

1952. Masked Kachinas in Spanish times. The Masterkey, vol. 26, pp. 17–20.
A brief summary of the evidence as given in Hackett, 1937.

HODGE, FREDERICK W., GEORGE P. HAMMOND, and AGAPITO REY (eds.)
1945. Fray Alonso de Benavides' revised Memorial of 1634. Albuquerque: University of New Mexico Press, 368 pp., illus.
A translation, with annotations, of the *Memorial* and related documents.

HOLIEN, ELAINE B.
1970. Kachinas. El Palacio, vol. 76, pp. 1–15, illus.
A well-illustrated popular account with legends related to some of the masked beings.

HOUGH, WALTER
1903. Archaeological field work in northeastern Arizona. The Museum-Gates Expedition of 1901. U. S. Natl. Mus. Ann. Rept. for 1901, pp. 279–358, illus.
This volume is a final summary of Hough's work on this expedition, with many illustrations in color.

JACKSON, A. T.
1938. Picture-writing of Texas Indians. University of Texas Anthropol. Papers, vol. II, 490 pp., illus.
Exhaustive treatment for the area, with many fine illustrations. Included are many parallels of pictographic work found farther west, of interest in any comparative study of pictographic art.

JAMES, HARRY
1951. Turtles for Tewaquaptewa. Desert, vol. 14, no. 14, pp. 22–23, illus.
Popular account of the sending of live turtles to a Hopi chief for his village to use in ceremonies—exemplary of contemporary influences.

1974. Pages from Hopi history. Tucson: University of Arizona Press., 258 pp.
An excellent compilation of the history of the people, arranged in chronological order. James was a participant in many of the events in the early 1900s, making this an especially valuable commentary.

JONES, VOLNEY H.
1950. The establishment of the Hopi Reservation, and some later developments concerning Hopi lands. Plateau, vol. 23, no. 2, pp. 17–25, map.
The most complete article on the subject. Later changes in the Reservation area are discussed as well as its establishment. A very good map is included.

KELLY, HENRY W.
1941. Franciscan Missions of New Mexico, 1740–1760. N. Mex. Hist. Rev., vol. 16, pp. 41–69, illus.
Discusses the problems of the missions during a troubled period, and is especially good concerning Hopi-Jesuit relations. Gives excerpts from Delgado's diary of his trip to the Hopi villages.

KIRKLAND, FORREST
1940. Pictographs of Indian masks at Hueco Tanks, Texas. Archaeol., Paleogr. Soc. Texas Bull., vol. 12, pp. 9–30, illus.
Of interest for purposes of comparing these painted pictographs with those of other areas.

KLETT, FRANCIS
1879. The Cachina: A dance at the Pueblo of Zuñi. *in* G. M. Wheeler, ed.,

Report upon U. S. Geographical surveys west of the one hundredth
meridian, vol. 7, pp. 332–336, illus.
    An early account of a masked dance, accompanied by a quaint illustration in
    color. Presents a careful description of ritual and costume, mentioning earlier
    witnesses (Ten Broeck and Davis). Valuable for its publication date, and for
    the early American use of the term 'Cachina' in the title.

McGREGOR, JOHN C.
1941a. Southwestern archaeology. New York: John Wiley and Sons, Inc.,
    403 pp., illus.
    Thorough and inclusive for the area. Particularly notable for fine illustrations
    and drawings, plus the several valuable appendices.
1941b. Winona and Ridge Ruin. Part I. Mus. N. Ariz. Bull. 18, 309 pp., illus.
    A very thorough account of one of the richest archeological finds in the South-
    west in recent years.
1943. Burial of an early American magician. Proc. Amer. Philos. Soc., vol.
    86, no. 2, pp. 270–298, illus.
    A summary of the *pièce de résistance* of the Ridge Ruin find; the color plates
    are especially valuable.

MAHOOD, RUTH I. (ed.)
1961. Photographer of the Southwest: Adam Clark Vroman, 1856–1916.
    Los Angeles: Ward Ritchie Press, 127 pp., illus.
    A beautifully produced survey of the artistry of Vroman, an important early
    photographer in the Southwest.

MARTIN, PAUL S. (ed.)
1962. Chapters in the prehistory of eastern Arizona, I. Fieldiana: Anthro-
    pology, vol. 53. Chicago Natural History Museum, pp. 69–74.
    The section *The Sacred Stone Image* details the circumstances of the discovery
    of the small carved figurine, including a photograph and excellent description.

MARTIN, PAUL S., and ELIZABETH S. WILLIS
1940. Anasazi painted pottery in Field Museum of Natural History. Field
    Mus. Nat. Hist., Dept. of Anthropol., Mem., vol. 5, 284 pp., illus.
    A descriptive catalogue, with excellent illustrations. Primarily useful for com-
    parison purposes.

MARTIN, PAUL S., GEORGE I. QUIMBY, and DONALD COLLIER
1947. Indians before Columbus. University of Chicago Press, 582 pp., illus.
    Excellent account of American archeology, north of Mexico. Very useful for
    quick-reference purposes.

MATTHEWS, WASHINGTON
1897. Navaho legends. Amer. Folklore Soc. Mem. no. 5, 299 pp., illus.
    One of the first important studies of the Navajo; still of primary value.

MERIAM, LEWIS (ed.)
1928. The problem of Indian administration. Baltimore: The Johns Hopkins
    Press, 872 pp.
    Findings of a commission, appointed by the Institute for Government Research
    in 1926, to investigate conditions of Indian administration and of the Amerind.
    Although little immediate reform resulted, the report is of value to anyone inter-
    ested in Government administration of minority groups.

MILLER, MAMIE RUTH TANQUIST
1941. Pueblo Indian cultures as seen by early Spanish explorers. University
    of Southern California, School of Research Studies, no. 18, 30 pp.
    A summary of the ethnographic content of the reports of various explorers,
    1540–1700.

MINDELEFF, VICTOR
1891. A study of Pueblo architecture: Tusayan and Cibola. Bur. Amer.

Ethnol. Ann. Rept. 8, pp. 3–228, illus.
    The best study yet made of the subject. Considers social and historical back-
    ground, as well as the architectural aspects of Pueblo culture. Richly illustrated.

MONTGOMERY, ROSS, WATSON SMITH, and JOHN O. BREW
1949. Franciscan Awatovi. Papers of the Peabody Mus. Amer. Archaeol.,
    Ethnol., Harvard Univ., vol. 36, 361 pp., illus.
    An exceptional monograph, both for its quality, and the cross-disciplinary
    qualifications of the several authors. Destined to become a classic in its field.

MORSS, NOEL
1931. The ancient culture of the Fremont River in Utah. Papers of the Pea-
    body Mus. Amer. Archaeol., Harvard Univ., vol. 12, no. 3, 81 pp.,
    illus.
    The section (pp. 34–42), treating the pictographs of masked dancers in the
    Fruitas region, is of especial interest.

NAGATA, SHUICHI
1970. Modern transformations of Moenkopi Pueblo. Urbana: University of
    Illinois Press, 336 pp.
    An excellent historical survey of the development of Moenkopi, with acute
    observations of the many changes that have taken place, and their impact upon
    the people.

NASH, PHILLEO
1937. The place of religious revivalism in the formation of the intercultural
    community of Klamath Reservation, in Eggan, 1937.
    The situation among the Klamath people, as discussed in this article, presents
    many parallels to what has developed in the Hopi area.

NEQUATEWA, EDMUND
1931. Hopi Hopiwime: The Hopi ceremonial calendar. Flagstaff: Mus. N.
    Ariz., Museum Notes, vol. 3, no. 9, pp. 1–4, illus.
    A summary discussion of the cycle of Hopi ceremonies.
1936. Truth of a Hopi and other clan stories of Shung-opovi. Flagstaff: Mus.
    N. Ariz. Bull. no. 8, 114 pp.
    Hopi stories by a Hopi. A delightful collection of legends from this Second
    Mesa village.
1943. Nampeyó, famous Hopi potter. Plateau, vol. 15, pp. 40–42.
    Sketch of the woman largely responsible for the Renaissance in Hopi pottery.
    written by a fellow tribesman.
1948. Chaveyo: the first Kachina. Plateau, vol. 20, pp. 60–62.
    Recounts the legend of the coming of Cháveyo and the introduction of the
    Kachina religion to the Hopis.

OAK, H. L. see Bancroft, Hubert Howe

ORTIZ, ALFONSO (ed.)
1979. Handbook of North American Indians. Vol. IX, Southwest. Washing-
    ton: Smithsonian Institution, 701 pp., illus.
    Compilation of various articles by many authors, related to the anthropology
    of the Southwest.

PARSONS, ELSIE CLEWS
1924. The religion of Pueblo Indians. Proc. 21st Internatl. Cong. Ameri-
    canists, Part I [1924], pp. 140–161.
    A brief discussion of various ceremonial patterns, listing parallel and variant
    customs.
1925. A Pueblo Indian journal, 1920–1921. Amer. Anthropol. Assoc., Mem.
    no. 32, 123 pp., illus.
    A "day-to-day" account of a Hopi's activities; concerned with First Mesa ac-
    tivities, and especially Hano. Valuable for its material on Tewa customs, about
    which little has been available.

1929. El uso de las máscaras en el suroeste de los Estados Unidos. Mexican
Folkways [México, D. F.], vol. 5, pp. 152–156.
Parsons here first expresses her theory of the alien origin of Pueblo masked ceremonies.

1930. Spanish elements in the Kachina Cult of the Pueblos. Proc. 23rd Internatl. Congr. Americanists [1928], pp. 582–603, illus.
A formal and much more complete presentation of her theory of the Catholic origin of the Kachina Cult in the Pueblos.

1933a. Hopi and Zuñi ceremonialism. Amer. Anthropol. Assoc., Mem. no. 39, 108 pp., illus.
An excellent study of the ritual customs of the two areas, pointing out parallel usages, and suggesting common origins. Emphasizes the Zuñi area.

1933b. Some Aztec and Pueblo parallels. Amer. Anthropol., vol. 25, pp. 611–631.
This study is based largely upon Sahagún, and includes a listing of many ritual parallels. In it, Parsons first began to retreat from her previous stand, and conceded certain elements of masking as pre-Columbian.

1939. Pueblo Indian religion. 2 vols. Chicago: University of Chicago Press, 1275 pp.
A classic volume, summarizing all that was known concerning the subject and still unsurpassed in its field. Her finest work and one which will remain the Bible of the Pueblo ceremonial scholar for years to come.

1940. A pre-Spanish record of Hopi ceremonies. Amer. Anthropol., vol. 42, pp. 541–542, illus.
Discusses, with illustration, a bowl found at Kawaika-a or Kokopnyama, bearing a design of two figures apparently performing the Snake Dance.

PATTIE, JAMES OHIO [R. G. Thwaites, ed.]
1905. Personal narrative, 1824–1830. Cleveland: The Arthur H. Clark Company, 379 pp.
A reprint of an 1831 account of a fur-trapping expedition which entered Tusayan—one of the first American groups to meet the Hopis.

REAGAN, ALBERT B.
1931. Some archaeological notes on Nine Mile Cañon, Utah. El Palacio, vol. 31, pp. 45–71, illus.
Useful for the several reproductions of pictographs found in this area.

1935. Petroglyphs show that the ancients of the Southwest wore masks. Amer. Anthropol., vol. 37, pp. 707–708.

ROBERTS, FRANK H. H. JR.
1932. The village of the Great Kivas on the Zuñi Reservation, New Mexico. Bur. Amer. Ethnol. Bull. no. 111, 197 pp., illus.
Of especial interest for the illustrations, and the discussion of mural paintings (p. 79f.) found at this site.

ROEDIGER, VIRGINIA MORE
1941. Ceremonial costumes of the Pueblo Indians. Berkeley: University of California Press, 252 pp., illus.
The most complete volume available on techniques and materials employed in the manufacture of Pueblo costume. Especially noteworthy for the many colored illustrations.

SCHAAFSMA, POLLY, and CURTIS F. SCHAAFSMA
1974. Evidence for the origins of the Pueblo Kachina cult as suggested by Southwestern rock art. Amer. Antqty., vol. 39, pp. 535–545, illus.
A review of the petroglyphic evidence of the possible early origin and development of masked ceremonies.

SCHOLES, FRANCE V.
1936. Church and State in New Mexico 1610–1650. N. Mex. Hist. Rev., vol.

192   11, pp. 283–349.
>An excellent account of the struggle between the civil and cleric officials which had a great deal to do with causing the Pueblo Revolt.

SCHOLES, FRANCE V., and LANSING L. BLOOM
1945. Friar personnel and mission chronology, 1598–1629. N. Mex. Hist. Rev., vol. 20, pp. 69–72. [This series of articles began in 1944, with vol. 19].
>A chronological listing of the establishment of the various New Mexican missions during this period, and a record of the individuals appointed to serve therein.

SCHOOLCRAFT, HENRY ROWE (ed.)
1854. Information respecting the history, condition and prospects of the Indian tribes of the United States. Philadelphia: Lippincott, Grambo & Co., Part IV, 668 pp., illus.
>An encyclopedic series, attempting to cover all that was then known of the Amerind civilization. Necessary to any study of the subject, it must be used with caution, for Schoolcraft often relied upon hearsay and used secondary sources without checking their accuracy.

SEKAQUAPTEWA, EMORY
1975. Preserving the good things of Hopi life. in Spicer, Edward H., and Raymond H. Thompson: Plural society in the Southwest. Albuquerque: University of New Mexico Press, 376 pp.; pp. 239–260.
>A colorful summary of recent sociopolitical activities in the Hopi area, with a perceptive commentary on Indian-White citizens; by a leading Hopi scholar.
1976. Hopi Indian ceremonies. in Capps, Walter H., Seeing with a Native eye. New York: Forum Books, 132 pp.; pp. 35–43.
>A general article on the various Hopi religious rites, from the point of view of a participant.

SIMMONS, LEO W. (ed.)
1942. Sun Chief. New Haven: Yale University Press, 460 pp.
>A classic autobiography of a Hopi Indian, Don Talayesva, particularly valuable to those who seek an insight into Hopi psychology.

SIMS, AGNES C.
1950. San Cristóbal petroglyphs. Santa Fé: Southwest Editions, 12 pp., illus.
>Contains a portfolio of illustrations, with notes, of petroglyphs of the region. Several masked dancers are shown, with interesting suggestions as to contemporary parallels.

SINCLAIR, JOHN L.
1951. The story of the pueblo of Kuaua. Papers of the School of American Research, no. 45, pp. 1–11, illus.
>A brief account of the history of Kuaua, with an excellent color plate of two of the murals found therein.

SMILEY, TERAH L.
1951. A summary of tree-ring dates from some southwestern archaeological sites. Tucson: University of Arizona, Bulletin, vol. 22, no. 4, pp. 1–32, map.

SMITH, WATSON
1952. Kiva mural decorations at Awatovi and Kawaika-a. Papers of the Peabody Mus. Amer. Archaeol., Ethnol., Harvard Univ., vol. 37, 363 pp., illus.
>A superb study of early Pueblo art. In this exhaustive monograph, Smith not only discusses the techniques of excavation and preservation of the murals, but thoroughly describes them, and suggests many interpretations and possible parallels in contemporary Hopi practices.

SPIER, LESLIE
1928. Havasupai ethnography. Amer. Mus. Nat. Hist., Anthropol. Papers, vol. 29, pt. 3, pp. 81–392, illus.
An excellent report, and one of the very few papers dealing with this isolated tribe. Because of their trade relations with the Hopis, the reference must not be overlooked in any study of culture influences or change.

STEPHEN, ALEXANDER M.
1893. Description of a Hopi ti-hu. Folk-Lorist, vol. 1, no. 2–3, pp. 83–88.
One of the earliest articles dealing with the Kachina doll, describing its manufacture and use.
1929. Hopi tales. Jour. Amer. Folklore, vol. 42, pp. 1–72.
A collection of legends gathered in 1883 and 1893. With Voth (1905), forms a major portion of all the Hopi legend material in print today.
1936. Hopi journal. 2 vols. Columbia University Contrib. Anthropol., vol. 23, 1417 pp., illus.
An exhaustive account of Hopi culture in the 1890's, it devotes much space to ceremonial activity, as well as including a wealth of material available nowhere else. The *Hopi Glossary*, by Benjamin Whorf, is the only extended vocabulary of the Hopi language in print.

STEVENSON, JAMES
1883a. Illustrated catalogue of the collections obtained from the Indians of New Mexico and Arizona in 1879. Bur. Amer. Ethnol. Ann. Rept. 2, pp. 307–422, illus.
Useful for the illustrations (many in color) and Hopi and Zuñi vocabularies which accompany the list.
1883b. Illustrated catalogue of the collections obtained from the Indians of New Mexico in 1880. Bur. Amer. Ethnol. Ann Rept. 2, pp. 423–465, illus.
As above, except that this article does not include Hopi material. Useful for comparing Río Grande-Acoma-Zuñi usages with Hopi material culture.

STEWARD, JULIAN H.
1929. Petroglyphs of California and adjoining states. Univ. Calif. Publ. Amer. Archaeol., Ethnol., vol. 24, no. 2, pp. 47–238, illus.
A thorough, well-written, and extremely useful illustrated "Catalogue" of the area.
1931. Notes of Hopi ceremonies in their initiatory form, 1927–1928. Amer. Anthropol, vol. 33, pp. 56–79.
Detailed notes by a competent observer, on initiation ritual and Kachina ceremonies during the initiation period.
1937. Petroglyphs of the United States. Smiths. Inst. Ann. Rept. for 1936, pp. 405–426, illus.
A general discussion, dealing with the presence of petroglyphs throughout the United States. Good illustrations.
1941. Archaeological reconnaissance of southern Utah. Bur. Amer. Ethnol., Bull. no. 128, Anthropol. Paper no. 18, pp. 275–356, illus.
Of especial interest are the petroglyphic figures reproduced on pp. 345–346, and Plate 52.

THOMAS, ALFRED B. (trans. and ed.)
1932. Forgotten frontiers. Norman: University of Oklahoma Press, 420 pp., map.
A scholarly study of the Indian policy of Gov. De Anza, 1777–1787, with documentary material and excellent notes.

THOMPSON, LAURA
1950. Culture in crisis: A study of the Hopi Indians. New York: Harper & Bros., 221 pp., illus.
A product of the new school of anthropological-psychological research, much

of the value is weakened by extensive use of specialized terminology. The historical background and factual reporting are good, but the sections attempting to analyse Hopi psychology are less satisfactory. Excellent photographs are included.

THOMPSON, LAURA, and ALICE JOSEPH
1944. The Hopi way. Chicago: University of Chicago Press. 151 pp., illus.
    Second in a series based on a coöperative project of the Bureau of Indian Affairs and University of Chicago. Applies White psychological tests to Hopi children, and attempts to draw conclusions therefrom.

TITIEV, MISCHA
1939a. The story of Kokopele. Amer. Anthropol., vol. 41, pp. 91–98, illus.
    A good discussion of contemporary appearances of Kókopölö which includes several legends concerning his activities.
1939b. Hopi racing customs at Oraibi, Arizona. Papers of the Michigan Academy of Science, Arts and Letters, vol. 24, pp. 33–42.
    The importance of racing in Hopi culture is considered in this article, as well as several activities connected with the Wáwas Kachinas. A brief list of the latter is included.
1944. Old Oraibi: A study of the Hopi Indians of Third Mesa. Papers of the Peabody Mus. Amer. Archaeol., Ethnol., Harvard Univ., vol. 22, no. 1, 277 pp., illus.
    An excellent report of two years' residence (1932–34) on Third Mesa. Valuable for its summary of Hopi social organization and kinship system, and most particularly for a penetrating study of the Oraibi split of 1906.
1950. The religion of the Hopi Indians. In Ferm, 1950, pp. 363–378.
    A concise, but thorough, analysis of the Hopi religion.

TOOR, FRANCES
1929. El uso actual de las máscaras. Mexican Folkways [México, D. F.], vol. 5, pp. 127–131, illus.
    Describes current practices in the use of masks in Mexico.

TWITCHELL, RALPH EMERSON (ed. and trans.)
1914. The Spanish archives of New Mexico. 2 vols. Cedar Rapids, Iowa: The Torch Press.
    A catalogue of the documents, now in the Library of Congress, which pertain to the early history of New Mexico. They cover, in varying degree of thoroughness, the period 1631–1821. Although most of the documents are merely listed, a few are translated in précis form.

UNDERHILL, RUTH
1944. Pueblo crafts: Wash: U. S. Indian Service, 147 pp., illus.
    An excellent handbook of the various Pueblo arts, very well illustrated throughout.

VICTOR, FRANCES FULLER
1870. The River of the West. Hartford: R. W. Bliss & Company, 602 pp., illus.
    Primarily a history of the Colorado River; useful for its mention of several expeditions into the area, some of which entered Tusayan.

VILLAGRÁ, GASPAR DE
1610. Historia de la Nuevo México. Tomo I. México, D. F.: Museo Nacional [reprint 1900] 183 pp.
    A history in verse form of an early expedition into New Mexico. Includes the earliest recorded mention of kiva murals—believed to be those excavated at Kuaua.

VIVIAN, GORDON
1935. The murals at Kuaua. El Palacio, vol. 28, pp. 113–119.
    A brief discussion of the murals and their excavation.

VOTH, H. R.   195

    1901. The Oraibi Powamu ceremony. Field Columbian Mus., Anthropol. Ser., vol. 3, no. 2, 97 pp., illus.
        A detailed account of this ceremony at First Mesa. Excellent for use in comparisons with descriptions of Powamú rites elsewhere, or at other times.

    1905. The traditions of the Hopi. Field Columbian Mus., Anthropol. Ser., vol. 8, 319 pp.
        The most extensive collection extant of Hopi legends, largely reported verbatim. Some Hopi texts are included, as well as scattered vocabulary material.

WASHBURN, DOROTHY K.

    1980. Hopi Kachina; spirit of life. San Francisco: California Academy of Natural Sciences, 158 pp., illus.
        An excellent catalog of a superb exhibition, profusely illustrated and accompanied by extensive notes.

WATERS, FRANK, and OSWALD WHITE BEAR FREDERICKS

    1963. Book of the Hopi. New York: Viking Press, 347 pp., illus.
        A fascinating, if somewhat naïve, volume detailing one Hopi man's account of the legendary traditions of his people. Although derided by many other Hopis as being inaccurate, it is nevertheless well written and offers one individual's point of view.

WEBB, WILLIAM, and ROBERT A. WEINSTEIN

    1973. Dwellers at the source. New York: Grossman, 214 pp.
        A selection of photographs of Indians of the Southwest, by A. C. Vroman between 1895–1904, with annotations.

WELLMANN, KLAUS F.

    1979. A survey of North American Indian rock art. Graz: Akademische Druck-u. Verlagsanstalt. 461 pp., illus.
        An encyclopaedic work with over 950 illustrations of petroglyphs and pictographs, with an excellent text, valuable bibliography, and thorough index.

WHITE, LESLIE A.

    1932a. The Pueblo of San Felipe. Amer. Anthropol. Assoc., Memoir no. 38, 69 pp., illus.
        A good study of this village; included is an illustrated discussion of San Felipe kachinas.

    1932b. The Acoma Indians. Bur. Amer. Ethnol. Ann. Rept. 47, pp. 17–192, illus.
        An exhaustive study of Acoma; the large amount of material on Acoma masked ceremonies is particularly useful in the present instance.

    1934. Masks in the Southwest. Amer. Anthropol., vol. 36, pp. 626–628.
        Primarily a reply to Parsons' arguments for the Catholic origin of masked ceremonies, White cites documentary evidence to the contrary.

    1935. The Pueblo of Santo Domingo, New Mexico. Amer. Anthropol. Assoc., Memoir no. 43, 210 pp., illus.
        A thorough, well-illustrated study. As with all of White's monographs, it contains considerable material on Kachina activities, hence is of especial value for comparisons with Hopi ceremonials.

    1942. The Pueblo of Santa Ana, New Mexico. Amer. Anthropol. Assoc. Mem., no. 60, 360 pp., illus.
        An excellent monograph, providing practically all of our knowledge concerning this village. Of especial value is the information concerning Santa Ana *katsina*.

WHITING, ALFRED H.

    1939. Ethnobotany of the Hopi. Flagstaff: Mus. N. Ariz., Bull. 15, 120 pp.
        The only complete ethnobotany of this tribe. Valuable not only for its thorough listing of plants in the Hopi environment and their uses, but also for the ethnological and linguistic material.

    1964. Hopi Kachinas. Plateau, vol. 37, pp. 1–7.
        An especially well-written account of the role of the Kachinas in Hopi life. Whiting was an informed, careful observer of Hopi culture.

WHITMAN, WILLIAM
1947. The Pueblo Indians of San Ildefonso. Columbia University Press, 164 pp.
    A thorough study of San Ildefonso, and of particular interest because of the attention given to the recent rise of factionalism in that pueblo.

WILDER, MITCHELL A.
1943. Santos. Colorado Springs: Taylor Museum, 49 pp., illus.
    A well-written, though brief, study of the religious folk art of New Mexico. Excellent illustrations.

WINSHIP, GEORGE P. (trans. and ed.)
1896. The Coronado Expedition, 1540–1542. Bur. Amer. Ethnol. Ann. Rept. 14, pt. 1, pp. 329–613.
    The standard English translation of the journal of Pedro de Castañeda, historian of the expedition. Includes the original Spanish text, notes by Winship, and a well-annotated bibliography.

WRIGHT, BARTON
1973. Kachinas; a Hopi artist's documentary. Illustrated by Cliff Bahnimptewa. Flagstaff: Northland Press, 262 pp.
    A greatly expanded version of an earlier catalog, which reproduces 237 paintings in full color, each accompanied by an explanatory text (see Bahnimptewa, 1971).
1975. Kachinas: the Barry Goldwater Collection at the Heard Museum. Phoenix: Heard Museum, 60 pp., illus.
    Although poorly designed and indifferently illustrated, this does catalog one of the largest *tihü* collections known.
1975. The legend of the Hopi Kachina. Phoenix magazine, vol. 10, pp. 40–43, illus.
    A popular account of Kachina traditions and legends.
1977. Hopi Kachinas; the complete guide to collecting Kachina dolls. Flagstaff: Northland Press, 139 pp., illus.
    A popular compendium, with 152 of the more commonly seen dolls illustrated by color plates, with a brief text.

WRIGHT, BARTON, and EVELYN ROAT
1962. This is a Hopi Kachina. Flagstaff: Mus. Northern Arizona. 28 pp., illus.
    A well-written museum guidebook, illustrated by examples from the fine Kachina collections of the Museum.

YAMADA, GEORGE
1957. The Great Resistance; a Hopi anthology. México, D. F.: Editorial Llamada, 75 pp., illus.
    A small pamphlet including various observations on the problem of Hopi-White relations. Although biased in tone, it is a fascinating and valuable document which places many passionate views on record.

YOUNT, GEORGE C.
1923. The chronicles of George C. Yount. Calif. Hist. Soc. Quart., vol. 2, pp. 3–66.
    The experiences of an early California fur-trapper. Among his trips was one to the Hopi villages in 1828, and the account of that trip is our earliest detailed description of Hopi life written by an American.

Index

This listing does not include the Glossary or Historical Summary. Italic numerals refer to Figures; Roman numerals refer to Plates; all other references are to pages.